Riches From The Word

Philippians:

Enduring Joy

Steven J. Cole

First Published: September 2014

Cover Artwork: Tricia Anne Walkowski

Unless otherwise identified, Scripture quotations are from The New American Standard Bible (NASB), © The Lockman Foundation 1960, 1962, 1963, 1968, 1971, 1972, 1973, 1975, 1977 and 1995.

CONTENTS

FOREWORD

The chorus of the bored, broken, confused and dying resounds, "Show me life! Take me to the place where I'll thrive in fullness!" Our heart's joy, peace, strength, love and life are found *fully* in God. The bull's-eye, along with the whole target and our only aim for that matter, is God. Only God, the Unshakable, can supply and sustain unshakable joy. Of all the proposed avenues to know and hear from God, I know of none better than His Word. The Bible.

"Your words were found and I ate them,
And Your words became for me a joy
and the delight of my heart."
        † Jeremiah 15:16

His word is an unexpected comfort in time of trouble, a sweet love letter and the true rescue story. This *letter to the Philippians* was written by a man in an ancient dungeon as death was breathing down his neck. There's no need to wait for the right mood, stage of life or suitable circumstance to read God's Word. Those who are away from the Word, "their heart is unfeeling like fat." (Psalm 119:70 ESV) May God's Word prick our fat numb hearts so we may feel God's joy, peace, strength, love and life! Let us be revived to joy.

Meditation on God's Word is precious in calm, jubilant days as well as in the dungeon, as uncertainty and chaos surround. Spurgeon notes, "When a true child of God is in trouble, the Bible becomes precious because in the text there are circumstances connected with God's dealings. True faith always loves the Word from which it springs. True faith feeds and grows on the Word" (*Beside Still Waters*, C.H. Spurgeon, p. 187). The longest chapter in the biggest book of God's Word is composed of one hundred and seventy-six testimonies of the life-changing, spiritually reviving, joy unleashing *power* of the Bible.

"O how I love Your law!
It is my meditation all the day."
        † Psalm 119:97

O the joy of seeing through God's Word to the Source of all goodness, joy, peace and strength. This book is an invitation to go deeper still, to mine the riches of the Word.

"His delight is in the law of the Lord,
And in His law he meditates day and night.
He will be like a tree firmly planted by streams of water,
Which yields its fruit in its season
And its leaf does not wither;
And in whatever he does, he prospers."
      † Psalm 1:2-3

May these writings stir up your meditations on His Word in order to see and know God, in whose presence is the fullness of joy, enduring joy.

Jacob Walkowski
Editor

The following chapters were written and preached
at Flagstaff Christian Fellowship
between April and November of 1995.

The audio is available at:
Fcfonline.org

Paul and Timothy, bond-servants of Christ Jesus, To all the saints in Christ Jesus who are in Philippi, including the overseers and deacons: Grace to you and peace from God our Father and the Lord Jesus Christ.

† Philippians 1:1-2

THE FOUNDATION FOR JOY
Philippians 1:1-2

If you want to build something of lasting value, you need to make sure that your foundation is solid. You could have an architect draw the most creative plans for a spacious dwelling. Order the finest construction materials available. Hire the most skilled craftsmen to build your home. Install the latest appliances and electronic systems throughout the house. Decorate it with the finest furniture. But if it's all resting on a faulty foundation, you're wasting your money.

It's the same spiritually. You can be a member of a church. You can even serve in that church. Outwardly, you can look like a good Christian by doing all the right things. But genuine Christianity is a matter of the heart before the God who knows our every hidden motive and thought. The joy He offers is not outward, superficial happiness based on good circumstances. It's a deep, abiding contentment that is restricted to those who are, to use Paul's frequent phrase, "in Christ Jesus." To be in Christ is to be in a vital, organic, indissoluble union with Him through faith. In this brief introduction (which we might be prone to skip) to this book that develops the theme of God's joy, the apostle gives us the solid foundation for that joy:

The foundation for joy is to be a slave of Christ and a saint in Christ in the fellowship of a local church by God's grace.

1. The foundation for joy is to be a slave of Christ.

"Paul and Timothy, bond-servants of Christ Jesus." Timothy did not write this letter with Paul, as seen by the fact that Paul consistently refers to himself in the first person and to Timothy in the third person. But Timothy may have been Paul's secretary, taking down his words as he spoke. Timothy had been with Paul, Silas, and Luke in the founding of the church in Philippi, some ten years earlier. Paul hoped to send Timothy from Rome to Philippi soon (2:19), so he wanted to give his backing to Timothy's ministry. So he included him in his opening greeting. This greeting, by the way, follows the common pattern of that day, in which the sender identifies himself, then states to whom he is writing, then sends a cordial wish such as "grace" (*charis*), a take-off on the Greek greeting (*charein*), or "peace," the common Hebrew greeting (*shalom*).

Immediately Paul identifies himself and Timothy as "bond-servants of Christ Jesus." It's the same word the demon-possessed servant girl used to identify Paul and his companions when they first visited Philippi: "These men are bond-servants of the most high God" (Acts 16:17). The word means a slave and has its roots in Israel's servitude to Egypt. When Paul refers to himself as the slave of Christ Jesus, the emphasis is on "the subordinate, obligatory and responsible nature of his service in his exclusive relation to his Lord" (R. Tuente, *The New International Dictionary of New Testament Theology*, ed. by Colin Brown, [Zondervan], 3:596).

So Paul identifies himself and Timothy right from the outset in the manner that all Christians must view themselves: "Do you not know that ... you are not your own? For you have been bought with a price: therefore glorify God in your body" (1 Cor. 6:19-20). To be a Christian is to be a slave, not to your own lusts, but to the Lord Jesus Christ. The foundation for knowing the abiding joy of the Lord is to recognize and submit to Jesus as your owner and Master, who has the right to command how and where you should live, how you should spend your time and money, and even how you should think. Your entire life must be focused on pleasing Him and doing His will as His slave.

James Boice points out (*Philippians, An Expositional Commentary* [Zondervan], p. 21) that in antiquity there were three ways a person could become a slave: by conquest; by birth; or, because of debt. He goes on to observe that we all are slaves of sin by the same three causes. Sin has conquered us, so that we are not free to do what we know is right. We are sinners by birth, being born with a nature that is hostile toward God and oriented toward pleasing self. We are sinners by debt, having run up an unpayable debt toward God who states that the wages of our sin is death.

But--and this is crucial--many people are not even aware of their condition as slaves to sin. Having been born in sin, living all their lives to gratify the selfish desires of their corrupt nature, and being unaware of the huge, unpayable debt they have run up before the holy God, they're like the Jews who argued with Jesus that they had never been enslaved to anyone (John 8:33). But Jesus replied, "Everyone who commits sin is the slave of sin.... If therefore the Son shall make you free, you shall be free indeed" (John 8:34, 36). Only Jesus Christ, by His substitutionary death, can set us free from bondage to sin. But He only does it when we recognize our need and call out to Him for deliverance. Then, having been freed from sin through faith in Christ, we become enslaved to God and begin to grow in holiness (Rom. 6:22).

You may not like the idea of being enslaved to anyone. But the fact is, you are enslaved to someone or something. As Bob Dylan sang, "You gotta serve somebody." Either you are enslaved to sin or you're enslaved to Jesus Christ (Rom. 6:16). But, while sin is a terrible master, because it destroys and leads to death, Jesus is a kind, gracious, and loving Master. Serving Him leads to eternal life.

So the question you need to ask yourself is, "Whom am I serving?" Slaves' lives were consumed with serving their masters. A slave didn't clock in at eight in the morning, put in his eight hours, and clock out for the night. He was the property of his master. He didn't have a life of his own. He was on call twenty-four hours a day, seven days a week, always ready to do what his master commanded, even if it was unpleasant or inconvenient. In Paul's case, his Master's will when he wrote Philippians was that he be in chains in prison in Rome. He could have chafed under that, complaining, "Is this any way to treat a faithful apostle?" But instead, Paul was content because he was in total submission as the slave of Christ Jesus.

Many people call themselves Christians, but the truth is, they live every day for themselves. They do not yield themselves each morning and say, "Master, I'm your slave. I'll do your bidding at work, at home, or at play." The starting place for experiencing God's joy is to yield yourself daily as a slave to Jesus as your Master; and to view yourself as being on duty for Him, listening for His voice, quick to obey His commands.

2. The foundation for joy is to be a saint in Christ.

Paul writes "to all the saints in Christ Jesus who are in Philippi." Maybe you're thinking, "There must have been a few outstanding Christians there who had already earned the reputation of being saints." The idea that sainthood is the state of a few exemplary believers comes to us from the Catholic Church, but it is contrary to the New Testament usage, which applies the word to every true Christian. Paul writes to the saints in Rome,

Ephesus, and even Corinth, referring to the whole church.

The word literally is "holy ones." The basic meaning of "holy" is to be set apart, especially, to be set apart unto God. It looks at the standing of every believer before God by virtue of the fact that when a person believes in Christ's sacrifice for his sin, God forgives all his sin and sets that person apart unto Himself. We are set apart from this evil world; we are set apart from serving ourselves; we belong to God, set apart by Him to do His will.

The late, well-known Bible teacher, Harry Ironside, in the days before airplane travel, used to spend many hours traveling by train. On one such trip, a four-day ride from the west to Chicago, he found himself in the company of a group of nuns. They liked him for his kind manner and for his interesting insights on the Bible. One day, Dr. Ironside began a discussion by asking the nuns if any of them had ever seen a saint. None of them had. He then asked if they would like to see a saint. They all said, yes, they would like to see one. Then Ironside surprised them greatly by saying, "I am a saint; I am Saint Harry." He took them to verses in the Bible, such as this one, to show that every Christian is a saint. (Told by Boice, p. 24.)

You may laugh at the idea of Saint Harry or Saint whatever-your-name-is. But it's an important New Testament truth that you view yourself as Saint whoever-you-are! As a saint, a person set apart unto God, you are not to withdraw into a monastery, or to withdraw from our culture, as the Amish folks do. You are to live in the culture, but to live distinctly from the culture, as one set apart unto God. Just as it would be odd for a wealthy man to live homeless on the streets, or it would be strange for an adult to spend great amounts of time playing as a child, because such behavior is opposed to their true identity, so it should be odd for a Christian, a saint, to live in the same manner as those who are not set apart unto God. Your attitudes, your values, your speech, your selfless focus, your humility, your love, your commitment to truth, should mark you as a saint in Christ Jesus.

Did you note the centrality and significance of Jesus Christ to the apostle Paul? He uses the name of Christ three times in these opening two verses, and 18 times in the first chapter. Martyn Lloyd-Jones wrote (*The Life of Joy* [Baker], p. 31),

> Paul has no gospel apart from Jesus Christ. The gospel is
> not some vague general offer, nor is it a mere exhortation
> to people to live a good life; rather it tells of the things that

have happened in Christ, because without Christ there is no salvation. And if Christ is not essential to your position, then according to Paul you are not a Christian. You may be very good, you may even be religious, but you cannot be a Christian. If Christ is not absolutely the core and centre, it is not Christianity, whatever else it may be.

To be "in Christ" means that all that is true of Christ is true of you. When Christ died to sin, you died. When He was raised, you were raised to newness of life in Him. Is He presently enthroned at the right hand of the Father, over all rule and authority? Then you are there in Him (Eph. 1:20-23). Just as the branch is organically connected to the vine and draws its life from it, so we are in Christ (John 15:1-6). We are to abide or live in Christ by keeping His commandments (John 15:10). After teaching this truth, Jesus said, "These things I have spoken to you, that My joy may be in you, and that your joy may be made full" (John 15:11). To be a saint in Christ Jesus is foundational for true joy.

3. The foundation for joy is to be in the fellowship of a local church.

Paul writes "to all the saints in Christ Jesus who are in Philippi, including the overseers and deacons." Being a Christian is an individual matter, in that you must personally trust in Christ as your Savior. But it is also a corporate matter, because you become a member, not only of Christ, but also of His body, the church. The church worldwide consists *spiritually* of all who have trusted Christ, but it gathers *locally* in congregations organized under the godly leadership of overseers and deacons. If you are not vitally connected to a local fellowship of Christians, you are lacking a crucial part of the foundation for joy in the Lord, because you are isolated from those who can stimulate you to love and good deeds, who can encourage you to godly living as the day of the Lord draws near (Heb. 10:24-25).

Relationships among believers can be a source of great joy, but, frankly, they can also be a source of great pain. As one wag put it, "To dwell above with the saints we love, O that will be glory; but, to dwell below with the saints we know, that's a different story!" If you've been a Christian for any length of time, I can predict with 100 percent accuracy that you have been hurt by fellow believers. Getting hurt, of course, makes you want to draw back from the church for fear of it happening again. But if you do that, you rob yourself of joy, because God doesn't call us to live in isolation, but in relation with other saints.

Remember, there were only two kinds of people in Philippi (or Flagstaff): the saints and the "non-saints." While it can be painful to relate to the saints, it's really tough to be cut off from the saints, surrounded by people who don't care about the things of God. There were tensions in the flock in Philippi, and Paul subtly begins to address those tensions even in this opening greeting with the little word "all" ("to all the saints"). He repeats the phrase "you all" in 1:4, 7 (twice), 8, and 25. In a gentle way he seems to be saying, "What I write, I write to all who are in Christ. What I pray, I pray for you all. What I think and feel, I think and feel towards all, because you all share in God's grace with me. You all must progress in God's joy together."

In the local church, God has ordained for leaders to have oversight and to serve. Two types of church officers are mentioned: overseers ("bishops"); and, deacons (the Greek word means "servants"). We don't know for sure why Paul singles them out, but perhaps it was because the gift he had received had been sent from the church through the overseers and deacons. Or, perhaps Paul wanted to call attention to their office so that the church would submit to their role in resolving the squabbles that were threatening their unity (Heb. 13:17; 1 Thess. 5:12-13).

Overseers are the same as elders (Acts 20:17, 28; Titus 1:5, 7). "Overseer" looks at the work, to watch over God's flock; "elder" looks at the man, that he must be a man of spiritual maturity. The qualifications for this office are given in 1 Timothy 3:1-7 and Titus 1:5-9, and are primarily godly character and the ability to exhort in sound doctrine and refute those who contradict. The primary task that the overseer/elder does is to shepherd God's flock, which involves protecting the flock from danger, leading by example, and feeding the flock from God's Word (Acts 20:28; 1 Pet. 5:1-4). Some elders are to devote themselves to the ministry of the Word and are thus worthy of financial support. Others concentrate more on oversight and administration ("rule well," 1 Tim. 5:17-18), and may also work in outside jobs.

The office of deacon arose in the early church because the apostles were being drawn away from their primary ministry of prayer and the Word into administering the distribution of food to the poor among the church (Acts 6:1-6). Thus the ministry of deacons is to serve the body in practical and administrative ways that free up the elders for the work of shepherding, teaching, and prayer. The qualifications for deacons are just as high as for elders, namely, that they must be men of godly character (Acts 6:3; 1 Tim. 3:8-13). But the point is, you won't know God's joy unless you are part of a local fellowship, under the oversight of godly men who shepherd and serve the flock under Christ.

Thus, God's joy is based on being a slave of Christ and a saint in Christ, in fellowship with the church of Christ. Finally,

4. The foundation for joy is to be the recipient of God's grace and peace in Christ.

"Grace to you and peace from God the Father and the Lord Jesus Christ" (1:2). As mentioned, this was a standard greeting, but it is far more than just a greeting. Perhaps Paul combined the Greek and Hebrew greetings to show that in Christ there is no distinction between Gentile or Jew. We are all one in Christ. This greeting also shows that God the Father and the Lord Jesus Christ (His deity is implicit in the equal association of Him with the Father) are the source of both grace and peace.

Grace is, quite simply, God's unmerited favor, shown to those who deserve His judgment. If you earn it, it's not grace, but a wage that is due. God's grace is extended to the ungodly who know it, not to those who think they're deserving (Rom. 4:4-5). God's grace is the only way to be reconciled to God. If you think you deserve a place in God's kingdom because you're a pretty good person, you don't understand and have not laid hold of God's grace. If you think things are right between you and God because you do good things for others and try to live a clean life, you have not grasped God's grace; you are, in fact, alienated from God. God resists the proud (those who think they're deserving), but He gives grace to the humble (James 4:6; 1 Pet. 5:5). The only way to receive God's unmerited favor is to see yourself rightly as an undeserving sinner and call out for His grace. If you don't know grace, you don't know God!

Peace is the result of experiencing God's grace. The order is important: You cannot know God's peace without first appropriating His grace. Where God's grace is lacking, peace will also be in short supply. Peace points to the inner well-being that comes from being reconciled to God through what He provided in Christ. Both grace and peace operate first vertically, but also horizontally. If you know God's grace and peace, you will become a gracious, peaceable person toward others. You will show grace to them because God's grace is real in your life. You will seek peace with them because God's peace floods your heart, and He commands you to live at peace with others, as much as it depends on you (Rom. 12:18).

Conclusion

If you're lacking God's joy, I encourage you to examine your foundation. Are you a *slave* of Christ Jesus, in total submission to Him, seeking at all times to please Him by doing His will? If you're living for self, you'll lack God's joy. Do you see yourself as a *saint* in Christ Jesus, set apart from this evil world unto Christ, living in union with Him? If you blend in with the world, you'll lack God's joy. Are you linked in fellowship with the *church* of Christ Jesus, serving together in the great cause of Christ? If you are isolated from the church, you will lack God's joy.

Have you received and do you live daily in the *grace* of Christ Jesus? Does the thought of God's unmerited favor, shown to you, cause you at times to well up in gratitude and love toward God? Because of His grace, does His *peace* flood into your soul, even in the midst of trials? If so, you're laying a solid foundation for lasting joy in the Lord. "Now may the God of hope fill you with all joy and peace in believing, that you may abound in hope by the power of the Holy Spirit" (Rom. 15:13). Amen!

Application Questions

1. Is there such a thing as knowing Christ as Savior, but not as Master? Can a Christian be a slave of sin (Rom. 6:16-22)?

2. Why is it crucial to view yourself as a saint? What if you aren't perfect? Are you still a saint?

3. Why is being connected to a local church not optional for the Christian?

4. Some say, "Christ died for you because you're worthy." Why is this totally contrary to God's Word?

I thank my God in all my remembrance of you, always offering prayer with joy in my every prayer for you all, in view of your participation in the gospel from the first day until now. For I am confident of this very thing, that He who began a good work in you will perfect it until the day of Christ Jesus.

†   Philippians 1:3-6

CONFIDENT ABOUT SALVATION
Philippians 1:3-6

One of the most important questions for every person to answer is, "How can I be confident that I am truly saved?" And, some follow-up questions are just as crucial, "If I am truly saved, can I know for sure that I will not lose my salvation?" "What about our loved ones? Can we know if they are truly saved and if they will persevere?"

These are crucial questions because they concern matters of our own and our loved ones' eternal destinies. If we are truly saved, but lack assurance, we will live in constant anxiety about the state of our souls. On the other hand, if we or our loved ones *think* we are saved when we are *not* truly saved, we will be in for the most rude awakening when we someday stand before the Lord only to hear Him say, "I never knew you; depart from Me, you who practice lawlessness" (Matt. 7:23). So we must be careful not to rest on false assurance, or to give it to others. But, if we can obtain true assurance from God about our salvation, then we need it.

Our text gives us some answers to these questions. It is not all that is written on this topic, of course. The entire epistle of First John was written so that those who had believed in Christ could know that they had eternal life (1 John 5:13). John gives a number of tests which we can both apply to ourselves and also to others, to make sure that we are in the faith. But Philippians 1:3-6 is an important text. James Boice calls verse 6 one of the three greatest verses in the Bible that teaches the perseverance of the saints, "the doctrine that no one whom God has brought to a saving knowledge of Jesus Christ will ever be lost," the other two texts being Romans 8:38, 39 and John 10:27, 28 (*Philippians, An Expositional Commentary* [Zondervan], p. 40).

It is tempting to develop these verses along the theme of joy (as I did the first two messages on Philippians), because Paul begins by mentioning his joy as he prayed with thanksgiving for these believers. It's certainly remarkable that Paul's focus was not on himself. He was in prison in Rome facing possible execution; fellow Christian leaders were preaching against Paul out of envy and strife (Phil. 1:15); but he was filled with joy because his focus was on God and His faithfulness and on what God was doing with the Philippian church.

If you are feeling down, a prescription for joy is to fix your thoughts on God's faithfulness. If He has used you in the past to lead someone to Christ or to minister to a fellow believer, think about them and pray for their continued growth. In other words, get your focus off of self and onto God and others and you'll be flooded with God's joy.

But to return to the other theme, of how we can be confident about our own or others' salvation, the apostle teaches us that ...

If there is evidence that God has begun the work of salvation in us, we can be confident that He will complete it.

My view on this subject will probably be different than the views many of you have heard or believe. Some teach that a person can be truly saved, but if he turns away from Christ, he can lose his salvation. This view is called Arminianism, and also was promoted by John Wesley. I believe this view is in error. Others teach that if a person professes faith in Christ, he is saved and, thus, eternally secure. One of the first things to share with this person is assurance of salvation. Even if he later falls away and goes back into the world, with no evidence of salvation in his life, this view teaches that he will be in heaven someday because, "Once saved, always saved." I believe that this view is incomplete and thus in error.

I believe that Scripture teaches that salvation is entirely the work of God, not of man. The God who is powerful to save is also powerful to keep the ones He saves. At the same time, the enemy is deceitful to counterfeit the work of God. Thus some, like the seed sown on the rocky ground and on the thorny ground, seem at first to be saved. But time proves that they were not truly saved, because they do not persevere by bearing fruit unto eternal life. Thus we must be careful to distinguish in ourselves and in others the true saving grace of God from the counterfeit work of the devil. If there is evidence that God has truly begun His work of salvation in us, then we can be confident that He will complete what He has begun. Let's develop this further:

1. God begins the work of salvation.

"He who began a good work in you" refers to God and the work of salvation which He began in the hearts of the Philippians. We have seen (in Acts 16) how the households of Lydia and the Philippian jailer responded to the gospel, and perhaps also the demon-possessed slave girl. It is the preaching of the good news that "Christ died for our sins according to the Scriptures, and that He was buried, and that He was raised on the third day according to the Scriptures" (1 Cor. 15:3, 4) that is "the power of God for salvation to everyone who believes" (Rom. 1:16).

We also saw in the first chapter that God is decidedly the author of salvation. He elected us to salvation in Christ before the foundation of the world (Eph. 1:4). He sent the Savior at the proper time. He ordained that Christ must die for our sins as the only acceptable substitute (John 1:29; Acts 2:23). He prohibited Paul and his companions from going into certain areas to preach and instead directed them to Philippi (Acts 16:6-10). When they obeyed God's leading and preached the gospel to Lydia, "the Lord opened her heart to respond" (Acts 16:14). As Jesus Himself stated plainly, "No one can come to Me, unless the Father who sent Me draws him"; "...no one can come to Me, unless it has been granted him from the Father" (John 6:44, 65). "Salvation is from the Lord" (Jonah 2:9).

We also need to understand that the *gospel* message is *not*, "If you've got some problems in your life and you'd like to have a happier life, trust in Jesus. He will give you an abundant life." We often hear variations of this theme presented as the gospel, but they miss the heart of the matter, which is of far greater consequence than enjoying a happy life here on earth. The *true gospel* confronts our fundamental problem, namely, our alienation from a holy God due to our sin and rebellion. If we die in this condition, we will be eternally separated from God, under His just wrath in hell. But God, who is rich in mercy, provided His substitutionary Lamb to make atonement for our sin, so that all who trust in Him are saved from God's judgment.

When that good news is proclaimed, the Holy Spirit bears witness to the objective truth of it in the hearts of those whom the Father is drawing to Himself. Apart from any human merit, God supernaturally imparts to that person an abiding change of nature through regeneration (the new birth). He grants them repentance leading to the knowledge of the truth (2 Tim. 2:25) and faith to believe it (Phil. 1:29). Thus salvation is not at all from man, but rather is "by grace through faith; and that not of yourselves, it is the gift of God; not as a result of works, that no one should boast" (Eph. 2:8, 9; see Titus 3:4-7; John 1:12-13).

It is important to affirm the true nature of the gospel and of salvation, because if we mistakenly think that salvation depends upon us, or upon a human decision, then that decision could be reversed or rescinded. The Arminian error is that God has given us a *free will*, so we can decide by ourselves either to choose God or reject Him. But Scripture is abundantly clear that the human will is *not* free, except to continue in sin and rebellion against God (Rom. 3:10-18; 8:7-8; Eph. 2:1-5). Even John Wesley sang his brother, Charles', great hymn which says, "Long my imprisoned spirit lay Fast bound in sin and nature's night. Thine eye diffused a quickening ray; I woke--the dungeon flamed with light! My chains fell off, my heart was free, I rose, went forth, and followed Thee."

If you want to read a powerful refutation of the idea of "free will," read Martin Luther's, *The Bondage of the Will* (translated by J. I. Packer and O. R. Johnson [Revell]). For over 300 pages, Luther relentlessly devastates the view that salvation depends on our "free will." He argues that if it depended on such a thing, we could never have assurance that we are right with God. He admits to his own misery in believing that for years before his conversion (pp. 313- 314). Then he states (p. 314),

> But now that God has taken my salvation out of the control of my own will, and put it under the control of His, and promised to save me, not according to my working or running, but according to His own grace and mercy, I have the comfortable certainty that He is faithful and will not lie to me, and that He is also great and powerful, so that no devils or opposition can break Him or pluck me from Him. "No one," He says, "shall pluck them out of my hand, because my Father which gave them me is greater than all" (John 10:28-29). Thus it is that, if not all, yet some, indeed many, are saved; whereas, by the power of "free-will" none at all could be saved, but every one of us would perish.

Please understand, a person is not saved apart from faith in Christ. But Scripture clearly teaches that when a person believes in Christ, that faith is not the product of his "free will," but rather comes from God who powerfully works faith in us. Salvation is totally from God.

2. God's salvation is always accompanied by evidence.

The "good work" which God begins works its way out as a believer grows to maturity and is progressively conformed to the image of Jesus Christ (Rom. 8:29). In other words, salvation is always accompanied and followed by sanctification, or growth in holiness. As Jonathan Edwards argued in his profound work, "A Treatise Concerning Religious Affections" (in *The Works of Jonathan Edwards* [Banner of Truth], 1:236), "True religion, in great part, consists in holy affections." He means that "love and the pursuit of holiness is *the* enduring mark of the true Christian" (*Jonathan Edwards, A New Biography* [Banner of Truth], by Iain Murray, p. 259).

The evidence in the Philippian believers to which Paul calls attention was their "participation in the gospel from the first day until now" (1:5). "Participation" is the word "fellowship" (Greek, *koinonia*), which means "sharing together in." The Philippians had shared with Paul in the gospel, first by believing it and being saved, then by devoting themselves to it and all that it entails. Like all who are truly saved, they were not just occasional dabblers in religion; rather, they were vitally joined together with the apostle in the great cause of Jesus Christ, so that he could rightly refer to them as fellow-sharers, participants, in the gospel. While there is far more evidence that could be compiled from the rest of the New Testament, I want to point out four lines of evidence of salvation contained in these verses.

A. Salvation is always accompanied by the evidence of fellowship with God.

To fellowship in the gospel is to fellowship with God Himself, who gave us the gospel. Christianity is not just believing a set of doctrines, as essential as doctrinal truth is. It is coming to know the living and true God, and that through His Son Jesus Christ. As Jesus prayed, "And this is eternal life, that they may know You, the only true God, and Jesus Christ whom

You have sent" (John 17:3). Or, as Paul wrote to the Corinthians, "God is faithful, through whom you were called into fellowship with His Son, Jesus Christ our Lord" (1 Cor. 1:9).

Thus if a person is genuinely saved, he enters into a personal relationship with the personal God. Relationships involve a *progressive knowledge* of the other person. We grow to know God as He has revealed Himself in His Word. A relationship involves *time spent together*, sharing our deepest thoughts, fears, and hopes with this God who knows us thoroughly. A relationship implies that we are interested in the things that concern the other person. Even so, an evidence of salvation is that a person becomes *interested in the things of God* as revealed in His Word. When a true Christian is around other Christians, he delights to talk about God and His Word. If there is no interest in the things of God and no evidence of personal fellowship with God, it is doubtful if a person is truly saved.

> B. Salvation is always accompanied by the evidence of fellowship with God's people.

By entering the fellowship of the gospel, the Philippians had entered into fellowship with Paul, Timothy, Silas, and Luke who brought the gospel to them. Paul shares his deep feelings of love for these people. His remembrance of them brought tears of joy to his eyes and a longing to his heart. There is nothing humanly to explain this bond of love between this Asian who was formerly a Jewish zealot and these mostly Gentile Europeans who were formerly worldly pagans. One evidence of salvation is that it brings us into genuine fellowship with the people of God, no matter how different our backgrounds.

I believe this is a powerful proof of the reality of the gospel. All of us who know Christ have had the experience of meeting someone we've never met before, and discovering that this person also knows Christ. In just a matter of minutes, even though the person was a total stranger, the fact that we both know the Lord draws us together into a bond of fellowship that often seems closer than you feel toward some family members who do not know Christ. One of the glories of the church is that people who otherwise would have nothing in common--people like Lydia, the businesswoman; the formerly demonic slave-girl; and, the career military man (the jailer)--suddenly become "partakers of grace" (1:7) together and join together in the great cause of the gospel (1:27).

C. Salvation is always accompanied by the evidence of a new focus and endeavor: the gospel.

The Philippians, from day one, joined with Paul in the fellowship of the gospel. Rather than living for self and pleasure, as they formerly did, they now lived to serve Jesus Christ, even in the face of opposition (1:27-30). This was also the experience of the early church in Jerusalem, as we read in Acts 8:4, "Those who had been scattered [by persecution] went about spreading the good news of the word" (lit.). That's not referring to so-called preachers only, but to all the believers. If your life has been transformed through the gospel, so that you have experienced the forgiveness of your sins by God's grace and you have been raised from spiritual death to life by God's power, then with the early apostles you must say, "We cannot stop speaking what we have seen and heard" (Acts 4:20).

God doesn't save anyone so that they can live a happy, self-centered life. When He saves you, you become a minister (servant) of the gospel. We have different spiritual gifts and we have different ways and situations in which to exercise those gifts. But there is simply no such thing as a saved person who is not supposed to be serving the Lord and His gospel in some capacity. You view all of life through the lens of the gospel (1 Cor. 9:23).

One way (not the only way) that the Philippians had fellowshipped with Paul in the gospel was by frequently sending him *financial* support (4:15-16). It's safe to say that if the gospel has not touched your money, it has not touched your heart, because your heart is bound up with your treasure (Matt. 6:21). So a powerful evidence of the new birth is when, quietly and without public notice (Matt. 6:1-4), out of a desire to please God, you begin giving generously to support the work of the gospel.

D. Salvation is always accompanied by the evidence of living in light of the Lord's coming.

Paul says that God will perfect His good work "until the day of

Christ Jesus" (1:6), that great day when He comes back in power and glory. We shall see Him and shall be like Him (1 John 3:2). We will give an account to Him of our management of what He has entrusted to us. Every true child of God will hear those joyous words, "Well done, good and faithful slave; ... enter into the joy of your master" (Matt. 25:21, 23). The Lord will then reveal "the motives of men's hearts; and then each man's praise will come to him from God" (1 Cor. 4:5). If you often think of the Lord's coming and our meeting Him in the air, it's a powerful evidence that He has begun the work of salvation in your heart.

3. God completes the work of salvation.

What God begins, He finishes. If salvation is, even in part, the work of man, there is the chance that it won't be finished. But if God has begun it, and we see evidences of it, then we can be confident, whether in ourselves or in others, that He "will perfect it until the day of Christ Jesus." As Paul states later in this letter, it is a process in which we never arrive in this life, and so we must press on toward maturity (3:12-14). Perfection in these evidences is not going to happen until we're with the Lord.

The fact that God does it does *not* imply that we are *passive*. God is at work, but we work with Him. We must work out our salvation with fear and trembling, for it is God who is at work in us, both to will and to work for His good pleasure (2:12, 13). But our assurance and confidence is never in ourselves or in our working, but only in God and in the evidences we see of His faithful working in and through us. If there is evidence that God has begun the work of salvation in us, we can be confident that He will complete it as we continue to participate in the gospel.

Conclusion

A message like this may have the effect of shaking the assurance of salvation that some of you formerly had. If that assurance was a false assurance because there is no evidence that God has truly begun His good work in you, then it needs to be shaken. Or, if your assurance was based on *your* decision to follow Christ (rather than on His sovereign, unmerited grace), or if it was based on what *you* have done for God through your good deeds (rather than on what God has done for you in the death of His Son), it needs to be shaken. You need to abandon your pride and call out to God for His saving grace.

But if you can see how God sovereignly, graciously has called you to Himself, and you see the evidence of His working through your fellowship in the gospel, then you can be confident that He who began the good work in you will complete it until the day of Christ Jesus.

Application Questions

1. What Scriptures counter the common notion that people have the "free will" to choose God? (Try Rom. 9:16; James 1:18.)

2. In light of the parable of the sower (Matt. 13:3-9, 18-23), is it wise to share "assurance of salvation" with someone who just professed faith in Christ? Why/why not?

3. Can a Christian who has turned away from the Lord have assurance of salvation? Should we share it with him?

4. Some argue, "If salvation requires evidence, then it is not by faith alone." Why is this fallacious?

I thank my God in all my remembrance of you, always offering prayer with joy in my every prayer for you all, in view of your participation in the gospel from the first day until now. For I am confident of this very thing, that He who began a good work in you will perfect it until the day of Christ Jesus. For it is only right for me to feel this way about you all, because I have you in my heart, since both in my imprisonment and in the defense and confirmation of the gospel, you all are partakers of grace with me. For God is my witness, how I long for you all with the affection of Christ Jesus.

† Philippians 1:3-8

TRUE CHRISTIAN FELLOWSHIP
Philippians 1:3-8

A family went to the movies. On the way in, the young man of the family stopped at the refreshment stand to pick up some popcorn. By the time he got into the theater, the lights were already dim and he couldn't find his family. He paced up and down the aisles in near darkness, peering down each row. Finally, in desperation, he stopped and asked out loud, "Does anyone here recognize me?"

Even though it's well-lit, there may be people who come into this church and feel like that young man--lost, isolated, disconnected from everyone. Deep down, they are silently crying out, "Does anyone here recognize me?" They're longing for true Christian fellowship.

While the local church ought to be the place where you can find genuine fellowship in Christ, all too often it is lacking. On vacation a couple of years ago, our family visited a small church in Colorado. It should have been obvious to the regular attenders that we were new. And yet, even though we arrived before the service began and stood around for quite a while after it was over, no one came up to talk with us. That doesn't incline you toward going back a second time.

The local church is not supposed to be like a theater, where you file in, find a seat next to folks that you don't have any relationship with, watch the performance, and file out. Part of our problem is that we've come to think of the church as the *building* you go to for church services. That idea is foreign to the New Testament, which clearly presents the church as *God's people*, a living body knit together by their union with Christ, the head. Coupled with the church as a building fallacy is the equally unbiblical notion that the *pastor* and perhaps *a few committed volunteers run the church*. The rest of the folks just come, sit, listen, and go home.

But the Bible is clear that *every member is a minister* of Christ, with a vital function to fulfill. If everyone here who knows Christ as Savior viewed himself or herself as a minister, here to serve Christ by reaching out in love to others, no one could walk into our services and feel like no one recognized him.

As you read our text, it is obvious that Paul had a relationship of close fellowship with this church. It wasn't what often goes by the label "fellowship" in American Christianity, the superficial chatting about sports or the weather over coffee and donuts. Even though they were miles apart, Paul's heart was tied up with these people, and their hearts were with him. There was no natural explanation for this closeness between this Asian Jew who was now in prison in Rome and these European people who themselves were no homogeneous group. What knit them together was true Christian fellowship.

True Christian fellowship means sharing together in the things of God.

There are five strands of true fellowship in these verses:

1. True fellowship means praying for one another (1:3, 4).

Though Paul was confined and could not be with the Philippians, his chains could not prevent him from thinking about them and praying for them. His remembrance of them filled him with thanksgiving and joy, as he thought about how God was truly at work among them. And those thoughts turned into frequent prayers on their behalf.

Our remembrance of other believers should not stop with warm feelings. Our remembrance should be turned God-ward, into heartfelt prayers for one another. I personally struggle with going over prayer lists, because I always think, "Lord, You can read my list. You know these needs." It always seems kind of mechanical and meaningless to me. The lists can be helpful, to bring to mind people I otherwise would forget. But I find it easier to pray for people as God brings them to my mind during the day. Turn your remembrances into prayer.

In Ephesians 6:18 we're told to "pray at all times in the Spirit, and with this in view, be on the alert with all perseverance and petition for all the saints." In 1 Thessalonians 5:17 we're told to "pray without ceasing." Romans 12:12 tells us to "be devoted to prayer." These verses do not mean that we are to quit our jobs and spend all day every day in prayer. The word translated "without ceasing" was used of a hacking cough. Someone with a hacking cough is always coming back to it after brief intervals. Thus, prayer is to be a frequent, common conversation between us and the Lord, and the subject of our prayers should often be other Christians and their walk with God (we'll look at the content of Paul's prayer in Phil. 1:9-11 in our next chapter.)

Sometimes you may wonder, "Why do I need to pray? God already knows everything, and He's going to accomplish His sovereign will anyway. So what's the point of praying?" But the prayers of the saints are part of God's method for accomplishing His sovereign will. And He uses prayer to change the heart of the one doing the praying, as well as to work in the hearts of others. As you bring your requests before God, your motives are exposed. You quickly realize that you can't honestly bring certain requests before God, because your thoughts about a brother or sister aren't pleasing to Him! If you're inclined to pray the imprecatory psalms against someone, God will convict you and ask, "Is that really what you want Me to do to this brother or sister in Christ?"

If you're having trouble with another believer, even if it's your mate or a family member, pray often for that person. It's hard to stay angry at someone you're praying for daily! James Boice states, "I think that ninety percent of all the divisions between true believers in this world would disappear entirely if Christians would learn to pray specifically and constantly for one another" (*Philippians, An Expositional Commentary* [Zondervan], p. 49).

2. True fellowship means serving God together (1:5, 7).

We've already seen how, from day one, the Philippians joined Paul in the cause of the gospel. They were active in serving the Lord. The concept of being a church member who just attends a church service once a week would have been completely foreign to them, and rightly so. It should be foreign to us! Christ never saves anyone so that they can just add church attendance to their list of weekly things to do. Nor does He save anyone so that they can live happier lives that are just as self-centered as they were before. Every believer is saved to serve God.

Americans have adopted a change in focus, in which they view the church like consumers who are shopping for a place that will meet their needs. So they try out this church and that church, and finally settle on one that seems to offer the services they're interested in. But if they have an unpleasant experience or if they hear of another church that seems to offer better programs, they change to it, much like they change department stores if another one better suits their fancy.

Sadly, a lot of churches cater to this mentality. Articles and books tell pastors how to market their churches to the "Baby Boomers." They warn that if we don't learn what the Baby Boomers want and re-design the church to give it to them, we'll lose them. Nervous pastors see the people going down the street to the church that offers a full-service program, and they get busy trying to design new programs to help their church compete in the marketplace.

I intend some time to write an article on why we're *not* a "full-service" church. The point of the church is decidedly *not* to meet the needs of folks who decide to give them their business! The church is a *fellowship* of those who serve Jesus because He bought them with His blood. That service sometimes includes being *persecuted*. Paul mentions how the Philippians were partners with him in his imprisonment and in the defense and confirmation of the gospel (1:7). He tells them, "For to you it has been granted for Christ's sake, not only to believe in Him, but also to suffer for His sake" (1:29) [it's a *gift!*]. Can you picture the Philippian church taking out an ad in the local paper to market the church: "Come, join our church! You'll love suffering with us! We have the best persecution program in town!"

When I was in the Coast Guard, I never had to serve in combat. But you who did can identify with this aspect of true Christian fellowship. Even though you probably served with pagans, fighting together against the enemy in life or death situations knit you together with those men. If you have a reunion of your company, seeing those men brings back memories of how you risked your lives for one another and for the cause.

The Christian church is engaged in mortal combat for the souls of men and women. The truth of the gospel is under attack, not only from outside the camp, but also from within. Thus it needs to be *defended*. There are many today who say that we should never be negative, that we should only emphasize loving one another. Those who dare to confront serious heresies get labeled as divisive and unloving. But Paul spent a good deal of time in his letters defending the gospel, often against false teachers in the church. So did John, Peter, and Jude. So must we, if we want to be faithful to Christ.

The gospel also needs to be *confirmed*. Defense focuses on the negative task of confronting error; confirmation focuses on the positive task of setting forth the truth of the gospel and its implications for how we should live. The gospel is confirmed through the church when our lives show the fruit of godliness (see 1 Cor. 1:6). Even though it is more positively focused, the confirmation of the gospel is also a battleground. The enemy hates it when God's truth is set forth in a clear, practical manner, because Christians start dealing with their sin and living holy lives. And so it draws fire and creates controversy.

The point is, every Christian has a role to fulfill by serving in Christ's army. The Lord saved you to serve, and serving Him isn't always easy or free from strife and conflict. But it knits us together in fellowship when we join in serving Him. True fellowship means praying and serving Christ together.

3. True fellowship means trusting in God's sovereign working in one another (1:6).

In the last chapter, we saw from this verse how salvation is God's doing from start to finish. But let's look at verse 6 from the angle of fellowship. It means that I can trust God to work in the lives of my brothers and sisters. God began their salvation; He will finish the job. Fellowship often breaks down because I see that another Christian isn't exactly where I'm at on some issue, whether it's how to interpret some doctrine or how to live on some issue. I'm threatened by Christians who are different than I am, and so I take it on as my task to change that person so he will be like me. He senses my rejection of him or my attempts to change him, and draws back. Fellowship is hindered.

Verse 6 means that I'm not responsible to change others. I am responsible to minister God's love and truth to others in a sensitive manner. If a brother is clearly wrong about a major truth or in sin or immature in the way he's living, I am responsible to come alongside and do all I can to help him change and grow. If it's a serious heresy or sin that he's involved in, I may eventually need to separate from him. But at the same time, I can trust that it's God's job to change that brother. If God has truly saved him, God will finish the job. So I can relax, accept him where he's at with the Lord, encourage him in areas of weakness, but also learn from him in areas where I need to grow. But I'm not the Holy Spirit, and it only serves to break fellowship when I take that role on myself. This applies also to husbands and wives and to parents and teenagers! You can and must trust God to change your mate, your kids, or your parents.

4. True fellowship means partaking together of God's grace (1:7).

Paul saw the Philippians as "partakers of grace" with him. Just as Paul, the persecutor of the church, had found God's undeserved favor at the cross, so had the Philippians. So have we all who have met Christ. Every true member of the church is a partaker of God's grace. The more I grow in Christ, the more I sense how much grace I needed to get saved and how much grace I need daily to go on with Christ. And the more I should view my fellow saints as fellow sinners who need not only grace from God, but also grace from me, as we labor together for Christ.

Viewing ourselves and other Christians as fellow-partakers of God's grace humbles us and puts us all on the same level. Paul could have viewed himself as God's greatest apostle to the Gentiles, and the Philippians as his converts. "Just think where you'd be at today if I hadn't come and given the gospel to you. And don't forget how much I suffered in the process!" It's interesting to trace chronologically how Paul referred to himself in three of his letters. In 1 Corinthians 15:9 he said that he was the least of the apostles. Later, in Ephesians 3:8, he said that he was the least of all saints. Finally, in 1 Timothy 1:15 he called himself the chief of sinners.

I've been around some Christians whose company, quite frankly, was difficult to enjoy. It's easy to become judgmental and impatient, where you think, "Why is this person so hard to be around?" And fellowship is strained. I had a secretary in my church in California who was that way. She tended to be abrasive and insensitive to people. One day I asked her to tell me how she met the Lord. She told me of a terrible childhood in which her father had abused and then abandoned her. Her succession of stepfathers had been equally abusive. She finally ran off with her boyfriend to escape this horrible home life, and only later had met Christ. Hearing her story changed my attitude toward her. I realized that she was a partaker of God's grace with me.

Of course, grace doesn't mean that we tolerate sin and shrug off sloppy living. We sometimes need to confront; we need to help one another face and overcome faults. But if we remember that we're all partakers of God's undeserved favor, we'll give one another more room to grow. We'll be more patient and forbearing with one another. True Christian fellowship is a sharing together in God's abundant grace.

Thus true fellowship means praying and serving together; it means trusting in God's faithfulness and grace.

5. True fellowship means heartfelt affection for one another (1:8).

Paul calls God as his witness of his longing and affection for the Philippian believers, not because they would be prone to doubt him, but because he felt it so deeply. "Affection" is the word for bowels or the inner vital organs. It emphasizes the emotional aspect of Paul's love for these people who were so dear to him. There was a popular Bible teacher a few years ago who used to say that *agape* love is a "mental attitude," not an emotion. I'm afraid that he and his followers often reflected his teaching, being some of the coldest people I ever care to meet. But the Apostle Paul was unashamedly emotional in his love for God's people. He told the Thessalonians that he had cared for them as tenderly as a nursing mother. Then he said, "Having thus a fond affection for you, we were well-pleased to impart to you not only the gospel of God but also our own lives, because you had become very dear to us" (1 Thess. 2:8).

Sin divides us from those who are different from us racially, culturally, or in other ways. But the love of Christ unites us, not just intellectually, but with heartfelt love. Such love isn't manipulative, trying to use the other person for our own advantage. It truly seeks God's best for the other person, even at personal inconvenience or sacrifice.

Now, here's the hard question (if you're honest, you wrestle with it at times): *How can I develop heartfelt love for a Christian whom I find it hard to be around?* Well, let's be honest, it's not easy! All of the factors of fellowship I've mentioned go into the solution: Pray diligently for the person; work with him in the gospel; trust God to do His work of sanctification in him; ask him to share his testimony or background, and recognize that you both are partakers of God's grace.

But there's another factor mentioned in verse 8: Love him or her with the affection of Christ Jesus. J. B. Lightfoot paraphrases, "Did I speak of having you in my own heart? I should rather have said that in the heart of Christ Jesus I long for you." Then Lightfoot comments, "A powerful metaphor describing perfect union. The believer has no yearnings apart from his Lord; his pulse beats with the pulse of Christ; his heart throbs with the heart of Christ" (*Saint Paul's Epistle to the Philippians* [Zondervan], p. 85). Jesus Christ loved that difficult brother or sister enough to go to the cross for him or her. He can love them through me. As I *obey* by judging my sinful thoughts toward the person and by *acting in love*, the feelings of love will almost invariably follow. But even if they don't, I need to obey!

Conclusion

I read about a man named Mohammed who lives in a North African country that is almost totally Muslim. He sent away for some literature he heard about on a radio broadcast and received in the mail a Gospel of Matthew and a Gospel of John. Through studying them he came to faith in Christ.

But there are no churches in his country. Mohammed longed for a Christian brother to fellowship and pray with. He prayed diligently for four years, wondering if he would ever have the joy of meeting another Christian. Then one day he received a letter from a British Christian he had never met, who was following up with those who had requested gospel literature. The man told Mohammed that he would be in his area and asked if they could meet. Mohammed was so excited that his prayer was finally going to be answered that he couldn't sleep for three nights before the scheduled meeting. When they met, Mohammed's first experience of Christian fellowship was more wonderful than he could have imagined. (Story in Operation Mobilization's "Indeed," April/May, 1994.)

Some of us take Christian fellowship for granted, don't we? What a great privilege it is to be able to share together in the things of God! If you just attend church, but aren't connected with other Christians during the week, you need to get plugged in with the fellowship! And we all need to see ourselves a servants of Christ with a responsibility to reach out in true Christian fellowship to our brothers and sisters and, especially, to new people, even to those who may be different than we are. We don't want anyone to come here and ask, "Does anyone here recognize me?"

Application Questions

1. How can we do a better job of including and incorporating new people in our fellowship?

2. How has the consumer mentality affected the church? Should the church see itself as being in the business of "meeting needs?"

3. How does the concept that every Christian is a minister affect the fellowship of a local body?

4. How can you develop heartfelt affection for a brother or sister you just can't stand being around?

And this I pray, that your love may abound still more and more in real knowledge and all discernment, so that you may approve the things that are excellent, in order to be sincere and blameless until the day of Christ; having been filled with the fruit of righteousness which comes through Jesus Christ, to the glory and praise of God.

† Philippians 1:9-11

DISCERNING LOVE
Philippians 1:9-11

We all must avoid two extremes in the Christian life if we wish to grow to maturity. On the one hand are those who are prone to *live by subjective feelings*, devoid of doctrine. They love to sing over and over, "Oh, How I Love Jesus" and other such songs, with hands lifted up, swaying with the music. They think that doctrine is divisive, that what we need is *life*, by which they mean a subjective feeling that comes over them when they "get in the spirit."

They also say that we *don't* need to *emphasize truth*, but rather, *love*. They're fond of saying, "Jesus didn't say the world will know that we are His disciples by our doctrine, but by our love." So they emphasize unity with anyone who names the name of Christ, no matter how erroneous their doctrine. They call for accepting all professing Christians, no matter what they believe or how they live. Such feeling-oriented Christians are not living in line with Scripture. They are imbalanced and will get into great trouble.

The other extreme we need to avoid is the precise opposite. These people *emphasize knowledge* and correct doctrine, but in practice they deny biblical love. They redefine love so narrowly that they can excuse their harsh attitudes toward those who disagree with them on some fine point of doctrine. They avoid confronting the coldness of their hearts toward God and His people by congratulating themselves on being "correct" doctrinally. In other words, they're *all head*, but *no heart*.

The Bible, however, presents a fine balance between head and heart. Biblical Christianity means loving God and others fervently, from the heart; but also, such love is in line with God's truth as revealed in His Word. Love for God or others that is not based on truth is just deluded emotionalism. But truth devoid of love leads to arrogance.

As I've mentioned before, my spiritual heroes are men who combine these two qualities: a fervent heart for God coupled with solid, biblical theology. John Calvin, Jonathan Edwards, Charles Spurgeon, and Martyn Lloyd-Jones were all men of this caliber. Their lives were dedicated to knowing and expounding God's Word of truth, but never in a cold, academic manner. They studied God's truth so that they and others would grow into a deeper love for God and others.

Of course, the Lord Jesus combined perfectly this balance between love and truth. In the very chapter in which He prayed that His followers would be unified, He also prayed that they may be sanctified by God's Word of truth (John 17:17, 21). The Apostle Paul also was a man marked by both love and truth. His prayer for the Philippian church, which was experiencing some friction between some of its members, is marked by a fine balance. He prays that they would abound in love; but, he adds that such love is inextricably bound up with real knowledge and all discernment. He is teaching us that:

Christians must grow in discerning love so that their godly lives give glory to God.

Paul's prayer shows us not only how we should be living, but also how we should be praying for other Christians. So often our prayers are devoid of solid or thoughtful content: "God bless the missionaries. God be with Aunt Suzy. God help Brother Bob." But Paul's prayers always reflect profound doctrine. They were never based just on feelings, but are always rich in theology as well.

Before we examine the content of this prayer, notice one other factor that gives needed balance to our Christian lives. In verse 6, Paul expressed his confidence that God, who began a good work in the Philippians, would complete the job. Those who are out of balance take such words and conclude, "Fine, then we don't need to do anything. God started it; God will complete it; we can sit back and watch Him do it apart from any effort on our part."

But Paul, who knew that it was God who started the work and God who would finish it, was still actively involved in the process of getting that work done! He prayed fervently for these people. He exhorted them and taught them. A proper belief in the sovereignty of God never leads to stoic passivity, but rather to diligent, fervent labor. And it never leads to prayerlessness. Rather, understanding God's sovereignty should move us to pray, since God uses prayer to accomplish His sovereign purpose. Let's examine Paul's prayer:

1. Biblical love for God and others is the supreme virtue of the Christian life.

You may have assumed that Paul's prayer is directed toward love of the brethren, but please notice that he does not state the object of love. Of course, love for God and love for others can't be separated. As John puts it, "God is love, and the one who abides in love abides in God, and God abides in him.... And this is the commandment we have from Him, that the one who loves God should love his brother also" (1 John 4:16, 21). Love is not optional for the believer. It is bound up with the very essence of being a Christian. As John again puts it, "We know that we have passed out of death in life, because we love the brethren. He who does not love abides in death" (1 John 3:14). Jesus summed up the Law with the two commandments, to love God and to love our neighbor (Matt. 22:37-40). If you are not growing in love for God and others, you're not growing.

But, what is biblical love? The word "love" conjures up warm, fuzzy, sentimental feelings of being nice all the time to everyone. But we must define love by Scripture, not by our cultural notions. Biblical love is never in opposition to truth, but rather is based on and is in line with truth. Biblical love is a caring, self-sacrificing commitment that seeks the highest good of the one loved. In our text, Paul says that ...

A.   Biblical love is bound up with knowledge and discernment.

We think of love as being undiscriminating. Discrimination and love seem like opposites. But Paul prays that the Philippians would grow in discerning love. Love is not blind. It does not close its eyes to reality. It is not a feeling devoid of content. Biblical love is related to true knowledge and it operates with careful discernment.

"*True knowledge*" is a single Greek word (*epignosis*) that refers to intensive or deep spiritual knowledge. The Greek scholar, J. B. Lightfoot, says that this word "is used especially of the knowledge of God and of Christ, as being the perfection of knowledge" (*St. Paul's Epistles to the Colossians and to Philemon* [Zondervan], p. 138. See Eph. 1:17; 4:13). Since God cannot be known except as He has revealed Himself, such true knowledge of God can only be obtained through His Word. Since God Himself is love, to grow in the true knowledge of God is to grow to understand what true love is.

This true knowledge of God as revealed in His Word is essential if you want to grow in love. We can't know love by looking at our culture. We can only know what love looks like by studying the character of God, especially as revealed in the Lord Jesus Christ, God in human flesh. Was Jesus always syrupy and sweet with people? Read Matthew 23, where He lays into the Pharisees! Notice how He sometimes confronts the disciples. Yet He is the epitome of love!

I've occasionally received criticism that I am lacking in love because I confront sin. A former elder's wife in California told me that I should get out of the pastorate because I was too much like Paul and not enough like Jesus! When I asked for clarification of that comment, she explained that Jesus was always nice and loving, but Paul was not like that! I'm not sure which translation she was reading! I don't deny that I need to grow in love. But confronting sin is not an evidence of a lack of love! Biblical love is based on the true knowledge of God.

Also, biblical love is bound up with *discernment.* This Greek noun occurs only here in the New Testament, but a related verb occurs in Hebrews 5:14: "But solid food is for the mature, who because of practice have their senses trained to discern good and evil." Since biblical love is both holy and based on truth, we cannot love properly if we lack discernment.

John MacArthur's recent book, *Reckless Faith* [Crossway Books], is a plea for discernment among American Christians, many of whom have abandoned this crucial quality. He shows how we have become anti-intellectual, trusting in feelings (as seen in the charismatic movement) or in tradition (as seen in the recent Catholic-Protestant rapprochement) and have thrown Scripture and sound reason to the wind. He defines discernment as "the ability to understand, interpret, and apply truth skillfully. Discernment is a cognitive act. Therefore no one who spurns right doctrine or sound reason can be truly discerning" (p. xv). Commenting on our text, he states,

> Those who think of faith as the abandonment of reason cannot be truly discerning. Irrationality and discernment are polar opposites. When Paul prayed that the Philippians' love would "abound still more and more in real *knowledge*

and all *discernment*" (Phil. 1:9, emphasis added), he was affirming the rationality of true faith. He also meant to suggest that knowledge and discernment necessarily go hand in hand with genuine spiritual growth.
Biblical faith, therefore, is rational. It is reasonable. It is intelligent. It makes good sense. And spiritual truth is meant to be rationally contemplated, examined logically, studied, analyzed, and employed as the only reliable basis for making wise judgments. That process is precisely what Scripture calls *discernment* (pp. *xv, xvi*).

The mood today is that if you are critical of anyone's doctrine or personal life, no matter how unbiblical it may be, you are not loving and you are arrogant to judge this person. Jesus' words, "Judge not, lest you be judged" (Matt. 7:1) are wrenched out of context and misapplied. If people would just keep reading, Jesus goes on to say, "Do not give what is holy to dogs, and do not throw your pearls before swine" (Matt. 7:6). How can you deter- mine if someone is a dog or swine if you don't make discerning judgments? A few verses later He warns us to beware of false prophets who come as wolves in sheep's clothing (Matt. 7:15). It takes a discerning sheep to see that this isn't a fellow-sheep whom we need to embrace, but a ravenous wolf we need to avoid!

Thus biblical love cannot be divorced from the true knowledge of God and from the discernment between truth and error and right and wrong that comes from a careful knowledge of Scripture.

B. Biblical love is a quality in which we must continually grow.

The Philippians were a loving people, as evidenced in their relationship with Paul. But he prayed that their love would abound still more and more. No one can say that they have arrived at perfect love for God and others.

This means that biblical love is something we need to work at constantly. Did you give any thought to it this week? Husbands, are you working at loving your wife? Wives, are you working at loving your husband? Parents, are you working at loving your kids? Kids, are you working at loving your parents? Singles, are you working at loving your roommate? It's a lifelong process.

One place to start is to study the many biblical references of the word "love." Jot down on a card and memorize Paul's great description of love in 1 Corinthians 13:4-7: "Love is patient, love is kind, and is not jealous; love does not brag and is not arrogant, does not act unbecomingly; it does not seek its own, is not provoked, does not take into account a wrong suffered, does not rejoice in unrighteousness, but rejoices with the truth; bears all things, believes all things, hopes all things, endures all things."

At the heart of biblical love is self-sacrifice. Christ loved us and gave Himself for us (Gal. 2:20; Eph. 5:25; John 3:16). So many sincere Christians have been sucked into the popular false teaching that we must build our own and our children's self-esteem. But this is diametrically opposed to Paul's prayer, that we may abound in biblical love, because self-sacrifice and self-esteem (or self-love) are opposites.

Don't misunderstand! To say that we should not build our children's self-esteem is not to say that we should be unloving toward them. In fact, we should esteem our children and others more highly than we do ourselves (Phil. 2:3-4). We should encourage them and give them proper affirmation, which is a part of biblical love. But the goal of such behavior is *not* to build their self-esteem, but rather to model Christ and encourage our kids to be like Him. If our children see us denying self to please our Lord, they will want to follow and serve Him by laying down their lives out of love for Him and for others. If our focus is to help our kids build their self-esteem, we're encouraging the inborn selfishness that dominates every fallen human heart.

Thus the heart of Paul's prayer is for us to grow in the supreme virtue of discerning love.

2. Biblical love results in godly living that gives glory to God.

Verses 10 & 11 are the result of verse 9 ("so that"). There are five aspects of godly living mentioned here:

A. Godly living involves proper priorities.

"... that you may approve the things that are excellent, ..." The NIV translates, "to discern what is best." Moffatt paraphrases, "Enabling you to have a sense of what is vital." Martyn Lloyd- Jones comments, "The difficulty in life is to know on what we ought to concentrate. The whole art of life, I sometimes think, is the art of knowing what to leave out, what to ignore, what to put on one side. How prone we are to dissipate our energies and to waste our time by forgetting what is vital and giving ourselves to second and third rate issues" (*The Life of Joy* [Baker], p. 54).

What is vital is that you focus your life on loving God and others based on true knowledge and discernment. If that is at the center of your life, everything else will fall into its proper place.

B. Godly living involves integrity.

"... in order to be sincere and blameless ...." These words do not imply perfection, which no one, including Paul, attains in this life (Phil. 3:13). Rather, the words mean to live with integrity. To be sincere means to be pure, unmixed, without hypocrisy. To be blameless means to walk without stumbling. Paul used the word "blameless" to describe his own conscience before God and men (Acts 24:16). Since God looks on the heart, to be sincere and blameless means to live openly before God, judging sin on the thought level. It means that you don't live a double life, putting on a good front around the church folks, but living another way when you're alone or with your family.

C. Godly living involves living in light of Christ's coming.

"... for the day of Christ; ..." The Christian who is growing in discerning love is living in light of Christ's soon coming, when we all must stand before Him. If you're living for personal happiness or fulfillment in this life, you will live for self and will not live in love for God and others. But if you realize that today you could be face to face with Christ, it motivates you to godly living, to self-sacrificing love.

D. Godly living involves bearing fruit through Jesus Christ.

"... having been filled with the fruit of righteousness which comes through Jesus Christ, ..." The instant we trust in Christ as Savior, God imputes His righteousness to our account, so that we have right standing with Him. But the Christian life is a process of growing in righteous character and deeds. As the word "fruit" implies, this is a process, not something instantaneous. The word picture also implies that it is the life of Christ working in and through us that produces the fruit (John 15:1-6). As we grow in the true knowledge of God and in discernment through His Word, the fruit of the Spirit, whose first characteristic is love, is produced in us. We will become "zealous for good deeds" (Titus 2:14). The final result will be:

E. Godly living results in glory and praise to God.

"... to the glory and praise of God." As we abound in discerning love, which leads to godly character and good deeds, God will be exalted in and through us, so that both we and others will praise Him for His grace and power. The ultimate goal of the Christian life is to glorify God and enjoy Him forever. He is glorified (made to look good as He truly is) when His people abound in discerning love.

Conclusion

Moffatt translates 1 Corinthians 14:1, "Make love your aim." Is your love for God and others abounding "still more and more in real knowledge and all discernment"? Is your growing love leading to godliness through proper priorities, integrity, living in light of Christ's coming, and bearing the fruit of righteousness, so that your life results in glory and praise to God? Let's all apply Paul's prayer first to ourselves, and then let's pray it for one another. If we grow in love rooted in true knowledge and discernment, we will avoid the winds of false doctrine that are blowing so many off course in our day.

Application Questions

1. Why must love be rooted in truth? What happens when it's not? Why must truth be coupled with love?

2. Can we have true Christian unity at the expense of truth (John 17:14-21; Eph. 4:3-6, 13)?

3. Why is it essential to determine what love is from Scripture rather than from our cultural ideas of love?

4. How can we know if we love God (John 14:21, 23; 1 John 5:3)?

5. How can we know if we love others properly (1 Cor. 13:4-7; 1 John 3:16-18; 4:7-21)?

Now I want you to know, brethren, that my circumstances have turned out for the greater progress of the gospel, so that my imprisonment in the cause of Christ has become well known throughout the whole praetorian guard and to everyone else, and that most of the brethren, trusting in the Lord because of my imprisonment, have far more courage to speak the word of God without fear. Some, to be sure, are preaching Christ even from envy and strife, but some also from good will; the latter do it out of love, knowing that I am appointed for the defense of the gospel; the former proclaim Christ out of selfish ambition rather than from pure motives, thinking to cause me distress in my imprisonment. What then? Only that in every way, whether in pretense or in truth, Christ is proclaimed; and in this I rejoice. Yes, and I will rejoice,

†   Philippians 1:12-18

HAPPINESS:
THROUGH CIRCUMSTANCES OR CHRIST?
Philippians 1:12-18

Everyone wants happiness, but most people seek it in the wrong way. They assume that happiness comes through good circumstances, so they set out to improve their circumstances. If they're single, they seek a spouse and a happy marriage. If they're married, but unhappy, they get a divorce and look for someone else who can make them happier. If they're married and childless, they seek to have children. If they're married with children who are giving them problems, they don't know what to do (since murder is not legal)! If they're poor, they seek to get rich. If they're rich, they discover that money doesn't give them what they're looking for. One wag said, "They say it's better to be poor and happy than rich and miserable. But couldn't something be worked out, such as being moderately wealthy and just a little moody?" (*Reader's Digest*, 9/82.)

Jesus explained how we can find lasting happiness, but in so doing He stood the world's way on its head: Lose your life for His sake and the gospel's and you'll find it. He said, "If anyone wishes to come after Me, let him deny himself, and take up his cross, and follow Me. For whoever wishes to save his life shall lose it; but whoever loses his life for My sake and the gospel's shall save it" (Mark 8:34, 35). He made the same point in the Sermon on the Mount, where He contrasted the pagans, who eagerly seek after the material comforts of life, with believers, who are to "seek first His kingdom and righteousness; and all these things shall be added unto you" (Matt. 6:33).

The Apostle Paul was a man who proved Jesus' words in the crucible of life. In our text, we find Paul in circumstances in which we could not fault him for being unhappy. Think of who he was God's chief apostle to the Gentiles. He was well-educated, experienced, influential. He had founded churches all over the Roman Empire. He had been used of God to pen much of our New Testament. He had endured much persecution and hardship in his labors for the Lord. By now he was over

60, at a time in life when a man looks forward to enjoying the fruits of his lifelong labors. Many American pastors by this time are looking forward to a relaxed schedule, a little more golf. If you're as successful in ministry as Paul was, you could expect to live off your book sales and speak at a lot of conferences and retreats.

But where was Paul? Instead of being out on the links or speaking under the pines at a retreat center, he was in prison in Rome, awaiting a trial that could result in his execution. He was not in the strictest confinement, in a dungeon (as he later was). He was in his own rented quarters, and his friends were allowed to visit him (Acts 28:30, 31). But he was chained to a Roman guard 24 hours of every day. He had already spent two years being confined in Caesarea without any crime on his part. He had suffered a shipwreck and near death on his trip to Rome. Not only that, but he was being unfairly criticized by a number of jealous pastors in Rome, who probably were saying things like, "If Paul had God's blessing in his life, do you think he would be in prison?" They were promoting their ministries at Paul's expense.

Paul's circumstances were enough to make any man unhappy, and yet we find him abounding with joy (1:18). What was his secret? How could Paul be filled with joy in these dismal circumstances? The answer is, he had put into practice the words of Jesus, that the way to find true life is to lose your life for the sake of Jesus and the gospel.

True happiness comes by proclaiming Christ in every situation.

Now maybe you're thinking, "That's a nice idea, but it doesn't apply to me. I'm not called to be an evangelist or preacher or missionary. I'm a simple layman. I try to earn a decent living and raise my family. But I'm not called to proclaim Christ as Paul was." But I contend that Jesus' words apply not only to the Apostle Paul, but to every Christian in every stratum of life. Whether you are a construction worker, a business executive, a housewife, a student, or whatever you do, your objective should be to lose your life for the sake of Christ and the gospel. In so doing, you will find the key to true life and happiness, no matter what trials or hardships you face.

There are two steps toward applying Jesus' words to your life, as

Paul did:

1. Say no to the self-life.

"Deny yourself and take up your cross" (Mark 8:34). "Lose [your] life for [Jesus'] sake and the gospel's" (Mark 8:35). Or, as Paul explains it (Gal. 2:20), "I have been crucified with Christ; and it is no longer I who live, but Christ lives in me; and the life which I now live in the flesh I live by faith in the Son of God, who loved me, and delivered Himself up for me." In Romans 8:12, 13 Paul put it this way: "So then, brethren, we are under obligation, not to the flesh [the old self], to live according to the flesh--for if you are living according to the flesh, you are about to die; but if by the Spirit you are putting to death the deeds of the body, you will live."

The Christian life is decidedly *not* a life lived for self, for personal fulfillment, for doing what we think will bring us pleasure and happiness. That is the way toward death! The Christian life is a life of daily, constant submission to the lordship of Jesus Christ in which, by the indwelling Holy Spirit, we say no to selfish desires and yes to the will of God. It means that we learn to submit every thought, desire, decision, attitude, action, and relationship to the question, "Does this please God?"

In our text, what is striking is Paul's almost total disregard of himself. The Philippians were rightly concerned about Paul's situation. They had sent Ephaphroditus to find out how Paul was doing. Was he suffering terribly in prison? Would he be acquitted and set free? Yet, as James Boice puts it, "In one deft sentence Paul shifts the legitimate interest of the Philippians from himself to the great undeterred purposes of God in history" (*Philippians: An Expositional Commentary* [Zondervan], p. 60). With Paul the main question was not, "What is happening to me?" but rather, "What is happening to the gospel?" His focus was not on self, but on Christ and the gospel.

It's amazing that Paul does not speak a word of complaint about his situation. He's not asking, "Why is this happening to me? I've served God faithfully all these years! I've always sought to do His will. Why this?" The modern approach would be to urge Paul to get in touch with his feelings: "How do you feel about the way God is treating you? Go ahead and be honest. Get out your anger and rage. God can take it! Tell Him how you feel!" If Paul answered, "I'm rejoicing and I'm determined to keep on rejoicing" (1:18) he would be accused of being in denial!

He would also be accused of being "in denial" about his feelings toward his critics! "How do you feel about the Christian leaders who are criticizing you, Paul? Don't you feel hurt, wounded? Don't you want to lash out at them?" "If they're preaching Christ, I rejoice that the gospel is going forth."

Who were these critics? Some commentators say that they were the Judaizers, those Jewish legalists who dogged Paul's steps, seeking to bring his converts under the Jewish law, especially circumcision, for salvation. Paul warns against this sect in Philippian 3. But these men Paul speaks of in 1:15a, 17 (the KJV reverses verses 16 & 17, but the strong weight of evidence is for the order in the NASB) could not have been the Judaizers, for several reasons.

These critics preached Christ (1:15a, 17), but the Judaizers preached another gospel, which is not a gospel (Gal. 1:6-9; 5:11). Paul rejoices in the message these critics were preaching (their message was true, even though their motives were wrong), but he wishes the Judaizers to be accursed because of their heresy (Gal. 1:8-9). Paul calls these men brethren, but he calls the Judaizers "false brethren" (Gal. 2:4). So these critics were apparently Christian pastors in Rome whose doctrine was correct, but whose hearts were wrong. They were jealous of Paul and selfishly ambitious to promote their own ministries. But, at least the message they preached was the true gospel. Paul would never rejoice at the preaching of false doctrine concerning something as crucial as the gospel.

I have found over the years that the most stinging criticism comes from fellow believers, not from the world. You expect the world to be hostile, but you also expect Christians to be on your side. Yet I have encountered the most hostility from those in the church, not from those outside. The Greek word translated "selfish ambition" was used of politicians building a personal following. Many in the church play politics to build a following. But it's not the way of self-denial and living for Christ.

So Paul was not complaining to God, and he shrugged off the criticism of these jealous preachers, because he was denying self. Also, as we'll see in our text for the next chapter (1:20, 21), Paul didn't even have a concern for whether he lived or died! If he got acquitted and lived, that would mean more useful service for Christ. If he got executed, he would be with Christ, which is better. But, he didn't consider his life of any account as dear to himself (Acts 20:24). Paul had said "no" to his self-life.

Lest you think that Paul was some sort of super-Christian, with a level of dedication that very few attain, I remind you that Jesus' words about denying yourself and taking up your cross apply to every person who wants to follow Him (Mark 8:34). Discipleship isn't an option for those who feel called to a life of hardship, who like a challenge. Discipleship is the *only option* for those who believe in Jesus. The only path for the true Christian is that of learning daily to say no to selfish desires and yes to the lordship of Jesus. The first step to happiness is to say no to the self-life.

2. Say yes to the gospel as first in your life.

Paul told the Corinthians, "I do all things for the sake of the gospel, that I may become a fellow partaker of it" (1 Cor. 9:23). The progress of the gospel must be our goal (note, "gospel" in 1:5, 7, 12, 16, 27 [twice]). If the progress of our happiness (comfort, success, etc.) is our goal, we will miss true happiness. With Paul, the progress of the gospel should be our main concern. Seek first to fulfill your own needs, and you'll come up empty. "Seek first the kingdom of God," and you will find that God meets your needs.

A. Saying yes to the gospel as first requires understanding and believing the gospel.

I'm amazed at how many people who attend evangelical churches cannot begin to explain the basics of the gospel to another person. It makes me wonder if they even understand, let alone believe in, the gospel. The gospel is not, "If you're having some problems in your life, invite Jesus into your heart and He will help you work out your problems." Nor is the gospel, "If you'd like a happier life, try Jesus." That kind of approach trivializes the gospel by missing the key problem the gospel addresses.

The main problem every person faces is that his sin has alienated him from a holy God and that he is under God's wrath or judgment. If he dies in this condition, he will spend eternity in hell, under the just condemnation of God. The good news ("gospel") is that God has not left us in this terrible situation. Nor does He expect us to earn our way back to

Him, which no one can do, because it requires perfect righteousness. Rather, "God demonstrates His own love toward us, in that while we were yet sinners, Christ died for us" (Rom. 5:8).

Jesus Christ, the sinless Son of God, met the requirement of God's Law in His perfect obedience to the Father. He went to the cross as the Lamb of God, to take away the sin of the world (John 1:29). God did not leave Jesus in the tomb, but raised Him bodily from the dead, victorious over sin, death, and hell. God offers to every person a full pardon from sin and total reconciliation to Himself based on what Christ did on the cross. The only way to receive this deliverance from God's judgment is to believe in the Lord Jesus Christ (Acts 16:31; Eph. 2:8, 9).

To believe the gospel is not merely to give intellectual assent to the facts of the gospel. To believe the gospel means to commit your life, both now and for eternity, to the Lord Jesus Christ as your Savior from sin. You can say that you believe that an airplane will carry you from Phoenix to Los Angeles, but you don't truly believe it until you get on board. Only then is your faith effective in transporting you from Phoenix to L.A. You can give mental assent to the truth of the gospel, but it is not effective in transferring you from Satan's domain of darkness to the kingdom of God's beloved Son, in whom you have redemption, the forgiveness of sins (Col. 1:13, 14) until you fully commit yourself by faith to the person and work of Jesus Christ.

Thus saving faith necessarily includes repentance (turning) from sin. It means entrusting yourself to Jesus as Savior and Lord. Saving faith is a commitment of all of myself of which I'm aware to all of Jesus whom I know. From that point, I grow in awareness of my own selfishness and sin, which I relinquish to Christ's lordship; and I grow in my awareness of the person and work of Christ, to which I yield. But there is no such thing as believing in Jesus as my Savior, and then living the rest of my life to please myself. We must understand and believe that the gospel is absolutely free, but it rightly demands total commitment.

B. Saying yes to the gospel as first requires proclaiming the gospel through your walk and words in every situation.

Here was Paul, under arrest, chained to Roman guards. Most of us would have thought, "What a restriction for proclaiming Christ!" But Paul thought, "What an opportunity! I've got a captive audience!" Every four hours or so the guard changed. They thought Paul was their captive, but Paul saw them as his captives!

These were rough, worldly Roman soldiers, used to guarding tough, accused criminals. Imagine the difference they saw in this prisoner! For one thing, his *attitude* was different. He never complained! He never bad-mouthed the system. Instead, he was always singing, praying, and praising God. All sorts of interesting people came to visit him, some from the far corners of the empire. They heard him dictate letters to churches, answering their questions with wisdom. They heard him talk about God and how God wants us to live. They heard him pray specific, heartfelt, personal prayers to a God who was very alive.

Besides, this prisoner took an interest in the guards as persons. He asked about their families, their backgrounds, and their thoughts about various issues. He prayed for their needs. And he told them how they could know the living God and have their sins forgiven through faith in His risen Son. Some of these rough soldiers began getting saved, and they talked to other guards. Word spread beyond the Praetorian guard even to the members of Caesar's household, some of whom believed (Phil. 4:22).

Paul's proclamation of Christ through his attitude and words in this difficult situation not only resulted in witness to these lost soldiers, but it also encouraged many of the Roman Christians. Previously, they had lacked the courage to bear witness of Christ for fear of being laughed at or persecuted. But when they saw the power of the gospel for salvation to these soldiers, and even to those in Caesar's household, they took courage and began to talk fearlessly to others about God's Word (1:14).

Our walk (especially, our attitude) always has an effect, not only on the lost, but also on the Lord's people. If we're cheerfully trusting in the loving sovereignty of God in the midst of trials, as Paul did, we proclaim the reality of faith in Christ both to the lost and to the saved. Lost people will want to know why we're different, why we don't complain like everyone else. The Lord's people who are discouraged will see our faith in God in the midst of trials and be encouraged to trust Him and bear witness for Him.

Many years ago I was praying for more of God's power in my life. I had in mind things like speaking in tongues, the power to see God do miraculous healings, and that sort of thing. In my Bible reading I came across Colossians 1:10-12, where Paul prayed (verse 10) that his readers would walk in a manner worthy of the Lord, pleasing Him in all respects, bearing fruit in every good work, and increasing in the knowledge of God. Then I read in verses 11 & 12, "strengthened with all power, according to His glorious might, for the attaining of all miracles, signs, and wonders"? Wait a minute! That's not what it says! "For the attaining of all steadfastness and patience; joyously giving thanks to the Father, who has qualified us to share in the inheritance of the saints in the light."

I thought, "The only time you need steadfastness and patience is when you're going *through* trials, not when you're instantly, miraculously delivered." God is saying that His mighty power is manifested by our having a thankful, joyous attitude in the midst of trials, not by being miraculously delivered from them.

Conclusion

Some of you, like Paul, are in situations you never planned to be in. He planned to go to Rome, but not in chains! Maybe you're in a confining situation where you feel bound by chains. It may be a difficult marriage which you didn't plan on. Maybe you're chained to a house full of kids. It may be a family problem. It could be a boring or a difficult job or the lack of a job. It could be a personal problem over which you have no control--a health problem or a situation that you've been thrust into with no choice on your part.

What should you do? *Make your chains a channel for proclaiming Christ.* How? First, *say no to the self life*, to seeking your own way, your own happiness, your own will. Say no to a grumbling, complaining spirit. Second, *say yes to the gospel as first in your life*; by understanding and believing it; and, by proclaiming Jesus Christ in every situation by your cheerful attitude of trust in Him and, as He gives opportunity, by your words of witness. You'll find that by so losing your life for the sake of Christ and the gospel, you'll find true happiness both for time and for eternity.

Application Questions

1. Does denying self mean that we can never do things we enjoy in life? What does it mean?

2. How can Christians break free from the pursuit of circumstantial happiness? Is it wrong to seek to improve our circumstances?

3. Why is the message, "If you've got problems, come to Christ" inadequate as the gospel? What is the core issue of the gospel?

4. How does "putting the gospel first" fit in with a job, family, etc.? Can every Christian seek first God's kingdom? How?

...for I know that this will turn out for my deliverance through your prayers and the provision of the Spirit of Jesus Christ, according to my earnest expectation and hope, that I will not be put to shame in anything, but that with all boldness, Christ will even now, as always, be exalted in my body, whether by life or by death. For to me, to live is Christ and to die is gain. But if I am to live on in the flesh, this will mean fruitful labor for me; and I do not know which to choose. But I am hard-pressed from both directions, having the desire to depart and be with Christ, for that is very much better; yet to remain on in the flesh is more necessary for your sake. Convinced of this, I know that I will remain and continue with you all for your progress and joy in the faith, so that your proud confidence in me may abound in Christ Jesus through my coming to you again.

† Philippians 1:19-26

WHAT ARE YOU LIVING FOR?
Philippians 1:19-26

A young man came to W. E. Gladstone when he was Prime Minister of England and said, "Mr. Gladstone, I would appreciate your giving me a few minutes in which I might lay before you my plans for the future. I would like to study law." "Yes," said the great statesman, "and what then?"

"Then, sir, I would like to gain entrance to the Bar of England." "Yes, young man, and what then?"

"Then, sir, I hope to have a place in Parliament, in the House of Lords." "Yes, young man, what then?" pressed Gladstone.

"Then I hope to do great things for Britain." "Yes, young man, and what then?"

"Then, sir, I hope to retire and take life easy." "Yes, young man, and what then?" he tenaciously asked.

"Well, then, Mr. Gladstone, I suppose I will die." "Yes, young man, and what then?" The young man hesitated and then said, "I never thought any further than that, sir."

Looking at the young man sternly and steadily, Gladstone said, "Young man, you are a fool. Go home and think life through!" (Told by Leonard Griffith, *This is Living* [Abingdon Press], pp. 48, 49.)

What are *you* living for? Your answer to that question will determine the direction of your life. If your purpose is wrong, your direction will be wrong. If your purpose is vague or fuzzy, your direction will be fuzzy. If you don't know your purpose, you'll just be swept along by the currents of our age, doing what seems to bring you happiness. It is crucial that you be clear and correct in answering the question, "What are you living for?" As the story of the young man and Mr. Gladstone illustrates, the correct answer to that question must include some thought about the fact of death and what lies beyond. It must also include consideration of the uncertainty of life, so that whenever death may come, it doesn't thwart your purpose.

The Apostle Paul was clear and focused on his purpose. I believe that the purpose for which he lived is the only purpose that takes eternity into account, so that whether we live a long life or whether it is cut short, that purpose will be fulfilled. In short, Paul's purpose is, "For to me, to live is Christ" (1:21).

As Martyn Lloyd-Jones points out (*The Life of Joy* [Baker], pp. 85, 86), that sentence is not only a statement of the apostle's true experience, but also it is a standard of judgment which confronts us with the most thorough test of our Christian faith we will ever encounter. Every person who professes Christ as Savior must grapple with the question, "Can I honestly say, 'For me, to live is Christ'?" If I can say, "Yes," then I have also answered that fundamental question, "What about death and what lies beyond?" It will be gain for me.

If for me, to live is Christ, then for me to die will be gain.

Paul's purpose statement means,

1. Every Christian should aim at being able to say truthfully, "For me, to live is Christ."

Can you truthfully say that? Can I? We need to be honest in examining our lives before the Lord. To bring this purpose into focus, we need to answer two questions: *What does it mean to "live Christ"?* and, *How do we "live Christ"?*

WHAT DOES IT MEAN TO "LIVE CHRIST"?

A. To "live Christ" means to live in union with Christ, so that He becomes my all in all.

The concept of being "in Christ" was vital to Paul's understanding of what it means to be a Christian. He addresses this letter "to all the saints *in Christ Jesus* who are in Philippi" (1:1). The instant a person truly believes in Jesus Christ as Savior, he is joined organically in a living, real union with Christ the Head as a member of His body, the church. To be "in Christ" means that all that is true of Christ is true of the believer. As Paul writes (Rom. 6:10, 11), "For the death that He died, He died to sin, once for all; but the life that He lives, He lives to God. Even so consider yourselves to be dead to sin, but alive to God in Christ Jesus." The believer is in union with Christ.

While that is our true standing before God, we must grow in our experience of the reality of that standing, so that in our daily lives, we live in *fellowship with Christ*, communing with Him and depending on Him for everything. It means growing to *know Christ* intimately (Phil. 3:10). It means growing to *love Christ* with all of my heart, soul, mind, and strength (Mark 12:30). It means submitting all of my thoughts, emotions, words, and deeds to the *lordship of Christ*, so that I seek to please Him in all respects (Col. 1:10). It means growing to experience Christ as my *"all in all"* (Eph. 1:23; Col. 3:11). Every aspect of life must be centered around the Lord Jesus Christ. The glorious *person of Christ*, and nothing less, *is* the Christian life.

Of course, our experience of "living Christ" is a process that is never fully realized in this life. As Paul says (Phil. 3:12), "Not that I have already obtained it, or have already become perfect, but I press on in order that I may lay hold of that for which also I was laid hold of by Christ Jesus." Even the most godly Christians have times when Christ seems distant and the soul is dull and sluggish. In this life we never reach a point where we are not tempted by sin, where we do not have to battle the lusts of the flesh, the lusts of the eyes, and the boastful pride of life (1 John 2:16). But, each of us who are truly children of God will have as our focus to live in an experiential way the fact of our union with Christ, so that He becomes our all in all.

In 1991 I was struggling with the issue of how psychology and Christianity fit together (if at all). I previously believed that the best insights of psychology could be integrated with Christianity ("all truth is God's truth"). In my devotional reading, I came across the chapter, "Christ is All," in J. C. Ryle's classic, *Holiness* [James Clarke & Co.]. Ryle hammers from every direction the practical truth that Christ is all for the believer, both in salvation and in sanctification.

As I read that chapter, it came into focus for me that one of the main problems with psychology (even the "Christian version") is that it undermines the all-sufficiency of Christ for the believer. It is saying that Christ is not enough to meet the needs of our soul, that we must add worldly wisdom. About the same time, John MacArthur's book, *Our Sufficiency in Christ* [Word] came out, and it clinched the point for me. Christ really is all we need. We must grow to know experientially what it means to "live Christ."

      B. To "live Christ" means to exalt Christ through everything we do.

      "... that with all boldness, Christ shall even now, as always, be exalted in my body, whether by life or by death" (1:20). This is just another way of stating the great goal of the Christian life, which is to glorify God by everything we are and do. To glorify God, in common language, means to make God look good, as He truly is.

      We may think, "Christ is the Almighty God, Creator of the universe. How can I possibly exalt or glorify Him?" Think of Him as being a distant star. It may be more brilliant than our own sun, but to the human eye, it is just a dim speck in the night sky. To many in this world, Christ is that way. He is the very splendor of God, brighter than a million suns. But the world doesn't see Him that way. The believer is to be a telescope to bring the truth about Christ into view for the unbeliever. Through us, and especially through how we handle trials, Christ is magnified to a skeptical, unbelieving world.

      In view of Paul's circumstances, it is remarkable that his main focus was not on getting released from prison, but rather on exalting Christ. Whether he lived or died wasn't the issue; all that mattered to Paul was that he exalted Christ. In verse 19, he says, "I know that this [situation] will turn out for my deliverance." The word "deliverance" is, literally, "salvation." Some interpret this to mean that Paul was hopeful of being released from prison. But verse 20 precludes this view, because Paul acknowledges that he may well be executed.

      Paul's words in verse 19 are verbatim from the Greek Old Testament of Job 13:16. In that context, Job was on trial by his "friends," and he wanted to be "saved" from being found to be a hypocrite, that is, he wanted to be vindicated. In the same way, Paul is saying that as the Philippians prayed for him and as God's Spirit enabled him, he would be delivered from denying Christ and disgracing the gospel at his trial before Caesar. Thus he would be vindicated in the ultimate court, before God, by exalting Christ, even through martyrdom if need be. The only cause for shame to Paul would be not to hear "well done" from Christ when he stood before Him.

Verse 26 does not mean that the Philippians would exalt Paul. It should read, "So that your reason for boasting [or, exulting] may abound in Christ Jesus in connection with me through my coming to you." Paul means that if their prayers are answered by Paul being released so that he can be with them, they will boast in Christ, not in Paul.

Note (1:20) that the way we exalt Christ is through our *bodies*. This is a comprehensive and practical concept. It means that we may either exalt Christ or bring shame to His name by our attitudes, our words, and our behavior. How do you use your eyes? A lustful glance at a woman or even at a sexy picture does not exalt Christ. How do you use your ears? Do you listen to music that defiles you or music that exalts Christ? Do you listen to gossip or slander? How do you use your tongue? Your hands? Your feet? Your countenance? Do you use your body in purity or for sensuality? What about your personal appearance? Do you dress to be seductive or to attract attention to yourself? Or, do you exalt Christ? To "live Christ" means to exalt Him through everything we do.

C. To "live Christ" means to die to selfish desires in order to live to serve others for Jesus' sake.

Paul's desire was to check out. He really wanted to depart and be with Christ. But, he also realized that the Philippians and others needed his ministry. So he was willing to deny his desires for the sake of serving others for Christ's sake. Of course, the final decision as to whether Paul lived or died rested with the Lord. But Paul was willing to live on in fruitful service if that's what the Lord wanted for him to do. Paul's focus suggests two applications:

First, if you're not denying self in order to serve Christ, you are not "living Christ"; you're living for self. Many people today have the notion that Christ is there to serve me, rather than that I am to serve Christ. They think the church is here to meet their needs, and if it doesn't they drop out of church or try to find one that better meets their needs. We need to get back to the biblical truth, that we have been saved to serve Christ. If everyone who attends this church had this mind-set, we'd have a waiting list to teach

Sunday School! What a radical thought!

Second, Christians should challenge the American notion of retirement. The idea that when you finally reach a point where you don't have to work, you're free to live for self and pleasure is contrary to Scripture. Any time the Lord gives us we are to manage for Him, seeking first His kingdom and righteousness. As long as He gives us health and strength, we should ask, "How can I serve Him?" Being freed from a job should mean that you're free to spend more time furthering the Lord's work. Give your time to the church or to a mission. Consider going to a foreign country to help out in the cause of Christ. Charles Simeon, a British preacher of the past century, worked long and hard for Christ. Late in life he said, "I cannot but run with all my might, for I am close to the goal" (cited by H. C. G. Moule, *Philippian Studies* [CLC], p. 75).

Thus, to "live Christ" means to live in union with Him, so that He is my all in all; to exalt Him in all I do; and, to die to self so as to serve Him.

HOW DO WE "LIVE CHRIST"?

I trust that the question has been answered for the most part by the answer to the first question. We "live Christ" by daily fellowship with Him, by seeking to exalt Him, by dying to self in order to serve Him. But also,

A. We "live Christ" by making that our constant aim.

Paul clearly was determined to "live Christ" as his sole aim. He expresses it elsewhere in slightly differing terms, but with the same idea: "I do all things for the sake of the gospel" (1 Cor. 9:23); "whatever things were gain to me, those things I have counted as loss for the sake of Christ" (Phil. 3:7); "... one thing I do: ... I press on toward the goal for the prize of the upward call of God in Christ Jesus" (Phil. 3:13, 14). Christ was Paul's constant aim.

As Christians, we need honestly to evaluate our lives in light of this aim. It's easy to fall into living for good things, but not for the best. God graciously blesses us with our families, friends, homes, possessions, work, leisure enjoyments. But if we're not careful, these good *things* become the things for which we're living. Even those of us in vocational ministry can begin living for our ministries. We need to keep asking ourselves, "What if this thing (person, activity) were taken from me?" Certainly, it would be difficult if, like Job, I lost my children, my health, and my possessions. But if I'm truly living for Christ, I will be able to come through any tragedy without despair, because He can't be taken from me. So I must constantly evaluate my life by asking, "Is Christ at the center? Is He my all in all?"

B. We "live Christ" through prayer and the provision of the Holy Spirit.

Paul was a man of prayer, but he also freely solicited the prayers of others for him (1:19). We tend to think of Paul as being naturally bold, but he often asked for prayer that he would be bold in his witness, because he knew that he was weak (see Eph. 1:19, 20; Col. 4:3, 4; 2 Thess. 3:1, 2). To "live Christ" we need much prayer!

But also, Paul needed "the provision of the Spirit of Jesus Christ" (1:19). The Christian life is impossible to live in the power of the flesh. We must walk by the Spirit every day, depending on Him for His strength. Why does Paul here say, "the Spirit of Jesus Christ"? He may mean, the Spirit who was given to us by Christ. Or, he may be describing the Spirit in this way because Jesus, in facing His trial and execution, bore faithful witness by relying on the Spirit. Paul was facing possible execution and wanted to be a faithful witness. This same Spirit is available to us so that we can "live Christ" in every situation, no matter how difficult. Living Christ must be our aim.

2. If we have sought to "live Christ," then to die will be gain.

In the next chapter, I'll deal more with the subject of how death will be gain for the believer. For now I'll make just a few comments. Note that for Paul, to go on living or to die is not a choice between the lesser of two evils. Paul didn't view life as a difficult trial to be endured, with death being a difficult thing as well, but at least a release. Rather, he viewed life as a progressive joy with Christ and death as even greater joy, because he would see Christ face to face and be with Him for eternity.

So a Christian has the best of both worlds! Even if we suffer now, we have Christ to strengthen, sustain, comfort, and encourage us. If Christ is real to our soul, what more could we want? And, the instant we die we are present with the Lord for all eternity, freed from all sin and pain and death! Sure, it is sad for those left behind. We miss our loved ones who have gone to be with Christ. But we have God's promise, that if "Jesus died and rose again, even so God will bring with Him those who have fallen asleep in Jesus. For this we say to you by the word of the Lord, that we who are alive, and remain until the coming of the Lord, shall not precede those who have fallen asleep. For the Lord Himself will descend from heaven with a shout, with the voice of the archangel, and with the trumpet of God; and the dead in Christ shall rise first. Then we who are alive and remain shall be caught up together with them in the clouds to meet the Lord in the air, and thus we shall always be with the Lord" (1 Thess. 4:14-17). If we have sought to "live Christ," then dying will be gain because we'll be with Him! We can't lose!

Conclusion

In Lewis Carroll's *Alice in Wonderland*, Alice asks the Cheshire Cat, "Would you tell me, please, which way I ought to go from here?" The Cat replies, "That depends a good deal on where you want to get to." "I don't much care where--" says Alice. "Then it doesn't matter which way you go," says the Cat. "You're sure to get *somewhere*--if you only walk long enough."

Where do you want to get to? If you want to get to heaven, then you need to consider the question, "What am I living for?" Complete the sentence: "For me, to live is _____." What? Money? Success? Happiness? Pleasure? Fun? Good times? Family? Self? If your answer is any of the above, then to die will be a terrible loss, not a gain. But if, with Paul, you can honestly say as you evaluate your life, "For me, to live is Christ," then you can also say with all the confidence of God's Word behind you, "to die is gain!"

Application Questions

1. Honestly complete the sentence: For me, to live is _____?

2. Is it overly simplistic to say, "Christ is all we need for our emotional and psychological wholeness"?

3. What are some of the implications of "exalting Christ" through our bodies?

4. Agree/disagree: If you aren't serving Christ, you're living for self?

...for I know that this will turn out for my deliverance through your prayers and the provision of the Spirit of Jesus Christ, according to my earnest expectation and hope, that I will not be put to shame in anything, but that with all boldness, Christ will even now, as always, be exalted in my body, whether by life or by death. For to me, to live is Christ and to die is gain. But if I am to live on in the flesh, this will mean fruitful labor for me; and I do not know which to choose. But I am hard-pressed from both directions, having the desire to depart and be with Christ, for that is very much better; yet to remain on in the flesh is more necessary for your sake. Convinced of this, I know that I will remain and continue with you all for your progress and joy in the faith, so that your proud confidence in me may abound in Christ Jesus through my coming to you again.

† Philippians 1:19-26

A CHRISTIAN PERSPECTIVE ON DEATH
Philippians 1:19-26

In our last chapter, I covered these verses with the emphasis on the great truth of the theme verse, "For to me, to live is Christ." In this chapter, I want to deal with the second half of the verse, "to die is gain." If I were to ask what word you associate with the word "death," and if you were not familiar with Philippians 1:21, I venture to say that the word "gain" would not come to mind. We think of death as a terrible loss, not a gain. Sometimes, if the person was suffering a great deal, we say that death was merciful, since it released them from their pain. But normally, we view death as tragic and we go to great effort and expense to hang on to life for as long as possible.

Also, we tend to avoid thinking or talking about death unless it is absolutely necessary. When author William Saroyan was within days of his own death from cancer in 1981, he issued this statement to the Associated Press: "Everybody has got to die, but I have always believed an exception would be made in my case. *Now* what?" No doubt he was speaking with his tongue in cheek, but he brought out what we all tend to think, that "somehow an exception will be made in my case." Since it is unpleasant to contemplate, we put off thinking about it until it seems inescapable.

But, as has often been stated, a person is not ready to live unless he is ready to die. To live properly, we must live purposefully, and always in view of both the certainty of death and the uncertainty of when it will occur. Many of the great Christians of the past thought often about death. Martin Luther said, "Even in the best of health we should have death always before our eyes [so that] we will not expect to remain on this earth forever, but will have one foot in the air, so to speak" (source unknown). Jonathan Edwards, as a young man, wrote down 70 resolutions which he read weekly to help keep his life focused. Number 9 was, "Resolved, to think much, on all occasions, of my dying, and of the common circumstances which attend death" (*The Works of Jonathan Edwards* [Banner of Truth], vol. 1, "Memoirs," p. xx). The Puritan preacher, Richard Baxter, who lived with chronic bodily illness, said, "I preach as though I ne'er should preach again, and as a dying man to dying men."

I submit that you cannot live the Christian life properly unless you understand the Christian perspective on death. Our views of death must be based on the truthfulness of God's revelation to us in His Word, not on the speculations of people devoid of God's Word.

As I developed in the last chapter, the apostle Paul was clear on his purpose: "For to me, to live is Christ." That is the only purpose that adequately takes into account the reality of death and the fact that it could occur at any moment. And, the person who can truly say, "For me, to live is Christ," can also confidently say, "to die is gain."

For the Christian, to die is gain.

But, what does this mean? We first must consider what ...

"TO DIE IS GAIN" DOES NOT MEAN:

1. "To die is gain" does not mean that a Christian should desire death because he hates life.

Paul did not hate life. To the contrary, he was filled with joy, even though his circumstances were difficult (1:18). He viewed life as sweet fellowship with Christ and the joy of serving Christ. So he was not viewing life as tough and death as escape or relief. Sometimes when life is difficult, or when a person suffers from a chronic, painful disease, he longs for relief and may be tempted even to take his own life. Sometimes even godly men get into such a state of depression that they would rather die than live. Moses (Num. 11:15), Elijah (1 Kings 19:4), Jeremiah (Jer. 20:14-18), and Jonah (Jon. 4:3, 8) all hit low points where they asked God to take their lives.

But suicide is never God's will for anyone. It does not exalt Christ, as Paul here wants his death to do. It is always a selfish act, done in disregard of those left behind to grieve. It usurps the sovereignty of God who has a fruitful purpose for every believer's life. Thus it would be grossly wrong to interpret Paul's words as a warrant for suicide.

Christians should love life and view it as an opportunity to serve the Lord thankfully. It is not wrong to seek to extend our lives through proper medical procedures when we face a life-threatening illness. Because of modern medicine, there are difficult decisions that we may have to face for ourselves or with loved ones. It's not always clear where to draw the line. As a general rule, if a medical procedure will not restore a person to life, but only prolongs the process of dying, then it probably should not be used. But as Christians, our motive for wanting to extend life should be so that we can further serve the Lord, not just so that we can enjoy ourselves.

But, the point is, God wants us to live life to the fullest, to serve Him joyfully as long as we have life. Paul was not suicidal or morbid. But he was expendable. He is saying here, that if God were to call him to heaven, that suited him just fine, because he knew he would be with the Lord.

2. "To die is gain" does not mean that a Christian should not grieve over the death of loved ones.

Until Christ returns, death is still our enemy that robs us of the presence of our loved ones. Scripture doesn't condemn grieving; in fact, it tells us to "weep with those who weep" (Rom. 12:15). Jesus wept with Mary and Martha at Lazarus' tomb, even though He knew He was about to raise him from the dead (John 11:35). As Christians, we do not grieve as those who have no hope (1 Thess. 4:13), but we still do grieve.

It is not unspiritual to grieve or weep at the death of a loved one. In two places in Scripture (that I know of) people were forbidden to grieve. When Aaron's sons disobediently offered "strange fire" on the altar, and the Lord struck them dead, Moses told Aaron and his surviving sons not to grieve for them, but to allow the rest of the people to grieve (Lev. 10:1-7). Apparently their grief would have given the impression that Aaron and his other sons were on the side of the sons who died, over against the Lord. The other occasion where grief was forbidden was when God suddenly took Ezekiel's wife. God told Ezekiel he could groan silently, but he was not to shed tears or grieve outwardly, as a sign of the impending judgment on Judah (Ezek. 24:15-24). But clearly, this was an exceptional situation. The norm is for Christians to grieve, and it is not a sign of weakness.

Thus when Paul says that "to die is gain," he does not mean that Christians should desire death because they hate life; nor, that we should not grieve over the death of loved ones.

"TO DIE IS GAIN" DOES MEAN:

1. "To die is gain" means that a Christian should view death as a means of exalting Christ.

Whether he lived or died, Paul's aim was to exalt Christ (1:20). If, by his faithful witness in dying, Paul could bear witness to the hope of the gospel, then he was ready to go. The time of death, for the believer, should be a time of bearing witness to the saving grace of the Lord Jesus Christ. Christians should "die well."

During the last four years of the reign of Bloody Mary in England (1555-1558), at least 288 people were burned at the stake because they refused to give up their Protestant beliefs and confess Mary's Catholicism. These faithful martyrs viewed their deaths as a means of exalting Christ. The first to die was a godly pastor named John Rogers. He had not been allowed to see his family while he was held in prison. On the way to his execution, his wife and ten children stood by the road. He was hardly allowed to stop and say farewell. As he marched to the stake, he calmly repeated Psalm 51. The French ambassador who witnessed the execution wrote that Rogers went to death as if he was walking to his wedding (J. C. Ryle, *Light from Old Times* [Evangelical Press], p. 23). In a sense, he was!

The second martyr, Bishop John Hooper, was entreated with many tears by a friend whom he had led to Christ, to recant and thus spare his life. The friend urged him to remember that "life was sweet and death was bitter." Hooper replied, "Eternal life is more sweet, and eternal death is more bitter" (p. 25).

The third Reformer to die, Rowland Taylor, was sent from London to the town where he had been pastor, to be burned in front of his former church members. When he got within two miles of the town, the sheriff asked him how he felt. He replied, "God be praised, Master Sheriff, never better. For now I am almost at home. I lack but just two stiles to go over, and I am even at my Father's house." As his church members lined the streets and greeted him with tears and lamentations, he repeatedly said, "I have preached to you God's Word and truth, and am come this day to seal it with my blood" (p. 27).

The fourth martyr, Bishop Robert Farrar, told a friend before his execution that if he saw him once stir in the fire from the pain of his burning, he need not believe the doctrines he had taught. By God's strength, he stood in the flames holding out his hands until they were burned to stumps, until a bystander in mercy struck him on the head to put an end to his sufferings (p. 29).

The fifth to die was John Bradford, age 35. At the stake, after kissing it, he held his hands toward heaven and cried, "O England, England, repent thee of they sins! Beware of idolatry; beware of false Antichrists! Take heed they do not deceive you!" Then he turned to a young man about to be executed with him and said, "Be of good comfort, brother; for we shall have a merry supper with the Lord this night."

I won't tell you of all 288, although I could tell of many others whose courage and witness exalted Christ in their deaths. But let me tell you of one other, the ninth, Archbishop of Canterbury, Thomas Cranmer. His story was different in that he stood firm through his trial and in prison for a long while. But, in the final month of his life, his courage failed. Under intense pressure, he signed a paper renouncing the doctrines of the Reformation and embracing Catholicism. But, his persecutors hated him so much that they made the mistake of resolving to burn him in spite of his recanting. But what they didn't know was that while he awaited execution, he repented of what he had done.

On March 21, 1556, he was brought to St. Mary's Church, like Samson before the Philistines, to make sport of him. I'm sorry to say that a man named Cole preached the sermon, and then Cranmer was invited to declare his Catholic faith. To the utter shock of his Catholic captors, he boldly renounced Catholicism, declared the Pope to be Antichrist, and rejected the doctrine of transubstantiation. In a frenzy, his enemies hurried him out of the church and to the stake. As the flames curled around him, he steadily held into the fire his right hand that had sinned by signing the recantation, and said, "This unworthy right hand." He held his left hand up toward heaven as he died (pp. 35-38).

We may not have to die a painful martyr's death, but we should view our death as a time to exalt the Savior, both by our attitudes and our words. Then, to die will be gain.

2. "To die is gain" means that a Christian's death leads to the return on his investment.

"To die is gain." Paul had counted everything else as loss for the sake of Christ (3:7), and had invested his entire life in the goal of knowing and serving Christ. Death would usher him into the Lord's presence where he would hear, "Well done, good and faithful servant. Enter the joy of your Master." In light of the reality of Christ's victory over death through His resurrection, Paul wrote (1 Cor. 15:58), "Be steadfast, immovable, always abounding in the work of the Lord, knowing that your toil is not in vain in the Lord." Death brings you to eternal rewards!

Toil for the things of this earth which will perish is in vain, because you won't take any of it with you. An unbeliever's life, even the life of a powerful, wealthy unbeliever, is like the wake of an ocean liner--impressive for the moment, but quickly gone. As a wall plaque we had near our front door when I was a child said, "Only one life, 'twill soon be past; only what's done for Christ will last." Death opens the door for us to receive the promised, rich returns on all that we have invested for Christ.

3. "To die is gain" means that a Christian's death frees him from earthly labors, trials, and temptations.

Paul had worked hard and suffered much for the cause of Christ. His body had endured one stoning, numerous beatings, several imprisonments, three shipwrecks, frequent dangers, many sleepless nights, often in hunger and thirst, in cold and exposure, plus the many concerns he bore for the work (2 Cor. 11:23-29). I don't doubt but what he was tired and was ready for the Lord to say, "Come on home to your rest."

Paul calls death "to depart" (1:23). The word was used of soldiers taking down their tents to move on. Paul says that at death our tent (our body) is taken down, while our spirit goes to be with the Lord (2 Cor. 5:1-8). Sailors used the word to describe a ship being loosed from its moorings to set sail. At death the believer sets sail from this world, but safely arrives at heaven's shore. It was also a political word, describing the freeing of a prisoner. This body holds us prisoner to various temptations and weaknesses, but death sets us free (Rom. 7 & 8). The word was also used by farmers, meaning to unyoke the oxen when their work was over. Death means laying down the burdens and concerns of our labors for Christ here, and to join Him in that place where there will be no death, no mourning, no crying, and no pain (Rev. 21:4). (The above word study adapted from Warren Wiersbe, *Be Joyful* [Victor Books], pp. 38, 39.)

Robert Moffatt, pioneer missionary to Africa in the last century, said, "We'll have all eternity to celebrate our victories, but only one short hour before sunset to win them." We should work hard for Christ now, but to die will be gain because our work will be over and we shall be like Jesus, because we shall see Him as He is (1 John 3:2).

4. "To die is gain" means that at death, a Christian goes immediately to be with Christ.

Paul says that when he departs, he will "be with Christ," which is "very much better" (1:23). In 2 Corinthians 5:8 Paul teaches that to be absent from the body is "to be at home with the Lord." This comforting truth shows that four commonly held ideas about death are in error because they contradict Scripture:

(1) *The doctrine of "soul sleep" is in error.* Some, notably the Seventh Day Adventists, teach that at death the soul sleeps while the body is in the grave until the future resurrection when Christ returns. They base this on the numerous places where the Bible refers to death as sleep. But Jesus' story of the rich man and Lazarus, plus Paul's clear statement that to be absent from the body is to be present with the Lord, show soul sleep to be wrong.

(2) *The doctrine of annihilation is in error.* Some believe that at death, we just cease to exist, like animals. This view is usually held by those who reject Scripture. But I have met professing Christians who think that we die and that's it; there's nothing after death. But Paul says, "If we have hoped in Christ in this life only, we are of all men most to be pitied" (1 Cor. 15:19).

(3) *The doctrine of reincarnation is in error.* One out of four Americans believe in some form of reincarnation, that the soul keeps being recycled, either in a better form of life if you've been good, or in a worse form as punishment for evil. But, Scripture plainly teaches, "It is appointed for men to die once and after this comes judgment" (Heb. 9:27).

(4) *The doctrine of purgatory is in error.* The Roman Catholic Church teaches that purgatory is a place of "purifying fire" where "the souls of those who died in the charity of God and truly repentant but who had not

made satisfaction with adequate penance for their sins and omissions are cleansed after death with punishments designed to purge away their debt" (from Vatican II, cited by Dave Hunt, *A Woman Rides the Beast* [Harvest House], pp. 475- 476). The church never defines what "adequate penance" is. Further, the church pronounces anathema (eternal condemnation) on anyone who denies this doctrine (The Council of Trent, cited by Hunt, p. 474).

The only support for purgatory comes from the apocryphal 2 Maccabees 12:46. The doctrine was invented by Pope Gregory the Great in 593, but it was not accepted as official Catholic dogma for nearly 850 years, in 1439 (Hunt, p. 477). It clearly contradicts the Scriptural teaching on the finished work of Christ, on the sufficiency of His atonement for sins, and salvation by grace through faith alone. It makes salvation depend on our works (indulgences) or suffering. It renders any assurance of salvation impossible.

Paul says, "To depart and be with Christ" is "very much better." The only way he can say that is if his soul goes immediately into Christ's presence, where he will be accepted on the basis of Jesus' shed blood and righteousness. Remember, "very much better" does not mean "better than life at its worst," but, "better than life at its joyous best" (based on, H. C. G. Moule, *Philippian Studies* [CLC], p. 78). The great joy of heaven is to be with Christ.

Conclusion

During the Boxer Rebellion in China a century ago, a missionary came as near to death as anyone could and live to tell about it. He felt the sword of the Chinese executioner on his neck before it was lifted for the final blow, when the executioner changed his mind and let him go. The missionary told a friend that his first emotion was disappointment that he would not see the Savior that day. Fanny Crosby, the prolific hymn writer, became blind as a young infant. She said later in life that she would choose blindness over sight, because the first face she would ever see would be that of her Savior.

For the Christian, "to die is gain." Can you say truthfully, "For *me*, to die is gain"? If not, you may need to go back one step and ask, "Is it true that for me, to live is Christ?"

Application Questions

1. How would you answer an advocate of euthanasia who appealed to Paul's seeming "death is better" perspective?

2. Is it possible for a Christian to grieve too much? How can we know if our grief is "normal" or if it goes too far?

3. If it's better to be with Christ in heaven, is it wrong to seek medical treatment for serious illnesses? Why/why not?

4. Which essential biblical truths are contradicted by the Catholic doctrine of purgatory?

Only conduct yourselves in a manner worthy of the gospel of Christ, so that whether I come and see you or remain absent, I will hear of you that you are standing firm in one spirit, with one mind striving together for the faith of the gospel; in no way alarmed by your opponents—which is a sign of destruction for them, but of salvation for you, and that too, from God. For to you it has been granted for Christ's sake, not only to believe in Him, but also to suffer for His sake, experiencing the same conflict which you saw in me, and now hear to be in me.

† Philippians 1:27-30

THE CHRISTIAN MISSION AND HOW TO FULFILL IT
Philippians 1:27-30

Imagine that we are correspondents sent out to a dangerous battle zone. We expect to see battle-weary soldiers in combat fatigues, dirt on their faces, living in the most difficult conditions, carrying their weapons at all times. But, instead, at the battlefront we're surprised to find the soldiers dressed in civilian clothes, playing volleyball and ping pong, lying around swimming pools, sipping cold drinks, with no weapons anywhere in sight. If such an army was defending our country from a hostile enemy, we'd have good reason to be alarmed!

The problem is, that army has forgotten its mission. It thinks that its mission centers around its own comfort and having a good time. Having forgotten its mission, it would easily fall to a hostile enemy. If that enemy attacked, the members of the army might try to desert, claiming, "I didn't sign up for this! I signed up for all the benefits, but I had no idea I might get shot at!"

I believe the American church is a lot like the army I've just described. We have promoted the Christian life for all its benefits: "Come to Christ and He will give you peace and happiness. He will help you overcome your problems. He will give you a happy marriage and family. He will give you an abundant life." So the recruits sign up, thinking about sitting poolside and enjoying the good life with Jesus. Then, the bullets start ricocheting. Bombs start dropping, shrapnel is flying everywhere. People are getting hurt and dying. And these laid-back recruits turn and run, thinking, "I didn't sign up for this!"

The Bible is clear that the Christian life is not a playground, but a battleground. God has not saved us so that we can live comfortably, happily, and self-centeredly in suburbia. He has conscripted us into His army. We have a mission given to us by our Commander-in-Chief, to take the message of His salvation and Lordship into enemy territory, to win captives from the forces of darkness. As in every war, our mission requires combat and struggle. If we forget our mission and get caught up with our own comfort, we will be quick to desert the cause when the enemy attacks.

We must both focus on and fulfill the Christian mission.

Paul describes the Christian cause in such combat terms in Philippians 1:27-30. There is a sense in which it would be easier to preach these verses to the church in China or Iran, where believers are threatened with daily persecution. They're quite aware of the cost of being a Christian. They're ready, if need be, to lay down their lives for the sake of the gospel. But few of us American Christians have ever had to endure severe persecution for our faith. We think of Christianity as something that increases the well-being of our daily lives. We focus on the benefits that come from being Christians. But, the danger is, in focusing on our own well-being, we forget our mission. If we forget our mission, there is no way we will fulfill it. And, we become an easy target for the powers of darkness.

1. We must focus on the Christian mission: to proclaim the faith of the gospel.

We've already seen that the gospel was the central focus of Paul's life. In 1 Corinthians 9:23 he says that he does "all things for the sake of the gospel." In Philippians 1, he uses the word "gospel" six times: verses 5, 7, 12, 16, 27 (twice). He alludes to it in other language several more times: "to speak the word of God" (1:14); "preaching Christ" (1:15); "proclaim Christ" (1:17); "Christ is proclaimed" (1:18); "Christ shall even now, as always, be exalted" (1:20); "to live is Christ" (1:21). Paul's focus should be the Philippians' focus, and ours: He charges them to stand firm and strive together "for the faith of the gospel."

To understand this mission, we must be clear on what Paul means by "the *faith of the gospel.*" By "the faith," he means the Christian faith, which points to the *content* of the gospel, that is, certain core doctrines which are essential to the gospel. Without these essential truths, the gospel is no longer the gospel. In 1 Corinthians 15:3, 4, Paul states the content of the gospel (see 15:1), "that Christ died for our sins according to the Scriptures, and that He was buried, and that He was raised on the third day according to the Scriptures."

This brief statement contains a wealth of essential truth. It tells us who Christ is, namely, the Christ revealed in the Scriptures. It is clear from the over 300 prophecies concerning Jesus in the Old Testament that He is both eternal God, who alone can atone for sin; and, fully human, capable of human death, and thus an acceptable substitute for our sin. Paul's statement tells us the central truth about the work of Christ, that He died for our sins, as our substitute. Anyone who denies the essential nature of the substitutionary work of Christ is denying the gospel.

Paul's gospel also affirms the fallen condition of the human race, that we are sinners in need of a Savior. Anyone who teaches the basic goodness of human nature is denying the gospel, because good people don't need a Savior. They just need a good example and a little encouragement to improve themselves. If we don't need a Savior, then Jesus died for no reason. The gospel also affirms the historical, bodily resurrection of the Lord Jesus Christ. As Paul goes on in that same chapter to state, "If Christ has not been raised, your faith is worthless; you are still in your sins" (1 Cor. 15:7). The resurrection is proof that God has made Jesus both Lord and Christ (Acts 2:36), and that in His death Jesus triumphed over sin, death, and hell. The gospel comes to us by grace through faith apart from any human merit or works (Eph. 2:8, 9).

In other words, "the faith of the gospel" involves certain core truths which must not be compromised. Since these truths are so essential, the enemy is always trying to get us to fudge on them in some way. But, to fulfill the Christian mission we must stand firmly for the faith of the gospel.

But, also, to fulfill our mission we need to get our focus back on the mission itself, namely, to strive together for the faith of the gospel. American Christianity has become too self-focused. We've turned inward-- to analyze our feelings, to "recover" from childhood abuses and "codependency," to fixate on having a more enriching marriage, to raise children with healthy self-esteem, etc. In other words, we're caught up with self-fulfillment and feeling good instead of with the mission our Lord gave us, to take the gospel to every people group.

I'm not denying the need to help hurting people deal with problems or to help get fractured families back together. Wounded people need some healing before they go out to the front lines. But it seems to me that we've shifted our focus onto ourselves to such a degree that, instead of viewing ourselves as God's army, the American church has come to see itself as a branch of the self-help movement. We need to keep the goal in view, that hurting people need healing so that they can be deployed into the battle of reaching lost people with the gospel. Thus, in order to fulfill our mission, first we must focus on it. The church is here to proclaim the faith of the gospel. Then,

2. We fulfill the Christian mission by walking consistently, working cooperatively, and warring confidently.

A. We fulfill the Christian mission by walking consistently as citizens of another country.

"Only conduct yourselves in a manner worthy of the gospel of Christ" (1:27a). The Greek word translated "conduct yourselves" is literally, "live as citizens." It was a word that meant a lot to the Philippians. Remember, Philippi was a Roman colony, and the people there took pride in their Roman citizenship. They lived in accordance with Roman customs. Even though they were about 800 miles from Rome, they were not under any regional authority, but answered directly to Rome, governed by Roman laws. They were a Roman outpost. These colonists lived differently than the barbarians surrounding them because they were citizens of a different country.

Paul is saying that Christians, no matter where we live geographically, must view ourselves as citizens of another country, namely, of heaven. Thus we should live differently than those around us who are citizens of this earth. Our lives must be worthy of the gospel of Christ. We seek to please our heavenly "emperor" and to live by His laws as revealed in His Word. We seek to conform our character to Christ. Though we are also citizens of this world, as the Philippian Christians were, we should be distinct because our primary citizenship is in heaven.

If you've ever visited or lived in a foreign country, you can identify with what Paul is saying. When you're there, you may eat some of their unique kinds of food. You may observe some of their customs, so as not to be needlessly offensive to them. When we visited the Orient, I learned that the way Americans pick their teeth is offensive to the people there, so we adopted the Chinese way of picking our teeth during the trip. But, unless your purpose is to be a missionary who completely blends in with their customs and ways, you probably will stand out as distinct. You're simply different than they are, so you're going to stand out.

As Christians, we want to blend in with the world in matters that do not violate any biblical principles, for the sake of not offending people and of opening the door for the gospel (1 Cor. 9:20-23). But, even so, our heavenly citizenship should mark us as distinct. We live for a different purpose. Instead of living for the things of this world, we live for the kingdom of God. We should be marked by different morals. We should display different character qualities, the fruit of the Spirit. Instead of living for self, as the world does, we live for Jesus Christ. As Paul puts it elsewhere (2 Cor. 5:20), we are ambassadors for Christ, representing His heavenly kingdom here on earth.

It's a sad thing when the church blends in with the world in matters where we should be distinct, and is distinct in matters where we should blend in. Polls show that there is no difference between the evangelical population and the rest of the country in the TV shows we watch or in the amount of time we spend watching them. That's terrible! There's not much difference between the church and the world in the rate of adultery or divorce. If we belong to Christ, it should make a difference in how we treat one another in our homes. There should be a difference in our business practices. Yet often I hear how a person got cheated in business by a professing Christian.

Yet, in matters where we should blend in, we go out of our way to look different. If the world's women are wearing makeup, Christian women don't use any. If the world's women stop using makeup, Christian women gob it on. In seminary, we got a lecture from a veteran pastor on how, as men of the cloth, we should adorn the gospel by always wearing a dark suit when we go out in public. We should always look ministerial. Once a fellow pastor told me at a pastor's luncheon that I didn't look like a pastor. I thanked him for the compliment! Why do we have to look weird to be Christians? We are supposed to be distinct, but we don't need to be weird!

So the first thing, if we want to fulfill our mission as Christians, is to walk consistently as citizens of heaven.

B. We fulfill the Christian mission by working cooperatively as contestants on the same team.

"... standing firm in one spirit, with one soul [lit.] striving together for the faith of the gospel" (1:27b). The Greek word translated "striving together" is *sunathleo*, from which we get our word "athletics." The prefix, *sun*, means "with" or "together." The picture is of an athletic team, working in cooperation and coordination toward a common goal. That goal, as we have seen, is "the faith of the gospel."

As Americans, we're prone toward competition and toward individualism. It affects us more than we sometimes realize. The test for me, as a pastor, is when I hear that the attendance is soaring at another church, while attendance at my church is not. I may need to stop and ask why my church isn't growing. But, I should rejoice if people are coming to Christ at the other church and if the other pastor is preaching God's Word, because we're all on the same team. But so often our tendency is to be competitive and jealous.

I read in a recent Wycliffe publication ("In Other Words," May/June, 1995) a story of a Bible translator in Brazil who was trying to paddle his canoe up river along with a group of natives in their canoes, but he just couldn't keep up. Finally, one of the natives, whose legs were disabled from a serious injury, but whose arms were strong, came back and told Steve, the missionary, to hang on to his canoe and he would paddle for both of them. When they caught up with the rest of the group, the others encouraged the missionary to paddle his own canoe, and offered pointers on what he was doing wrong. He would try for a while, and when he fell behind, one of them would tow him again.

Then, just before they got to the final bend in the river, while they were still out of view of the waiting crowd, two men came alongside Steve and pushed his canoe to the front so that he was the first to land. They had gone to get thatch for their huts, and they shouted out, "We have the thatch! Steve paddled his own canoe!" Those words expressed their philosophy, "Together we have done it." That should be our Christian attitude, of working together as teammates in the great cause of Christ. A united team can win. A team divided against itself, with the teammates bickering or fighting over the glory, will lose.

But a word of caution: There is a strong movement in our day to break down every doctrinal difference between professing Christians and to proclaim our unity in Christ. If this means uniting in gospel efforts with those who truly know Christ and hold firmly to the essential truths of the gospel, that's fine. We should not separate from brothers in Christ over minor doctrinal differences. But, we dare not join forces for evangelism or fellowship with those who deny essential Christian doctrine, or we simply confuse the truth of the gospel.

Some people wonder why I do not promote the "unity" services that are held here in town each year. The reason is that I'm not comfortable proclaiming my "unity" with men who deny essential biblical truth, nor do I wish to proclaim my "unity" with the Roman Catholic Church, as if it were just a different flavor of Christianity. This is not to say that there are not some true Christians in these churches. It is to say that the churches themselves are denying essential biblical truth, and it is wrong to do anything to imply to the world that we are no different than they are. Our cooperation must be limited to those who stand firm for the faith of the gospel.

Thus we fulfill our mission of proclaiming the faith of the gospel by walking consistently and working cooperatively.

C. We fulfill the Christian mission by warring confidently as combatants in the same army.

"... in no way alarmed by your opponents--" (1:28a). We should not create enemies because we are abrasive or cantankerous people. But, if by your life and words you oppose sin and challenge the illicit ways of the world, especially, the sinful ways people in the world make money, you will have enemies. We don't know for sure who the Philippians' enemies were-- perhaps the city magistrates who opposed Paul; perhaps the Judaizers. But they had enemies, and so will we if we stand for righteousness.

For some reason, Christians are often surprised when people don't like them. The word "alarmed" was used of a startled horse rearing in fright. But Paul says, "Don't be alarmed, because our side is going to win." The same God who granted faith to you has also given you another gift: suffering! Twice Paul emphasizes that we suffer "for Christ's sake" (1:29).

If Christ, the Son of God suffered, and if Paul, the great apostle to the Gentiles suffered, then we're in good company if we suffer for the sake of the gospel. Someday soon God will save us and will condemn those who persecute His church. Stand confidently for the Lord and rest in Him.

I have never experienced anything close to the persecution Paul went through. But a few years ago, I was being attacked and falsely accused by some people. I was tending toward discouragement until I read Jesus' words, "Blessed are you when men hate you, and ostracize you, and cast insults at you, and spurn your name as evil, for the sake of the Son of Man. Be glad in that day, and leap for joy, for behold, your reward is great in heaven; for in the same way their fathers used to treat the prophets.... Woe to you when all men speak well of you, for in the same way their fathers used to treat the false prophets" (Luke 6:22, 23, 26).

Conclusion

When I was in boot camp in the Coast Guard, a recruit showed up who was the laughingstock of the entire base. He came to boot camp with his fishing pole and water skis, because the recruiter had explained to him that the base was on an island where you could do those things. That poor guy had been sold a phony bill of goods! They took every personal possession away from us, including our combs. They took every privilege from us. We couldn't watch TV or read the newspaper, except for the front page which they posted on the bulletin board. We were in harsh, difficult conditions. Why? Because they wanted to shape us into a tough, combat-ready unit.

When you trusted Christ, you didn't join a country club. You got drafted into God's army! Your mission is to proclaim the faith of the gospel. You fulfill that mission by walking consistently as a citizen of heaven; by working cooperatively with your fellow teammates; and, by warring confidently with your fellow soldiers. Are you facing hardship or criticism or ridicule because you're a Christian? Remember, it's for the sake of Christ who someday soon will triumph over all His enemies and reign as King of Kings and Lord of Lords. And, if you endure, you will also reign with Him (2 Tim. 2:12).

Application Questions

1. Agree/disagree: American Christians have lost sight of the mission.

2. How do we know where to draw lines of division over doctrine? Which truths are essential?

3. Where is the balance between focusing on our mission versus dealing with personal emotional problems?

4. Should we cooperate with religious groups (Mormons, Catholics, etc.) on common causes such as pro-life or anti-pornography?

Therefore if there is any encouragement in Christ, if there is any consolation of love, if there is any fellowship of the Spirit, if any affection and compassion, make my joy complete by being of the same mind, maintaining the same love, united in spirit, intent on one purpose. Do nothing from selfishness or empty conceit, but with humility of mind regard one another as more important than yourselves; do not merely look out for your own personal interests, but also for the interests of others.

† Philippians 2:1-4

HARMONIOUS RELATIONSHIPS
Philippians 2:1-4

An ad in the Lawrence, Kansas, *Journal-World*, purported: "We will oil your sewing machine and adjust the tension in your home for only $1." (In *Reader's Digest* [5/85], p. 190.) Who cares if they oil the sewing machine-- if only someone could adjust the tension in our homes, I'll bet we'd all gladly pay $100!

We all crave harmonious relationships, but they seem to be a rare commodity. We enter marriage with high hopes for harmony: "This adorable creature I'm marrying is so easy to get along with! We're in love, so we won't have any serious problems!" But then a few months into reality, I discover that she's not quite as adorable as I had thought! In fact, she's got a few problems that I need to help her work on. One of her main problems is that she doesn't see things my way! As I seek to help her with her problems, I discover that she has another problem, namely, that she is stubborn and won't change.

We want harmonious relationships with our children, and yet the alienation between parents and their teenagers is proverbial. We want harmony in our church, but those people at church are so unloving! "Why, do you know what so-and-so said to me? I don't know who she thinks she is! After all the times I've helped her, and then she acts like that toward me! See if I ever do anything for her again!"

I'm glad that the Bible was written to real people with real problems. It doesn't paper over their problems and offer superficial answers. The church at Philippi was a good church, but it wasn't perfect. None is. If its first three converts were any gauge, it was a motley crew that gathered for worship in Philippi: a sophisticated, wealthy businesswoman; a career Roman military man; and, a former slave girl who had been into the occult. It was a built-in formula for conflict, and some tensions were surfacing among the members (4:2). So Paul gently urges them to work through their differences and he gives some principles for harmonious relationships that apply both to the church and to the home.

But, I'll warn you: It's a painful, difficult cure! Like chemotherapy, you may wonder at times if the cure is worth it. But it's the only cure and if you don't take it, the disease will ultimately cause great suffering and result in death. Briefly stated, the principle is:

The key to harmonious relationships is to put self to death and to regard others more highly than myself for Jesus' sake.

As Pogo observed, "We have met the enemy and he is us." The source of quarrels and conflicts is self (James 4:1-3). The cause of divorce, according to Jesus, is hardness of heart (Matt. 19:8). And, before you say, "Yes, my ex-mate really did have a hard heart," Jesus says, "You hypocrite, first take the log out of your own eye, and then you will see clearly to take the speck out of your brother's eye" (Matt. 7:5). Alexander Maclaren put it, "To live to self is the real root of every sin as it is of all loveless life" (*Expositions of Holy Scripture* [Baker], 14:252). If we want harmonious relationships, each of us must confront self, put self to death, and live to build up others. In any conflict, I need to examine self from four directions:

1. In any conflict, I need to look to my own relationship with Christ: Am I motivated by His great love (2:1)?

The only force powerful enough to motivate us to crucify self (and it is a lifelong process) is the great love of God in Christ. So Paul begins his plea for unity with an appeal to think about their experience of the love of Christ. The word "if" which begins each clause is not, in the original text, a word of doubt or uncertainty. Rather, it can be translated "since." To paraphrase,

Therefore, in light of our mission to proclaim Christ, if you have ever received encouragement at a time of need because of your union with Christ, and I know you have; if Christ's love has ever given you comfort in trials, as I know it has; if you've known that common bond with God and others that comes from the Holy Spirit--in fact, we've known that bond together; if you've ever felt deep down inside the tender concern Christ has for you, as every Christian has; then, top off my joy by working through any conflicts until you come out at the place of true oneness of heart.

There are four facets of Paul's appeal here:

(1) *Encouragement in Christ*--This is the Greek word *paraklesis*, a

compound word meaning "one called alongside to help." Jesus used it as a name for the Holy Spirit (John 14:16). Sometimes it has the meaning of exhortation, at other times encouragement. I think the context favors encouragement. Relational conflicts can be a source of great discouragement. Sometimes we feel as if we've tried everything, but nothing seems to work. At such times, our union with Jesus Christ, His all-sufficiency, and His promise never to leave us or forsake us, are a source of tremendous hope. Even if the other person is not responsive to my attempts at reconciliation, I can rely on Christ for the strength I need to live in a Christ-like way in the situation. The encouragement Christ gives motivates me to live to please Him.

(2) *Consolation of love in Christ--*"Consolation" is used of comforting someone in grief. When a relationship is strained, you often feel grief, a sense of loss. When you lean upon Jesus, He gives you comfort through His love. Since He loved me when I was rebellious and not deserving, I can extend that same love to others, even if they aren't deserving. When someone sins against God, He doesn't cut them off. Instead, He ups the intensity of His love by going after that person, as the good shepherd went after the one lost sheep. Even so, my love shouldn't depend on the other person's response; it depends on the comforting love of Christ for me. I need to allow His love to flow through me to the one who has offended me.

(3) *Fellowship of the Spirit--*The Holy Spirit indwells every believer and draws us into fellowship with God and with all who love God. The instant you believe in Christ, the Holy Spirit baptizes you into the one body of Christ (1 Cor. 12:13). This fellowship of the Spirit is always two-way: toward God and toward other Christians. In fact, John says that if we claim to love God, but do not love our brothers and sisters in Christ, we're lying (1 John 4:20). In any conflict with a fellow Christian, I must rely on the indwelling Spirit to be the "oil" to lubricate the friction so that I can love and get along with the other person.

(4) *Affection and compassion in Christ--*"Affection" is translated "bowels" in the King James Bible. It and "compassion" both point to the emotional element in God's love. Jesus looked on the multitude and "felt compassion for them, because they were distressed and downcast like sheep without a shepherd" (Matt. 9:36). Thank God that He didn't look at me and

say, "Stupid sheep! It serves you right to be suffering, because you're such a sinner!" Thank God He had compassion on me! And now, having received His compassion and tender mercies, I must show the same to other sinners, even if they don't deserve it.

We should view every relational conflict or problem as an opportunity to learn more of Christ. Did someone treat me in an offensive manner? Jesus was treated offensively, but He still loved. Did they run roughshod over my feelings? Jesus knew that kind of treatment. Did my friends desert me at my time of need? The disciples deserted Jesus at His trial and crucifixion. Did a close associate betray me? Jesus was betrayed by Judas. Maybe you feel mistreated, unloved, or betrayed by a family member or fellow Christian. Draw near to Jesus and enter into His heart of love for you, even though you put Him on the cross. In any relational conflict, I must first look to my relationship with Christ and ask, "Am I motivated by His great love?"

2. In any conflict, I must look to my attitude: Am I seeking unity or am I seeking my own way (2:2)?

The word "mind" is actually a verb that can be translated, "that you *think* the same thing." It occurs again at the end of the verse, "that you think the one." Ten out of 26 New Testament uses of this verb, which has the nuance of "attitude," are in Philippians. There is a direct correlation between attitude and joy (the other dominant theme of this letter)! Paul's joy would be filled to the brim, not if he got out of prison, but if he heard that the Philippians were minded toward love and harmony.

There is also a correlation between attitude and harmonious relationships. We sometimes err by thinking that good relationships happen by accident. We see a happy couple or a family where everyone seems to get along and we think, "They're sure lucky!" Or, a couple is having conflict and they think, "Maybe we ought to just find someone more compatible." But harmonious relationships aren't a matter of luck or natural compatibility. They are built on a mind-set that works at seeking unity. There are four facets of this attitude:

(1) *The same mind*--literally, "that you think the same thing." Obviously, Paul doesn't mean that we all must see every matter exactly the same. Nor does he mean that we're supposed to set aside essential truth for

the sake of unity. As we saw in 1:27, we must stand firm for the faith of the gospel. Rather, he means that we must have our minds geared toward Christian love so that we seek the highest good of one another; and, that we must be growing to experience what we possess--the mind of Christ, revealed to us in His Word (1 Cor. 2:16). As believers grow in their understanding of Scripture, they share a common way of approaching problems. The world offers all sorts of conflict resolution techniques to help people work through differences, but they're all built on self. They teach you how to get what you're after. But God's way is to teach us to deny self as we seek to please God and love others. If two people have this same mind, there is a basis for working through conflicts.

(2) *The same love*--The love of Christ, revealed in His incarnation and in His death, as Paul goes on to illustrate (2:5-8). It is a love that yields its rights for the sake of others. Christians must have that love in mind in every relationship.

(3) *United in spirit*--literally, "one in soul." True unity is not organizational or outward; it is a matter of the heart. This is not automatic or a matter of luck. I must deliberately set my mind on being one with those who truly know Christ, even if I don't particularly like them or agree with them on everything.

(4) *Intent on one purpose*--literally, "being minded on the one thing," which is the faith of the gospel (1:27). The corporate witness of the body of Christ rides on our outwardly visible love. If I am minded toward the gospel, I will also be minded toward getting along with fellow Christians, and especially with those in my own family. So in any conflict, I must ask myself, "Is my focus on happiness and pleasing myself, or is my focus on exalting Christ?" If both parties are intent on exalting Christ by honoring His Word of truth and by living for each other's highest good, there is a solid basis for resolving conflict.

Thus, in any conflict, I must first look to my relationship with Christ: Am I motivated by His love? Then, I look to my attitude: Am I oriented toward love or toward my own way?

3. In any conflict, I must look to my view of myself: Am I being selfish and conceited or humble (2:3)?

The world's way for resolving conflicts is to teach you to stand up for your rights, to be assertive, to negotiate for what you want, to have proper self-esteem, etc. Some of these techniques work by balancing one person's needs against the other's so that a working harmony can be achieved. Christian psychologists have imported this stuff wholesale into the church. But the problem is, the world's ways do not deal with the root problem, which is pride or self.

Several studies done over the past few years show that the American public consistently defines their ultimate goals in terms of self-fulfillment. They view marriage, work, and even the church, as ways toward personal fulfillment. It's not surprising that the general public is self-seeking. But David Wells did a survey of American seminary students that revealed that they "are oriented toward self-fulfillment, self-expression, and personal freedom to a degree that often exceeds" that of the general population. In his 1993 survey, "40.2% of the respondents affirmed that 'realizing my full potential as a human being is just as important as putting others before myself.'" Wells goes on to observe, "Had Christ held this belief, for example, it would have ended all prospects of the incarnation" (*God in the Wasteland* [Eerdmans], p. 201).

In contrast to these worldly ways, Paul says that Christians must "do nothing from selfishness or empty conceit" (2:3). *Selfishness* means to have a party spirit, or to campaign for office. A politician tries to build a following for himself by building himself up and, if need be, by putting his opponents down. It's the same word Paul used in 1:17 of those who were preaching out of "selfish ambition." In Galatians 5:20 it is a deed of the flesh, "disputes." Many churches suffer because some of the leaders view their position as a way of promoting self. Some husbands misuse their authority in marriage in the same way. But, Christians are not to do anything from this self-seeking motive.

Empty conceit is literally, "vain glory," to be puffed up with a sense of our own importance, to think that we're really great. A. B. Bruce, in his classic *The Training of the Twelve* (Kregel, p. 180) observed, "The whole aim of Satanic policy is to get self-interest recognized as the chief end of man." In the garden, Satan's appeal to Eve was to build her self-esteem by getting her to think she could be like God. All this self-esteem teaching that has flooded the church is not from Scripture, but from Satan. It does not help you to have harmonious relationships; it is directly opposed to harmonious

94

relationships because it feeds pride.

Thus, we are not to act from selfishness or empty conceit. Instead, with *humility of mind*, we are to regard others as more important than ourselves. "Humility of mind" is literally, lowliness of mind. Our problem is not that we think too lowly of ourselves, but that we regard ourselves too highly. Even the person who goes around dumping on himself is too self-focused. He needs to get his thoughts off himself and onto the needs of others. The non-Christian philosopher, Allan Bloom, saw this when he wrote, "Everyone loves himself most but wants others to love him more than they love themselves" (*The Closing of the American Mind* [Simon and Schuster], p. 118).

Maybe you're wondering how we can practically apply verse 3. You think, "I study my Bible and try to obey it. But the person I have conflict with doesn't know the Bible or live by it. How can I honestly regard him as better than myself? Am I supposed to see myself as a doormat?"

First, we all need to recognize that all that we are and have is due to God's grace (1 Cor. 4:7). I deserved hell; He has shown me mercy. If I am intelligent, it is a gift from God to be used for His glory, not mine. If I have money, even if I earned it by hard work, I am not to boast in it, but to use it as God's steward. If I am not enslaved to various sins, it's not due to me, but to God's grace. I must use my gifts to help others, not to boast.

Also, I need to recognize the awful depravity of my own heart apart from God's grace. If you're not growing to see your own sinfulness more and more, you're not growing. Apart from God's grace, I could be a murderer or be enslaved to sexual sin. Rather than condemn another person for his sin, I need to deal with the log in my eye; then I can come alongside and help the other person with his sin (Matt. 7:5; Gal. 6:1).

Just as I need God's grace, so does the other person. Maybe his problem isn't one I struggle with. But, I have problems he doesn't struggle with. Rather than proudly looking down on my brother, as one sinner to another I need to show him God's grace and help him toward victory in Christ. And, not thinking too highly of myself (the tendency) but truthfully, I also need to recognize the other's unique giftedness (Rom. 12:3-8). Thus, in any conflict, I must lower my view of myself and esteem others.

4. In any conflict, I must look to my view of others: Am I putting their interests above my own (2:4)?

Why is it that when the other guy in front of me in the express check out lane has five items over the limit and writes a check instead of paying with cash, he's inconsiderate, but when I do it, it's because I'm in a hurry and have a good reason? When my wife is late getting ready, it's because she didn't plan her time well, but when I'm late it's because of circumstances beyond my control. When my kids lose something, it's because they're irresponsible, but when I lose something, it was because I had a lot on my mind.

We're so selfish that we're like fish in the water who don't know they're wet! I read of a new husband who went up to a ticket counter and only bought one ticket. When his new bride pointed it out, he made a quick comeback by saying, "You're right, dear, I'd forgotten myself completely!" Yeah, right!

Paul does not mean that we are never to say no to the demands others place on us. Jesus sometimes said no to the needs of the crowds so that He could spend time alone with the Father (Mark 1:35-39). At times, He drew away with the twelve so that He could train them (Matt. 15:21; 16:13; 17:1). We all have responsibilities that demand our time (Gal. 6:5). So Paul does not mean that we let others walk all over us.

But he does mean that we need to think about the other person and his needs and interests rather than just think about things from our own perspective. It's the golden rule principle--how would I feel if I were him? How would I want to be treated? That's how I need to treat the other person. Consider others, not just yourself.

Conclusion

A secular psychologist did a study in which he asked his subjects to list ten people he knew best and to label them as happy or not happy. Then they were to go through the list again and label each one as selfish or not selfish, using the following definition of selfishness: "A stable tendency to devote one's time and resources to one's own interests and welfare--an unwillingness to inconvenience one's self for others." The results showed that all of the people labeled *happy* were also labeled *unselfish*. He wrote that those "whose activities are devoted to *bringing themselves happiness* ... are far less likely to be happy than those whose efforts are devoted to making others happy" (emphasis in original, cited by Martin & Deidre Bobgan, *How to Counsel from Scripture* [Moody Press], p. 123).

The key to harmonious relationships is not to esteem self, assert self, or stand up for self. It is, rather, to put self to death and to regard others more highly than myself for Jesus' sake. If we would apply this to our homes and church, we would experience much more harmony and much less conflict. It's a painful cure; but it's the only cure given by God's Word of truth.

Application Questions

1. If my mate is living for self and I deny self, won't I get taken advantage of? Doesn't this only work if both parties do it?

2. How do I apply verse 2 with someone who is doctrinally wrong or who is not seeking to live by Scripture?

3. When does "holding to right doctrine" become a matter of pride? How can we seek to be doctrinally correct, yet be humble?

4. How do we know when to say "no" to the demands of others without being selfish?

Have this attitude in yourselves which was also in Christ Jesus, who, although He existed in the form of God, did not regard equality with God a thing to be grasped, but emptied Himself, taking the form of a bond-servant, and being made in the likeness of men. Being found in appearance as a man, He humbled Himself by becoming obedient to the point of death, even death on a cross.

† Philippians 2:5-8

SUPREME HUMILITY
Philippians 2:5-8

We live in a day when Bible doctrine is commonly despised, even among God's people. I've heard people say, "We want life, not doctrine," as if the two were in opposition to each other. A young woman once told me that the wonderful thing about her experience-oriented church was that they didn't have any doctrines; they just had Jesus! The term "air-head" was not yet in existence, or it might have popped into my mind on that occasion. Christian people proclaim that doctrine is divisive and that what we need is unity. Often that unity is built on a common experience that people have had, supposedly through the Holy Spirit, even though these people often hold to seriously erroneous doctrine. We tend to think of theology as impractical, academic stuff that seminary students and professors like to debate. But it doesn't have anything to do with how we live.

But when we buy into this anti-intellectual approach to the Christian life, we are forgetting that the Apostle Paul did not write his profound doctrinal sections of Scripture to theologians. He wrote Romans, Galatians, and the other great theological portions of his letters, including our text, which is one of the most profound Christological portions of Scripture, to common people--business people, working people, soldiers, housewives, and even slaves--to help them live their daily lives in a manner pleasing to God.

It is significant that Paul is not using our text to combat some heresy or theological error. He is writing about a most practical subject-- how Christians can get along with one another. It applies to how we relate to one another in the church, but also in our homes. As we saw in the last chapter, at the heart of our relational problems is self. To live in harmony, we must learn to die to self and humbly live for others for Jesus' sake. To illustrate this point, Paul sets before us the person of our Lord Jesus Christ as the example of supreme humility. Solid theological understanding about Jesus Christ is the foundation for how we can get along with one another. Paul is saying that ...

To promote harmonious relationships, we must grow in the humility Jesus modeled in His incarnation and death.

Since the early 1970's there have been dozens of books and hundreds of articles written from a supposedly Christian perspective that tell us how to build our self-esteem, our mate's self-esteem, and our children's self-esteem. We have been assured by the supposed "experts" on human behavior that low self-esteem is at the root of all our emotional and relational problems. I'm sad to confess that for many years I was influenced by this teaching and even taught it myself. But I came to realize that there is not a single verse in the entire Bible that tells us that we need to build our self-esteem. There are many verses that tell us we need to lower our view of ourselves and grow in humility (the biblical word for humility means "lowliness of mind"). How many recent books or articles have you read on how to lower your self-esteem and grow in humility? Yet that is what Paul is clearly teaching here. His teaching is built on the great doctrinal truths of the incarnation and death of Jesus Christ.

1. To grow in humility, we must understand the incarnation and death of Jesus Christ.

Although many volumes have been written on these verses, the basic thought is quite simple and clear: That Jesus Christ voluntarily left the highest position in the universe and went to the very lowest position on earth in order to rescue from God's judgment people who did not in any way deserve it. There can be no greater example of lowering oneself than what Jesus did on our behalf. If your heart is cold toward the things of God, think on who Jesus is and on what He did in leaving the splendor and purity of heaven and coming to this wicked world to be made sin on your behalf. It should fill our hearts with love and devotion and make us realize that no personal sacrifice we make, no humiliation we go through, can ever match what our glorious Savior did for us!

A. To grow in humility, we must understand Christ's incarnation, that the eternal Son of God left His glory to take on human flesh.

When Paul states that Jesus existed in the form of God (1:6), he is referring to His preexistence before He was born of the virgin Mary. Jesus is not a created being, but rather is the second person of the triune God. As John opens his gospel, "In the beginning was the Word, and the Word was with God, and the Word was God. He was in the beginning with God. All things came into being by Him, and apart from Him nothing came into being that has come into being" (John 1:1-3). A few verses later John explains further, "And the Word became flesh, and dwelt among us, and we beheld His glory, glory as of the only begotten from the Father, full of grace and truth" (John 1:14). Or, as Jesus said to the Jews who challenged His claims, "Before Abraham was born, I am" (John 8:58).

When Paul states that Jesus existed in "the form of God," "form" refers to that which is intrinsic and essential to the being of God, that is, to God's attributes (J. B. Lightfoot, *Saint Paul's Epistle to the Philippians* [Zondervan], pp. 132-133). Thus Paul is saying that Jesus in His preexistence shared the essential attributes of deity. He is God! Before He came to this earth, Jesus dwelled in the indescribable glory and perfection of heaven, one with the Father and the Spirit, in the blessedness of the divine being. But He willingly left that glory to come to earth!

The next phrase has been variously translated and interpreted. The King James Version reads that He "thought it not robbery to be equal with God." The NASB translates, He "did not regard equality with God a thing to be grasped." John Calvin explains the sense: "There would have been no wrong done though he had shewn himself to be *equal with God*" (*Calvin's Commentaries* [Baker], on Philippians 2:6, p. 55).

Lightfoot, following the early Greek fathers, gives the sense as, "Be humble as Christ was humble: He, though existing before the worlds in the form of God, did not treat His equality with God as a prize, a treasure to be greedily clutched and ostentatiously displayed: on the contrary He resigned the glories of heaven." He goes on to observe, "For how could it be a sign of humility in our Lord not to assert His equality with God, if He were not divine? How could such a claim be considered otherwise than arrogant and blasphemous, if He were only a man?" (pp. 134, 137).

Paul goes on to say that Jesus "emptied Himself" (NIV = "made Himself nothing"). Clearly, God cannot cease to be God, and so Jesus did not, as some have asserted, give up any of His divine attributes. He limited the independent use of certain attributes and prerogatives while on this earth. And, His preincarnate glory was veiled (John 17:5), except for the brief time on the Mount of Transfiguration, and perhaps when the soldiers in the garden fell backwards after a flash of His glory (John 18:6). Paul explains the main sense of how Christ emptied Himself in the rest of verse 7 and in verse 8: by taking the form of a servant and being obedient to death on the cross.

When Paul says that Jesus took on the form of a bond-servant (2:7), he means that He voluntarily adopted the very nature of a servant. He did not cease to be God in any sense, but added to His divine nature a true human nature. Jesus' human nature was exactly like ours, except that it was joined to a divine nature (not mixed or blended); and, it was without sin, although His body was subject to the results of the fall, such as weariness, aging, and death. When Paul says that Christ was "found in appearance as a man" (2:8), he means that if you had looked at Jesus, you would not have thought, "There is a superman or a god," but rather, "There is a normal-looking man." He was born into a family as a baby, grew to maturity as we all do, and in every other observable way was completely human.

Thus the orthodox statement concerning the person of Christ is that *He is undiminished deity and perfect humanity united without confusion in one person forever.* To deny either the full and perfect deity of our Lord or His complete humanity is to veer into serious heresy. So what Paul is showing is that the Lord Jesus went from the highest place in the universe, as eternal God, to take on human existence, and that, not as a king or powerful warrior, but as a lowly servant. But, He went even lower:

B. To grow in humility, we must understand Christ's death, which was the most shameful death imaginable.

It would have been amazing enough for the eternal God to come to this earth as a mighty king. It was even more amazing that He came as a humble servant. But it's almost beyond comprehension that He would even go lower and die. And, even more staggering, His death was not a noble death, but a horrible, ignoble death of a common criminal. For the Jew, whoever was hanged on a tree was accursed of God (Deut. 21:23). For Gentiles, death by crucifixion was the lowest, most despicable form of death imaginable. Roman citizens were exempt from crucifixion. The

Roman poet, Cicero, said, "Far be the very name of a cross, not only from the body, but even from the thought, the eyes, the ears of Roman citizens" (cited by R. P. Martin, *Philippians* [IVP/Eerdmans], p. 103).

So, Paul is saying that Jesus went from the height of heights to the depth of depths. We will never begin to know what glory He gave up or what humiliation He suffered on our behalf until we are with Him in glory. But, to grow in humility, we must think about the staggering implications of what it meant for the holy, glorious, eternal Son of God to take on human flesh; and, not the flesh of a king, but of a servant; and, stooping even lower, He willingly and obediently went to the cross for our sins.

2. To grow in humility, we must allow the truth of Christ's incarnation and death to affect the way we act toward one another.

In our day humility is hardly ever emphasized as a Christian virtue that we must pursue. In fact, we extol the opposite, self-love, as a healthy quality that we need to work on! I began to see how far off I was on the self-esteem issue by reading John Calvin and Jonathan Edwards. In Calvin's *Institutes* (ed. by John McNeill [Westminster] II:II:11), he mentions how Chrysostom, the church father, viewed humility as the foundation of Christianity; and how Augustine said that the precepts of the Christian religion, first, second, third, and always are humility. Calvin rightly argues that due to the fall, self-love is innate in all humans. He says that we are quick to listen with applause to anyone who extols human nature in favorable terms. Even those who take a more modest attitude and give God credit for some things, he says, "so divide the credit that the chief basis for boasting and confidence remains in themselves" (II:I:2).

Edwards, in his "A Treatise Concerning Religious Affections" (*The Works of Jonathan Edwards* [Banner of Truth], 1:294-303) points out that there is a false and inadequate sort of humility which professing, but unconverted, people can have. But, he argues that anyone who is truly converted will display what he calls "evangelical humiliation." Listen to his words:

> Evangelical humiliation is a sense that a Christian has of his own utter insufficiency, despicableness, and odiousness, with an answerable frame of heart....

> The essence of evangelical humiliation consists in such

humility as becomes a creature in itself exceeding sinful, under a dispensation of grace; consisting in a mean [= worthy of little regard] esteem of himself, as in himself nothing, and altogether contemptible and odious; attended with a mortification of a disposition to exalt himself, and a free renunciation of his own glory.

This is a great and most essential thing in true religion. The whole frame of the gospel, every thing appertaining to the new covenant, and all God's dispensations towards fallen man, are calculated to bring to pass this effect. They that are destitute of this, have no true religion, whatever profession they may make, and how high so ever their religious affections may be;..." (p. 294).

When I first read this about four or five years ago, the first thing it did was make me question my own salvation. The second thing it did was draw a line in the sand and confront me with the question, "Which side are you on? The side of Scripture (and Edwards heaps up verses to prove his case) or on the side of modern psychologized Christianity?" I realized that both cannot be truly Christian. I had to repent of my former errors.

Granted, then, that we must pursue humility, what does it look like? Christ's humility teaches us several aspects of true humility:

(1) *True humility is a proper attitude toward self that results in proper actions toward others.* "Have this attitude in yourselves ...." Jesus Christ could rightly have thought, "I'm the eternal God. I'm not about to become a human being, let alone be a servant, let alone die!" I'm glad He didn't think like that!

Who are we? According to Scripture, we are rebellious sinners at heart, who have gone our own way and despised the God who created us. But, by His undeserved favor, we have become His children through faith in Christ. By grace, He has forgiven all our sins and has made us members of Christ's body. He has entrusted spiritual gifts to us to use for His kingdom and glory (*not* our own kingdom and glory!). As a result, we have the great privilege of serving others for Jesus' sake.

(2) *True humility means renouncing self for the sake of others.* Jesus had to renounce any self-will when He came to earth and went to the cross. In the garden, He prayed, "Not My will, but Yours be done" (Luke 22:42). Of

course, He had no sinful will to renounce, whereas we fight it every day. But humility means dying to self daily so that we can do God's will.

(3) *True humility means lowering myself to lift others up.* That's what Jesus supremely did in giving up the splendor of His glory in heaven to hang naked on the shameful cross for our sins. It would be impossible for us to go to that extreme. But we do need to lower our view of ourselves so that we can serve others. If you ever find yourself saying, "That task is beneath me," you'd better check your pride.

(4) *True humility yields any rights for the sake of serving others.* Did Jesus have a right not to come to this earth in the humble way He did? Of course He did! Did He have a right not to go to the cross? Of course! But, He yielded all His rights and became a bond-servant for our salvation. A bondservant was the extreme bottom of the ladder when it came to rights, because he had none. He didn't have a right to his own time. He didn't even have a right to his own life.

This doesn't mean that we become the slaves of everyone else's whims or desires. Jesus was obedient to the Father, not to what others thought He should do. Even so, we become enslaved to do what God wants us to do. Jesus told the disciples that when a slave comes in after a day of working in the field, his master doesn't serve the slave dinner. The slave has to fix dinner and serve the master, and only then is he free to eat. Jesus concluded by saying, "So you too, when you do all the things which are commanded you say, 'We are unworthy slaves; we have done only that which we ought to have done'" (Luke 17:10). The only right I have is the right to hell. Any privileges I enjoy are by God's undeserved favor.

(5) *True humility serves others in obedience to God, even at great personal cost.* The cross was painful beyond description for Jesus, not just because of the physical pain, but because He who was totally without sin endured the wrath of God by becoming sin for us (2 Cor. 5:20). Any personal cost we have to bear in serving Christ is nothing by way of comparison, even if it means laying down our lives. As Isaac Watts put it, "Love so amazing, so divine, demands my soul, my life, my all" ("When I Survey the Wondrous Cross").

Conclusion

If you're experiencing friction in your relationships, whether at home or anywhere, chances are you need to grow in humility. C. S. Lewis saw this. He wrote,

> ... Pride ... has been the chief cause of misery in every nation and every family since the world began.... Pride always means enmity--it is enmity. And not only enmity between man and man, but enmity to God.
>
> In God you come up against something which is in every respect immeasurably superior to yourself. Unless you know God as that--and, therefore, know yourself as nothing in comparison-- you do not know God at all. As long as you are proud you cannot know God. A proud man is always looking down on things and people: and, of course, as long as you are looking down, you cannot see something that is above you (*Mere Christianity* [Macmillan], pp. 110-111).

Calvin sums up the practical application of our text: "Since, then, the Son of God descended from so great a height, how unreasonable that we, who are nothing, should be lifted up with pride!" (*Calvin's Commentaries*, p. 55). But, the fact is, we must fight pride all our lives. In 1985, a Spanish bullfighter made a tragic mistake. He thrust his sword a final time into the bull, which then collapsed. Thinking that the bull was dead, the bullfighter turned to the crowd to acknowledge the applause. But the bull was not dead. It rose and lunged at the back of the unsuspecting matador, piercing his heart with its horn.

Pride is like that. Just when we think we've conquered it and we turn to accept the congratulations of the crowd, pride stabs us in the back. It won't be dead before we are. Fight it by focusing on what the Savior did for you by leaving the glory of heaven and coming to die for your sins. Have that same mind in you which was in Christ Jesus: "Do nothing from selfishness or empty conceit, but with humility of mind let each of you regard one another as more important than himself; do not merely look out for your own personal interests, but also for the interests of others" (2:3, 4). That's the way toward harmony in our church and in our homes.

Application Questions

1. Why is proper theology essential for proper conduct?

2. Those who teach self-esteem say that they're not promoting pride, but only a proper self-concept. Are they?

3. How can a proud person grow in humility? What steps should he take?

4. How does a humble person keep from becoming a doormat?

For this reason also, God highly exalted Him, and bestowed on Him the name which is above every name, so that at the name of Jesus every knee will bow, of those who are in heaven and on earth and under the earth, and that every tongue will confess that Jesus Christ is Lord, to the glory of God the Father.

† Philippians 2:9-11

EVERY KNEE SHALL BOW
Philippians 2:9-11

Suppose you had been out of the country during the recent NBA play-offs between Houston and Orlando. You had not heard that Houston swept it in four games. You had asked me to videotape the series so that you could watch the games after you returned. When you got back, I proposed that we place a $100 bet on the series. Would you take me up on it? Only if you wanted to give me $100! Why? Because the outcome is not in any doubt. Betting against a game where the outcome is certain would be utterly foolish.

And yet millions of people bet their eternal destiny against an outcome that God has declared absolutely certain. Jesus Christ has been raised from the dead and is ascended to the right hand of God the Father where He awaits all of His enemies to be made His footstool (Ps. 110:1). God's Word assures us that every knee will bow to acknowledge Jesus Christ as Lord. And yet people go on betting their eternal destiny against this sure word from God, living as their own lords and saviors, as if God's Word were uncertain or not true. In our text, the apostle Paul assures us that ...

Because Jesus humbled Himself through the cross, God has exalted Him above all, so that all will submit to Jesus as Lord.

I want to set forth what this text of Scripture teaches; deal with some potential objections to that teaching; and, offer some applications.

THE TEACHING:

1. The crucified, risen, and ascended Jesus is now at the place of supremacy over all creation (2:9).

"Therefore" takes us back to verse 8: Because Jesus was willing to humble Himself and be obedient to death on the cross, God highly exalted Him and bestowed on Him the name above every name. As we saw in the last chapter, Jesus willingly left the height of heights, laid aside His glory

109

that He had with the Father from before the foundation of the world, and took on the form of a lowly servant, adding genuine humanity to His eternal deity. His deity was not diminished or laid aside, but rather was veiled during His earthly ministry, like an eclipse of the sun. But verse 9 tells us that after that time of veiling, God restored Him to that place of supremacy (John 17:5). "Highly exalted" is a word that occurs only here in the New Testament, and may be translated "super-exalted." Thus Jesus went from the height of heights to the depth of depths and back again to the height of heights.

Jesus did not exalt Himself (although He could have), but the Father exalted Him, thus putting His stamp of approval on Jesus' death as the satisfaction of the penalty for our sins. As Peter proclaimed to the Jewish Sanhedrin (Acts 5:30, 31): "The God of our fathers raised up Jesus, whom you had put to death by hanging Him on a cross. He is the one whom God exalted to His right hand as a Prince and a Savior, to grant repentance to Israel, and forgiveness of sins." The exaltation of Jesus proves that He defeated Satan, who could not keep Jesus in the grave (Col. 2:13-15).

Men did not exalt Jesus. They cast insults and abuse at Him. They jeered and spit upon Him and called Him names. But the Father gave Jesus the name above all names, the name "Lord," which is equivalent to the Old Testament name of God, Yahweh, a name so sacred that the Hebrews would not even pronounce it. When they were reading the Scripture and came to Yahweh, they would read, "Adonai," which means "Lord." "Jesus is Lord" means "Jesus is Yahweh," eternal God.

That this is Paul's meaning becomes obvious when you compare Philippians 2:9 with Isaiah 45:22, 23: "Turn to Me, and be saved, all the ends of the earth; for I am God, and there is no other. I have sworn by Myself, the word has gone forth from My mouth in righteousness and will not turn back, that to Me every knee will bow, every tongue swear allegiance." To whom? To God! Citing these verses, Paul says that every knee will bow to Jesus. Jesus is God, Yahweh, Lord!

Peter affirmed the same truth on the Day of Pentecost (Acts 2:33-36): "Therefore having been exalted to the right hand of God, and having received from the Father the promise of the Holy Spirit, He has poured forth this which you both see and hear. For it was not David who ascended into heaven, but he himself says: 'The Lord said to my Lord, "Sit at My right hand, until I make Your enemies a footstool for Your feet."' Therefore let all the house of Israel know for certain that God has made Him both Lord and Christ--this Jesus whom you crucified."

Thus any teaching, such as that of the Mormons and Jehovah's Witnesses, which diminishes or denies the full deity of Jesus Christ, goes against the clear apostolic witness to Jesus. The Jesus who humbled Himself to the death on a cross has been raised up, ascended into heaven, and placed at the right hand of God the Father, in the place of supremacy over all creation.

2. Every creature will bow before the exalted Lord Jesus Christ (2:10).

To emphasize the universality of Christ's exaltation and lordship, Paul adds, "of those in heaven, and on earth, and under the earth." Every created being will submit to Jesus Christ. In heaven, the angels will bow willingly before Jesus. The angels are awesome creatures of great power and glory. The mighty angel Gabriel, who brought visions from God to the prophet Daniel, struck such fear into Daniel that he fell on his face (Dan. 8:17). On another occasion when Daniel saw the angel, he grew pale and lost all his strength. When the angel's hand touched Daniel, it set him trembling on his hands and knees and rendered him speechless (Dan. 10:8, 10, 15). But the mighty Gabriel bows before the Lord Jesus Christ.

On earth, those who have tasted His sovereign grace will bow willingly before Jesus. Others, including many of the mightiest, most powerful men who have ever lived--great kings, wealthy tycoons, evil drug lords--will bow against their wills, but they will bow. *Under the earth*, Satan and all his powerful demonic forces will bow before the Lord Jesus Christ. These demons have been granted tremendous power. The Book of Job shows how Satan can move wicked people to commit slaughter, he can cause a powerful wind to knock down a house, and he can inflict a man with illness (Job 1:15, 19; 2:7). Certain demons apparently have territorial power over entire nations (Dan. 10:13). But they all will bow before the Lord Jesus Christ.

Years ago the well-known missionary, Don Richardson, spoke at our church in California. Over lunch after church, he shared an interesting theory he has about hell. He said that often hell is pictured as the demons and the damned blaspheming and cursing God. But, Don said, God isn't going to allow that to go on throughout eternity. Rather, those in hell will forever acknowledge the lordship of Jesus.

He explained by using the analogy of the threshold of pain. Some people can endure only a small amount of pain before they will submit to anyone torturing them. Others can endure much more pain before they are broken. As a boy, you may have wrestled with a bigger boy who got you in a painful hold and increased your pain until you would agree to do or say what he wanted. If he let up on the pain, you would defy him and say, "I'm not going to do it." So, he would increase your pain until you said, "Okay, I'll do what you want!"

Don speculates that in hell, God is going to inflict on every person or demon the amount of pain necessary to bring that being into submission, where under duress he cries out, "Jesus is Lord." If God were to lessen the pain, the person would defy God. So God increases the pain to the point where they submit and then holds them at that level throughout eternity. I don't know that you can prove his theory from Scripture, but it does make sense. However God does it, there isn't a rebellious creature on earth or in hell who will not acknowledge that Jesus Christ is Lord. It will be a forced confession, but every knee shall bow before Jesus.

3. Every tongue will confess the lordship of Jesus Christ to the glory of God the Father (2:12).

I've just alluded to this fact. But also we need to understand that to honor Jesus is to honor the Father, because Jesus is God. As Jesus told His Jewish critics, "For not even the Father judges anyone, but He has given all judgment to the Son, in order that all may honor the Son, even as they honor the Father. He who does not honor the Son does not honor the Father who sent Him" (John 5:23, 24). Because Jesus and the Father are one, to glorify Jesus is to glorify the Father. God's glory is the aim of His eternal purpose in Christ. If people will not willingly give glory to God in this life, they will do so against their will throughout eternity.

That's the teaching: Because Jesus humbled Himself through the cross, God has exalted Him far above all, so that all will submit to Jesus as Lord, to the glory of God the Father. This teaching raises some questions or objections. Perhaps there are more, but I can think of two:

OBJECTIONS TO THE TEACHING:

1. If Jesus is exalted as Lord, why does He allow evil and suffering? Why doesn't He squash all rebellion now?

Of course, this is the age-old problem of evil that theologians and philosophers have wrestled with. We can't ultimately answer the question, "Why did God allow evil and sin in the first place?" except to say, "It was a part of His inscrutable plan and it results in greater glory to God than any other plan." To attribute evil to the fact that God gave freedom of choice to the angels and later to human beings does not really solve the problem, because obviously God knew the sinful choices that would be made. He even ordained the cross before the foundation of the world (Eph. 1:4; Rev. 13:8). And yet the Bible clearly affirms that God is not responsible for sin and that He is apart from all sin (1 John 1:5).

The Bible is equally clear that the current reign of Satan as god of this world and the abundance of evil in no way disproves the absolute lordship of Jesus Christ. The Book of Revelation makes it clear that evil will abound and seemingly be winning the war right up to the end. Saints will be martyred (Rev. 6:9-11), wicked Babylon will be prospering (Rev. 17 & 18) right up to the end. And then, "in one day, in one hour" (Rev. 18:8, 10, 17, 19) God's judgment will destroy her. That final book of the Bible shows that the fact that evil abounds does not in any way thwart the plans of God or the triumph of Christ.

The Bible is also clear that any delay of God's judgment is only because of His great patience, in not wanting any to perish, but to bring all of His elect to repentance (2 Pet. 3:9). The final salvation of God's elect and condemnation of the wicked will demonstrate God's perfect justice and bring glory to Him (see 2 Thess. 1:6-10).

So, the Bible acknowledges the presence of evil, but also clearly affirms that it in no way disproves the lordship of Jesus, who in God's perfect timing, will suppress all evil and reign in absolute triumph. That leads to the second question or objection:

2. How can we be sure that Jesus will ultimately triumph, especially when we see evil winning in our day?

As I pointed out, Scripture is clear that evil will seemingly be winning right up to the final hour. Then God's axe will fall. But, how can we know that those prophecies about the future will come true?

Look at the many prophecies that were fulfilled in the birth, life, death, and resurrection of the Lord Jesus. Peter mentions how the Old Testament prophets sought to know what time or manner "the Spirit of Christ within them was indicating as He predicted the sufferings of Christ and the glories to follow" (1 Pet. 1:11). The risen Jesus told the men on the Emmaus road, "O foolish men and slow of heart to believe in all that the prophets have spoken! Was it not necessary for the Christ to suffer these things and to enter into His glory?" Then, "beginning with Moses and with all the prophets, He explained to them the things concerning Himself in all the Scriptures" (Luke 24:25-27).

Not only do we have the witness of the Old Testament prophets who spoke of Christ's sufferings and glory, but also the witness of the many apostles, men of integrity, who saw the risen Lord Jesus, who saw Him ascend into heaven and heard the witness of the angels to His promised second coming (Acts 1:11). Those witnesses went out and gave their very lives based upon what they had seen and heard. We can trust their witness.

So we can know that even though it seems as if evil is winning, Jesus is risen and He is Lord. His kingdom will be established and every knee in heaven, on earth, and under the earth will bow before Jesus as sovereign Lord.

APPLICATION OF THE TEACHING:

1. The exaltation of the Lord Jesus Christ is an encouragement to humility.

This is Paul's primary application in the context. If Jesus is the exalted Lord, we've got to dethrone self. We are to follow our Lord in His example of laying aside His rights and taking the form of a servant. Because He humbled Himself, God highly exalted Him. Jesus taught, "For everyone who exalts himself shall be humbled, and he who humbles himself shall be exalted" (Luke 14:11). It would be wrong to think that Jesus was motivated to go to the cross by the thought of being exalted afterwards. He went to the cross out of love and obedience to the Father and love for you and me.

But being exalted was His reward. Our motivation to humble ourselves should be love for God and others, because of His great love for us. But, if we humble ourselves under God's mighty hand, He will exalt us at the proper time (1 Pet. 5:6).

2. The exaltation of the Lord Jesus Christ is an encouragement in trials.

Jesus endured the cross, and the Father strengthened Him and gave Him grace for that awful ordeal. The cross, the resurrection and subsequent exaltation of Jesus shows that God can transform the most grotesque of human sins against us into the greatest of divine triumphs. Any suffering or tragedy we face can redound to the glory of God.

The great British preacher, Charles Spurgeon, knew this encouragement from Christ's exaltation. When he was only 22, his popularity had spread throughout London. Thousands were flocking to hear him preach. To accommodate the crowds, his church rented the Surrey Gardens Music Hall, which seated at least 10,000. The opening service there was Sunday, October 19, 1856. Word spread and when they opened the building, people crowded in, taking every seat, packing the aisles and stairways, while thousands more stood outside, hoping to hear through the open windows. When Spurgeon arrived and saw the crowd, he was almost overwhelmed. The service began, and everything seemed to be going well.

But just after Spurgeon began to pray, the place was thrown into confusion. Some in a gallery shouted, "Fire!" Another on the ground floor shouted, "The balconies are falling!" A third voice cried, "The whole place is collapsing!" People panicked and began rushing for the exits, but there was no room. Some fell through the balcony railings to the floor below. As some rushed out the doors, the crowd outside saw it as their opportunity to get a seat and began rushing in. Spurgeon tried to calm everyone, but before it was over, seven people had been crushed to death, and 28 others had been severely wounded. The whole thing had been orchestrated by enemies who were jealous of Spurgeon's popularity and wanted cause to bring him down.

Spurgeon himself was devastated by what had happened, so much so that a man who knew him well reported that 25 years later, when the event came up, Spurgeon was overcome with emotion. His critics used the event to bring all sorts of slander against the young preacher. Spurgeon withdrew for over a week, unable to preach or do anything. But as he walked in a friend's garden, our text flashed into his mind: "Therefore also God highly exalted Him, and bestowed on Him the name which is above every name." As he meditated on the exalted Christ, he found strength, and when he returned to the pulpit, he spoke on these verses. Let them comfort you in a time of tragedy.

3. The exaltation of the Lord Jesus Christ is an encouragement to evangelism.

The fact that every knee shall bow before Jesus as Lord, either willingly in this life, or forcibly at the judgment, should impel us to warn others to flee the wrath to come. The ultimate lordship of Jesus is the culmination of what God is doing in history, and we have a part in the work of His kingdom. Lost people need to see the serious consequences if they continue in rebellion. They need to repent of their sins, trust in Christ as Savior, and yield to Him as Lord.

4. The exaltation of the Lord Jesus Christ is an encouragement to salvation.

If you have not bowed before Jesus as your Lord and Savior, do not delay! Today is the day of salvation; tomorrow you may have to face Him as Judge! Believing in Christ as your Savior and Lord requires that you humble yourself, because you must let go of the proud notion that you can save yourself. Your good works are not good enough. Only Christ can save. Let go of any thoughts that you're good enough for the holy God. Turn from your sin and flee to Jesus.

"Turn to Me and be saved, all the ends of the earth; for I am God, and there is no other. I have sworn by Myself, the word has gone forth from My mouth in righteousness and will not turn back, that to Me every knee will bow, every tongue will swear allegiance. They will say, 'Only in the Lord are righteousness and strength.' Men will come to Him, and all who were angry at Him shall be put to shame. In the Lord all the offspring of Israel will be justified, and will glory" (Isa. 45:22-25).

The outcome is certain. The question is, On which side are you?

Application Questions

1. How can we minister to a believer who has gone through some tragedy and asks, "Where was God when this happened?"

2. If Jesus is highly exalted over all, why is there so much evil in this world?

3. Jesus said, "Why do you call me 'Lord, Lord,' but do not do what I say?" (Luke 6:46). Can a professing, but disobedient, Christian have assurance of salvation?

4. Why is it impossible to separate belief in Christ as Savior from submission to Him as Lord?

So then, my beloved, just as you have always obeyed, not as in my presence only, but now much more in my absence, work out your salvation with fear and trembling; for it is God who is at work in you, both to will and to work for His good pleasure.

† Philippians 2:12-13

WORKING OUT OUR SALVATION
Philippians 2:12-13

Christians have often been confused over the relationship between God's sovereignty and human responsibility in the matters of salvation and sanctification. Some have emphasized God's sovereignty in salvation to the exclusion of human responsibility. For example, when William Carey planned to go to India as a missionary, he was told by one minister, "Young man, sit down. When God pleases to convert the heathen, He will do it without your aid or mine." Others have stressed human responsibility to the exclusion of divine sovereignty. These folks lay a guilt trip on you by saying, "If you don't witness to your neighbor, his blood will cry out to God against you on judgment day!" They put all the emphasis for salvation on us.

On the matter of sanctification, or growth in salvation, some teach that we are to be passive: "Let go and let God." If you struggle or strive against sin, they say you're operating in the flesh, because the Christian life is an effortless experience of "not I, but Christ." Others stress obedience and effort to the exclusion of God's power, so that people end up trying to live the Christian life in their own strength.

Where's the biblical balance? I contend that the Bible teaches both/and, not either/or. God is absolutely sovereign and yet we are responsible, both in salvation and in sanctification. If the scale is tilted, it is in the direction of God's sovereignty, since He initiates, sustains, and brings the whole plan to completion. But, even so, we have a responsibility in the process. The apostle Paul brings out both emphases in our text, which teaches that ...

We must work out the practical implications of our salvation because God Himself is working in our midst.

To understand this text, we must take note of the context and of several facts brought out by the Greek text. In the flow of thought, these verses introduce the conclusion of an appeal for unity that began in 1:27 and runs through 2:18. "So then" (2:12) in Greek indicates a conclusion from what precedes. Also, all of the words used here are plurals in Greek.

Paul is not telling individual Christians to individually work out their personal salvation, as is often taught. Rather, he is appealing to the church, based on the example of humility seen in Jesus Christ, to work out the practical implications of their salvation in their relationships with one another. Because God Himself is at work in their midst as a church, they need to lay aside personal rights and humbly serve one another, putting others ahead of self. In so doing, they will stand out as lights in this dark, selfish world (2:15).

So Paul is especially concerned about these dear people ("my beloved") working out the relational implications of their salvation, with a view to their corporate testimony to the lost. If we talk about salvation but can't get along with one another, either in the church or in our homes, the world laughs off our message. But when the world sees Christians laying aside selfishness and regarding one another as more important than self (2:3), they will be more inclined to listen to the gospel. That's Paul's main message here, that we need to work out the practical implications of our salvation, because God Himself is working in our midst. There are four important things about salvation that we need to understand from this text:

1. We must possess salvation before we can work it out.

"Salvation" is a theological word we sometimes toss around without thinking much about its implications. It's a radical word because it points to a situation where someone is in dire straits. The American pilot who was recently shot down in Bosnia needed to be saved, because he could not get out of his predicament by himself. The Marines who rescued him saved his life. A person who is drowning needs a savior, because he is about to perish. Someone who is mortally ill needs a doctor or some medicine to save them, or else they will die.

The Bible tells us that the condition of every human being outside of Jesus Christ is that we are perishing, under God's wrath and condemnation. Unless we are saved, we will go into eternity bearing the penalty for our sins, which means eternal separation from God and punishment in the lake of fire. Unless we see our desperate condition, we will not call out to God to save us from our sins. Jesus described His mission as "to seek and to save that which was lost" (Luke 19:10). So we will not understand "salvation" if we think it just means that Jesus can give you a happier life. It refers to God's rescuing us from Satan's domain of darkness and transferring us to the kingdom of His beloved Son, in whom we have redemption, the forgiveness of sins (Col. 1:13, 14).

Paul was not writing to people who lacked salvation, telling them that they needed to work in order to obtain it. Rather, he was writing to people in whom God had begun the good work of salvation (1:6), telling them to work out the practical implications of the salvation they already possessed. The Bible is clear that we can never work for salvation, to earn or merit it, since it is the free gift of God (Eph. 2:8-9). Good works can never gain heaven for anyone, because no amount of good works can ever eradicate our sin, and God's holiness and justice demand that the penalty for sin be paid. If anyone could earn heaven by good works, he would boast in himself, which God will not allow. We are not saved by our good works, and not even by our faith. We are saved by Jesus Christ. Faith is simply the hand that receives the life ring of salvation that He throws to us.

I can't emphasize this point too strongly, because by far the most prevalent error people make about salvation is to think that God will accept them because of their good works. The world operates on the merit system. Every religion in the world, except biblical Christianity, is built on that system: If you're good enough, you'll earn salvation. I've sometimes been amazed at how deeply this is ingrained in us. I've had people sit under my preaching when I have labored to make it clear that we are not saved by any works that we have done. But then they've told me that the reason they think God will accept them into heaven is because they've tried hard to be good and to love others.

Because the point is so crucial, let me be blunt: If you think that you're going to heaven because you're a pretty good person, you are not going to heaven! The only ones going to heaven are those who have recognized that they were lost and who called out to God to save them through the blood of His Son Jesus.

Once we possess salvation, then it's necessary to work it out in its practical, everyday implications. Paul here mentions how the Philippians had always obeyed, not only when Paul was present; but now, in his absence, he was sure they would also obey, not just him, but God. If their obedience had just been to please Paul, it would not have been evidence of a genuine work of God in their hearts. Those truly saved by God want to please and obey Him in all respects. Since God looks on the heart, we need to learn how to please Him each day with our thoughts as well as with our words and deeds.

Once we possess salvation, we must learn to hold in tension two seemingly contradictory truths that the Bible clearly affirms: that salvation, from start to finish, is God's work; but, also, that at the same time, salvation requires diligent effort on our part.

2. Salvation, from start to finish, is God's work.

The reason the Philippians needed to work out their own salvation was that it was God who was at work among them, both to will and to work for His good pleasure. That sounds contradictory, doesn't it? But the Bible puts both together.

We're not saved because we choose God; we're saved because God willed to save us. He begins the good work in us (1:6). John 1:12-13 says, "As many as received Him, to them He gave the right to become children of God, even to those who believe in His name, who were born not of blood, nor of the will of the flesh, nor of the will of man, but of God." James 1:18 says, "In the exercise of His will He brought us forth by the word of truth, so that we might be, as it were, the first fruits among His creatures." Jesus said, "You did not choose Me, but I chose you, and appointed you, that you should go and bear fruit" (John 15:16).

One of the most prevalent errors in Christendom today is the idea that lost people can choose God by their own free will. The fallen human will is bound by sin. Jesus said plainly, "No one can come to Me, unless the Father who sent Me draws him" (John 6:44). "No one can come to Me, unless it has been granted him from the Father" (John 6:65). "All things have been handed over to Me by My Father, and no one knows who the Son is except the Father, and who the Father is except the Son, and anyone to whom the Son wills to reveal Him" (Luke 10:22). Left to ourselves, we all choose to go our own way. Salvation depends on God's choosing us and irresistibly drawing us by His grace according to His good pleasure.

God not only *wills* our salvation; He *works* it. Salvation is not through any human effort. It comes from the mighty power of God imparting spiritual life to those who were dead in their sins (Eph. 2:1-5), resulting in a new creation (2 Cor. 5:17). Not only in its inception, but throughout the whole process, God must be the energizing power of the Christian life (our English word "energy" comes from the Greek word translated "work" in 2:13). Jesus said, "... apart from Me you can do nothing" (John 15:5). We cannot live the Christian life in our own strength or effort, but must walk each day in the power of the indwelling Holy Spirit. Salvation, from start to finish, is God's work.

"If that's true," you say, "then let's kick back and not sweat it. If God wants to do it, He will do it without our effort." Not so:

3. Although salvation is God's work, it requires diligent effort on our part.

Maybe this sounds like double-talk, but it is clearly what God's Word declares. We are dead in our sins, in bondage to sin, unable to escape. Yet God calls on us to be saved and He commands us to call others to salvation. As Peter "solemnly testified and kept on exhorting" his hearers on the Day of Pentecost, "Be saved from this perverse generation!" (Acts 2:40).

You say, "How can you exhort someone to be saved when he can't be saved by his own will or effort?" Perhaps an illustration from the ministry of Jesus will help. On one occasion, Jesus encountered a man in the synagogue who had a withered hand. Apparently he had nerve damage which made it impossible for him to move or use his hand. Jesus commanded that man to stretch forth his hand (Matt. 12:13). Humanly, that was an impossible command. But Jesus told him to do it and when the man obeyed, his hand was restored. On another occasion Jesus told a man who had not been able to walk for 38 years to get up, take up his pallet, and walk (John 5:8). The man did it!

In both cases, the Lord called those men to do something they could not do in their own strength. He imparted to them the supernatural power required to fulfill His command. But they still had to do it. If they had said, "I can't do it," they would not have been healed. God worked mightily, but they had to work, too.

Hear me carefully on this, because I could easily be misunderstood: There is a sense in which receiving God's salvation requires diligent effort on your part. If you sit back and say, "Well, I'm not sure whether I'm one of the elect, and there isn't much I can do about it anyway," you'll be lost!

Complacency about your soul is deadly! You must have a desperate concern for your eternal well-being that moves you, in the words of 2 Peter 1:10, to "be all the more diligent to make certain about His calling and choosing you." Jesus talked about men taking the kingdom of God by force (Matt. 11:12; Luke 16:16). He urged His hearers, "Strive to enter by the narrow door; for many, I tell you, will seek to enter and will not be able" (Luke 13:24). If you are uncertain about your standing before God, do not give rest to your soul until you know that God has saved you.

There's a good illustration of this truth in the Old Testament. Six cities were designated as cities of refuge, where a man who had accidentally killed another man could flee so that a relative of the dead man could not avenge his death. If you were guilty of such an act, you wouldn't sit around, hoping that the avenger would not get you. You wouldn't have complacently shrugged your shoulders and said, "I can't do anything about saving myself." You would have taken off on the run for the nearest city of refuge, knowing that if you didn't make it inside, you would be killed. The avenger is in hot pursuit, and you're exhausted. But you don't stop until you're safe inside the gates of that city.

Those cities are a picture of salvation in Jesus our Refuge. God's wrath will surely come upon you for your crimes. If you die outside of Christ, you will have to pay with your life. But, God has provided a place of refuge. So there is an urgency, if you have not done so, for you to flee to Christ, who alone is our Refuge against sin and hell. In that sense, coming to salvation requires our diligent effort.

Continuance or growth in salvation also requires our effort. There is a popular teaching, known as the Keswick teaching (it was popularized at some Bible conferences held in Keswick, England), that we are not to exert any effort in the Christian life, that any striving proves that we are operating in the flesh, not in the Spirit. It is built on verses like Galatians 2:20, "I have been crucified with Christ; and it is no longer I who live, but Christ lives in me; and the life which I now live in the flesh I live by faith in the Son of God, who loved me, and delivered Himself up for me." That's a blessed truth which we all must learn to apply!

But there are also many verses in the New Testament which show that even the Spirit-filled life requires that I must strive against sin (Heb. 12:4); I must fight the good fight of faith (2 Tim. 4:7; Eph. 6:10-18); I must run the race so as to win (1 Cor. 9:24); I must be active in cleansing myself from defilement of flesh and spirit and perfecting holiness in the fear of God (2 Cor. 7:1). As our text says, because God is at work, I must work out my salvation. Doing it "with fear and trembling" implies both a reverent fear of God and an awareness of my own weakness and propensity toward sin that leads me to judge myself.

So the point is, even though God sovereignly wills and works all things after the counsel of His will, at the same time each of us is responsible to exert effort to work out the implications of our salvation each day. Yes, we must rely on the Holy Spirit and His power, not on our flesh. But, yes again, we must work. As Paul says (1 Cor. 15:10), he labored more than all of the other apostles; then he adds, "yet not I, but the grace of God with me." So we can't excuse our laziness or lack of obedience by saying, "God didn't move me to do it!" We must work with God.

We've seen that we must possess salvation to be able to work it out; and that while salvation is completely God's work, yet we must work out our salvation in dependence on God.

4. Salvation always has practical relational implications.

This is the main point of Paul's appeal here, that if we are truly saved by God's working in us, then we are under obligation to work out relational differences by following Christ's example of self-denying love. Just as Jesus laid aside His rights, just as He did not live for Himself and His own pleasure, just as He put others ahead of Himself, even to the point of death on the cross, so we must learn to die daily to self and live for others for Jesus' sake. If you claim to be saved, but you persist in selfishness, in refusing to yield your rights, in demanding your own way, whether at home or in the church, your life isn't backing up your claim. If the living God ("God" is emphatic in the Greek of 2:13) truly is at work in our midst, we must work out relational differences in a spirit of Christ-like humility and love.

As Americans, I think we sometimes put too much emphasis on the individual aspect of salvation and not enough emphasis on the corporate side of it. Of course, salvation is intensely individual; if you're not saved individually, you're not saved. But being saved individually of necessity affects how you relate to others. As I said, all the words in verses

12 & 13 are plurals. You can't live the Christian life in isolation. You've got to work out your individual salvation in your relationships with other Christians, both in your family and in the church. And, I might add, it is work! It's a lifetime process, and it isn't automatic. But as we work through such problems or differences, we learn more of Christ. We grow in humility and servanthood.

I also add, the reason we work out our salvation in terms of good relationships isn't primarily so we'll be happy, but rather for God's good pleasure, that is, to please God, whose pleasure is that His people love one another. As we work out our salvation in loving relationships, lost people will see the difference God makes in our daily lives and so be drawn to Him.

Conclusion

John Wesley and George Whitefield were both used of God to bring thousands of people to faith in Christ in the 18th century. They were good friends although they differed greatly on the matter of God's sovereignty versus man's responsibility in salvation. Wesley put such an emphasis on human responsibility that he was unsure of his own salvation on his deathbed, after a life of preaching the gospel. Whitefield, on the other hand, was a firm believer in God's sovereignty in salvation.

A man who was trying to find a juicy bit of gossip once asked Whitefield if he thought he would see John Wesley in heaven. Whitefield replied, "No." "Do you mean that you do not believe that John Wesley is converted and thus won't be in heaven?" the man asked, hoping to procure his bit of gossip. "You asked me if I would see John Wesley in heaven," Whitefield replied. "I do not believe I will, because John Wesley will be so close to the throne of God and I will be so far away, that I will not get a glimpse of him."

George Whitefield was applying what Paul is here teaching. If, by God's grace, we have been saved--if it is none other than God who is at work among us, both to will and to work for His good pleasure--then, we must then be diligent to work out the practical implications of that salvation in our relationships with one another in obedience to God.

How are your relationships at home? With other Christians? If God has saved you, you've got to follow the example of the Lord Jesus

Christ, who laid aside His rights and went to the cross on our behalf. Work out your salvation by dying to self and loving others for Jesus' sake.

Application Questions

1. Discuss: One of our main problems in evangelism is trying to get people saved who don't even know that they're lost.

2. What are some of the practical dangers if we camp too hard on either God's sovereignty or human responsibility in salvation?

3. How can we know when to "let go and let God" or when we need to exert more effort on a matter?

4. How can we hold to essential truth without sacrificing love? Is all division among professing Christians wrong?

Do all things without grumbling or disputing; so that you will prove yourselves to be blameless and innocent, children of God above reproach in the midst of a crooked and perverse generation, among whom you appear as lights in the world, holding fast the word of life, so that in the day of Christ I will have reason to glory because I did not run in vain nor toil in vain. But even if I am being poured out as a drink offering upon the sacrifice and service of your faith, I rejoice and share my joy with you all. You too, I urge you, rejoice in the same way and share your joy with me.

† Philippians 2:14-18

GRUMBLE, GRUMBLE--NOT!
Philippians 2:14-18

Complaining is probably one of the sins most tolerated by Christians. We tolerate it and perhaps don't even think of it as sin because we're all so prone to do it. I remember when God began convicting me of my grumbling spirit. I was in seminary in Dallas, where it is hot and humid. My apartment did not have air conditioning and there was no shower, only a bathtub. We had a rubber showerhead hooked to the tub faucet, so you could take a sit-down shower. On a hot and humid day I was taking my sit-down shower and I was grumbling to myself about the inconvenience of it and about how hot this crummy apartment was. This was during the Vietnam war, and it suddenly hit me: I could be over there in that sweltering jungle, getting shot at, in conditions a lot worse than my Dallas apartment! I had to confess my grumbling spirit to the Lord and give thanks to Him for the blessings of a sit-down shower.

After telling the Philippians to work out their salvation with fear and trembling, because it was none other than God who was at work in their midst, both to will and to work for His good pleasure (2:12-13), Paul goes from preaching to meddling: He applies it specifically by telling them (and us) to do *all* things without grumbling and disputing. In the context, he is especially exhorting us against grumbling and disputing against one another in the church, because he has been urging us to adopt the humble, self-sacrificing, servant ways of the Lord Jesus. But to grumble against any person or any circumstance is really to grumble against the sovereign God who wills and works all things in our lives (2:13). So Paul's exhortation means that we have to confront our grumbling and griping as sin. I still struggle with the problem, as most of us do!

I wish Paul had been a bit more realistic and down-to-earth. He could have said, "Try to do *most* things without grumbling or disputing." That's realistic, isn't it? I can give it a try. But *all things*? In fact, the word translated "all things" is emphatic in the Greek text. Paul isn't going to let us off the hook! And, his reason for this commandment concerns our individual and corporate testimony before the world (2:15, 16). Paul's own example (2:17) shows that not only are we not to grumble and dispute, but positively, we are to be marked by joy, even in the midst of difficult trials. So he is saying,

Our testimony as children of God requires that we be marked, not by grumbling and disputing, but by joy, even in trials.

To explain and apply Paul's words, I want to consider 4 things:

1. Our testimony of Christ should be uppermost in our thinking so as to affect all our attitudes and behavior.

What is the chief end of man? To glorify God and enjoy Him forever. What does it mean to glorify God? To make Him look good, as He truly is. To glorify God means that when people look at our lives as Christians, they should extol and exalt our God whom they see shining through us. So as children of God our testimony--what our lives communicate about our Savior--should be uppermost in our thinking so that our attitudes, our behavior, and our words bring glory to God.

Paul here refers to Christians as "children of God." A specific Old Testament passage is behind Paul's words. In Deuteronomy 32:5, in the song of Moses, in referring to the grumbling and unbelief of the children of Israel in the wilderness, Moses says, "They have acted corruptly toward Him, they are not His children, because of their defect; but are a perverse and crooked generation." Paul turns that around and says that we are God's children, living in the midst of a crooked and perverse generation, and thus we must be careful not to grumble and dispute, as Israel did in the wilderness, because as God's people we are supposed to shine forth in this dark world as lights, holding forth to people the word of life, the gospel of Christ.

Children reflect on their parents, don't they? Of course all children are selfish, rebellious sinners by nature. They all are immature and express themselves in inappropriate ways. They all grumble at times. No child is sinless. But, even so, children will take on the behaviors, attitudes, and words of their parents. I worked with the Boys Brigade program when Daniel was younger. A boy came to that program whose parents went to a liberal church where the gospel was not preached. This boy had the habit of taking the Lord's name in vain as a word of exclamation. I took him aside once and explained to him that God's name is holy and that we shouldn't use it carelessly, as he was. Then the dad came one evening, and I immediately saw where the boy learned to take the Lord's name in vain!

Children's attitudes reflect on the parents. If a child is sullen, unhappy, and always complaining about life, it doesn't speak well of the parents. It may be that the parents are truly loving, caring, people who provide well for their kids. But the child's bad attitude makes people think poorly of the parents, no matter how good of parents they really are.

That's the point we have to keep in mind as children of the Heavenly Father. He is perfect in all His ways. But, let's face it: Sometimes His ways lead us into the wilderness, where there are hardships. When you read Exodus, you see how God delivered Israel from Egypt in a powerful way. He sent the plagues, then He led Israel to the edge of the Red Sea and brought Pharaoh's army on their heels. He miraculously parted the sea so that Israel could march through on dry ground, and then brought the sea back on top of the Egyptian army.

Then, after this mighty demonstration of God's power and of His care for His chosen people, we read next that they came to a place, three days journey into the wilderness, where there was no water (Exod. 15:22). Coming right on the heels of their mighty victory, and just after the Song of Moses celebrating that victory (Exod. 15:1-18), when you read about their lack of water, you think, "So what? God who just parted the sea can provide water." But instead we read, "The people grumbled at Moses" (Exod. 15:24). Then we read how they grumbled because there was no food (16:2), so the Lord provided manna. Then they grumbled because there was no meat, so the Lord provided quails (16:8-13). Then they ran out of water again, and grumbled again, and the Lord again provided water (17:3).

But, in their grumbling against Moses and disputing with him (17:2), they were really grumbling and disputing against the Lord (16:8). It was a bad testimony to the nations around them, that the God who had provided a mighty deliverance for Israel would not also provide for their basic needs. It reflected badly on His love, His care, and His power to provide. The pagan nations around them, who were looking for a pretext to justify their rebellion against the living God, would scoff at God when they heard the grumbling and complaining of His people.

That's Paul's point in our text. We live in the midst of a crooked and perverse generation that refuses to submit to the Lordship of Jesus Christ. It's a world marked by grumbling and complaining. In the original temptation, Satan got Eve to doubt the goodness of God, and ever since he seeks to do the same. People won't trust in a God whose goodness is in question. So here are God's people, delivered from bondage to sin by God's mighty salvation through the death and resurrection of the Lord Jesus. They have seen His power. Then they get into a wilderness situation, a trial where they run out of some basic resource and don't have a clue where it's going to come from.

What do they do? Do they grumble and dispute with God: "How could You do this to me when I've faithfully followed You?" Or, filled with joy in the Lord, do they shine forth as lights in the darkness? The testimony of Christ is at stake, especially when you're going through a difficult trial.

Paul says that three things should mark children of God (especially in trials): We should be blameless, innocent, and above reproach. *Blameless* has the nuance of *moral integrity as seen by others*. It points to our outwardly observable behavior, including our attitudes. Nothing in our lives should give an occasion for scandal, where unbelievers can look at how we live and say, "I thought he was a Christian! How can he be a Christian and live like that?" A great example of a blameless man is Daniel, who lived in Babylon and served in that pagan government. When his enemies wanted to find some charge against him to bring him down, because they were jealous of his position, they finally concluded, "We shall not find any ground of accusation against this Daniel unless we find it against him with regard to the law of his God" (Dan. 6:5). Daniel lived with integrity.

Also, we are to be *innocent*. This word focuses on *inward* moral integrity, which is the proper root of outwardly blameless behavior. It focuses on what we are in our thought life before God. It's possible to put on a good front at church, but to be leading a double life. You can be an upright man at church, but be filled with lustful thoughts, always checking out the women. You can be a nice, smiling man at church, but be an angry tyrant with your family. All sin starts in our thoughts or mind (Mark 7:20-23). Thus we have to judge our sinful thoughts and take every thought captive to the obedience of Jesus Christ (2 Cor. 10:5) so that we will be not only blameless, but innocent.

Then we also must be *above reproach*. It's a summary of the other two and means, *without blemish*. It's an interesting Greek word, *amoma*. In Greek, the letter "a" negates something. So the word means, the opposite of *moma*. "Momus" was a carping Greek god who did nothing himself and found fault with everybody and everything. So those who gripe and find fault came to be called "Moma." But Paul says that the children of God are not to be fault-finders and gripers. We are to be without the blemish of complaining because we want this crooked and perverse generation to know that our Heavenly Father is a good, loving, and caring God. Our testimony of Christ should be uppermost in our minds so that we glorify Him by how we live.

2. Our testimony of Christ is tarnished by grumbling and disputing.

As I said, in the context Paul especially means grumbling and disputing against one another. But all grumbling and disputing is really against God who is sovereign over all our circumstances. "Grumbling" is used repeatedly of Israel in the wilderness, both in their complaining about Moses, as well as about their circumstances. Moses wasn't a perfect leader; no human leader is. But God had appointed him. So God said that their grumbling was against Him (Exod. 16:8). When we grumble, whether about a church leader we don't like or about some trial we're going through, we're really saying, "God, you're not doing a very good job of directing my life. Why am I out here in this wilderness? Why don't we have any water? Why did you appoint this man to lead us into this mess?" We're wrongly questioning God.

"Disputing" can either mean inward questioning or outward dissension (1 Tim. 2:8). Paul's command not to dispute does not stifle honest discussion of differences on matters of doctrine or practice. Nor does it mean that it is wrong to question church leaders about problem areas. But it does confront our attitude in how we raise questions or disagreements. To dispute means to challenge in a selfish rather than submissive spirit. It means to assert your authority in an attempt to resist God and the leaders He has appointed, so that you don't have to submit to His Word. Satan was disputing when he said to Eve, "Indeed, has God said, ...? You shall not surely die!" (Gen. 3:1, 4). As Matthew Henry put it, "God's commands were given to be obeyed, not to be disputed" (*Matthew Henry's Commentary*, on Phil. 2:15, [Revell], p. 734).

The most appropriate example of grumbling and disputing I have ever experienced was when I was in the military. They think something's wrong if you're not complaining! Everyone gripes about the food, about the regulations, about the commanding officer, about the no-good guys in your company who don't carry their share of the work. If you don't complain, but do your work cheerfully as unto the Lord, you stick out like a sore thumb, or, in Paul's words, you shine as lights in the world.

We've seen that our testimony should be uppermost in our thinking so that it affects all our attitudes and behavior, to bring glory to our Heavenly Father. Grumbling and disputing tarnish that testimony. Thirdly,

3. Our testimony of Christ shines forth when we are filled with joy even in the midst of trials.

"Lights" means luminaries, things that shine. When do stars shine the brightest? When the night is the darkest. They shine, but not as brightly, when the moon is full. The stars shine during the day, but we can't see them because the light of the sun blocks them out. But on a dark night, they shine the brightest.

When can you bear the most effective witness for Jesus Christ? When you're in the darkest place! It may be a place of personal trial, where you radiate with God's joy in spite of your situation. Maybe you're in a dark situation at work or school, surrounded by crooked and perverse people. If you do all things without grumbling or disputing, but rather are blameless, innocent, and above reproach, filled with joy in the Lord, you're going to shine! Many people will never read the Bible, but they do read you.

As Paul wrote, he was in a dark place, in prison, facing possible execution from the pagan Nero. Christian preachers in Rome were slandering him out of envy and strife. But Paul says that if his life is poured out as a drink offering on the altar, if it was upon the sacrifice and service of the Philippians' faith, he rejoiced and shared that joy with them. And he urges them to rejoice in their trials and to share that joy with him (2:17, 18).

Our lives shine as we put off grumbling and disputing and live in joy, especially during trials. But, also, we have a message we hold forth: "*the word of life*" (2:16). The gospel--that Christ died for our sins, that He arose victorious over sin and death, that He offers a full pardon from the wages of sin to all who will receive it by faith--that good news is the power of God to salvation for all who believe. The gospel is not just a set of propositions or doctrines to subscribe to, although it involves certain non-negotiable doctrines. The gospel brings the very *life* of God to those who are dead in their transgressions and sins (Eph. 2:1-10). Those apart from Christ are not pretty good people who just need a little help to solve some of their problems. According to Scripture, they are spiritually dead, separated from the life of God. But when we hold forth to them the word of life, God can use it to raise them from the dead, to give them eternal life.

Thus our testimony is built on our life in Christ, a life free from grumbling and disputing, a life filled with the joy of Christ and the salvation He has given us, even in trials. But our testimony also involves the verbal witness of telling people the word of the gospel that imparts new life to all who believe. Every Christian should have this two-fold witness: a life of joy, which often opens the door to the second part, the message or word of life. Paul's witness in Philippi illustrates what he is teaching here. He had been unjustly beaten and thrown into prison and locked in the stocks. He had good cause to complain, but instead he and Silas sang hymns of praise to God. God sent an earthquake to open the jail. The jailer was prevented from taking his own life and asked, "What must I do to be saved?" Paul shared the gospel message with him and his family. That's how we should bear witness of the Savior.

"But," you say, "how can I have joy when things aren't going well? My life is filled with problems. I've prayed, but the problems seem to get worse, not better. I live and work with difficult people. How can I have God's joy in such trials?"

4. Our testimony of Christ can reflect joy even in trials if we live in view of Christ's coming.

Paul could joyfully let his life be poured out as a drink offering because his focus was on "the day of Christ" when he would be rewarded because he did not run or labor in vain (2:16). The very words, "run" and "labor" point to the difficulty of serving Jesus Christ. It's no Sunday School picnic! The imagery of being lights in the world also points to the difficulty of ministry, because lights give off light by being expended themselves. The candle is burned up by giving off light. Every servant of Christ has to die to self in obedience to Christ. You may ask, "Why do that? Why endure hardship, why have people malign you, why wear yourself out serving Christ?" Because the day of Christ is coming, when He will render His rewards to every person. If people are there in heaven on that day, rescued from hell, gathered before the throne of Christ to sing His praises for all eternity because of your witness, don't you think that you will say, "Any suffering I went through for the sake of the gospel was worth it"?

Living in the light of the day of Christ means that we must daily submit ourselves in every situation to a sovereign God. He is working all things after the counsel of His will (Eph. 1:11). At present, He is allowing evil to go on. Living in this evil world, we often will suffer for the sake of righteousness. But we believe that He is sovereign, that His plan for the ages will be fulfilled, that Christ will return in power and glory to reign on His throne. So we can submit joyfully, without grumbling or disputing, to whatever He brings into our lives, knowing that He is in charge, and that His plan will not be thwarted.

Conclusion

A little old lady walked into a department store one day and was surprised when a band began to play and an executive pinned an orchid on her dress and handed her a crisp $100 bill. She was the store's millionth customer. Television cameras were focused on her and reporters began interviewing her. "Tell me," one asked, "just what did you come here for today?"

The lady hesitated for a minute and then sheepishly answered, "I was on my way to the Complaint Department." How embarrassing!

But I wonder, if there had been a secret video camera recording your life this past week, how much grumbling would have been captured on film? Maybe you even came to church like that lady went to the department store, ready to air your complaints or to give someone a piece of your mind. But God meets you at the door and pins His Word on you: "Do all things without grumbling or disputing, that you may be blameless and innocent, a child of God above reproach in the midst of this crooked and perverse generation, among whom you shine forth as a light in the world." Grumble, grumble--NOT!

Application Questions

1. The psalmists sometimes complained to the Lord. Is this okay? How does it fit in with Paul's command in Phil. 2:14?

2. If you're in a bad situation (work, home, etc.) is it wrong to complain to those in charge? To complain to a friend?

3. If a Christian's life isn't what it should be, should he give verbal witness of Christ? How "perfect" must we be to bear witness?

4. Why is affirming the sovereignty of God in all things so important in learning to live with joy rather than with grumbling?

But I hope in the Lord Jesus to send Timothy to you shortly, so that I also may be encouraged when I learn of your condition. For I have no one else of kindred spirit who will genuinely be concerned for your welfare. For they all seek after their own interests, not those of Christ Jesus. But you know of his proven worth, that he served with me in the furtherance of the gospel like a child serving his father. Therefore I hope to send him immediately, as soon as I see how things go with me; and I trust in the Lord that I myself also will be coming shortly. But I thought it necessary to send to you Epaphroditus, my brother and fellow worker and fellow soldier, who is also your messenger and minister to my need; because he was longing for you all and was distressed because you had heard that he was sick. For indeed he was sick to the point of death, but God had mercy on him, and not on him only but also on me, so that I would not have sorrow upon sorrow. Therefore I have sent him all the more eagerly so that when you see him again you may rejoice and I may be less concerned about you. Receive him then in the Lord with all joy, and hold men like him in high regard; because he came close to death for the work of Christ, risking his life to complete what was deficient in your service to me.

† Philippians 2:19-30

TWO MEN WORTH IMITATING
Philippians 2:19-30

At St. Bede's Episcopal Church in Santa Fe, New Mexico, there is only one door into the sanctuary. Over that door is a hand-lettered sign that reads, "Servant's Entrance." There isn't any way in or out of that church except through the servant's entrance! That's not a bad reminder of the fact that every believer is called to serve our Lord and Master, Jesus Christ. Unlike most sports teams, the Lord's team does not have any bench warmers. Every Christian is given a first-string spot on the team, with a vital role to fulfill. A non-serving Christian is a contradiction in terms.

After the doctrinal high water mark of this letter, where Paul speaks of the person and work of the Lord Jesus Christ who left the glory of heaven to take on the form of a servant and to become obedient to death on the cross for our sakes (2:5-11), Paul turns to some seemingly mundane matters about sending Timothy and Epaphroditus to the Philippian church, and about his hope of coming personally if he is released from prison. This is one of those sections of Scripture that, at first glance, you may wonder why God took up the pages of the Bible with the travel schedules of these three men. But as we examine it, I hope you will see that the Holy Spirit uses it in a marvelous way to illustrate for us the truths that Paul has been presenting in this entire chapter. These choice men whom Paul commends to the Philippian church, Timothy and Epaphroditus, are two men worth imitating as we seek to serve our Lord. Along with Paul himself, they have much to teach us about Christian servanthood. They show us that ...

If we cultivate a servant's heart and endure a servant's hardships, we will receive a servant's honor.

1. We must cultivate a servant's heart.

Our Savior did not come to be served, but to serve and to give His life a ransom for many (Mark 10:45). Every Christian is the blood-bought servant of the Lord Jesus Christ. Being a servant of Christ is not an option if you want to be more dedicated; it is the calling of every believer. If you are not a servant of Christ, you cannot rightly call yourself a Christian. But, because we all are selfish by nature, we must cultivate the heart of a servant as we grow in Christ. Paul, Timothy and Epaphroditus illustrate men who had servant's hearts, as seen in two dimensions:

A. A servant's heart is centered on the things of Jesus Christ.

The Apostle Paul was a man whose focus was on the Lord Jesus Christ. In 2:19 he says, "But I hope *in the Lord Jesus* to send Timothy to you shortly." In 2:24 he says, "I trust *in the Lord* that I myself also shall be coming shortly." It is Paul's way of saying, "If it be the Lord's will." It shows that he did not make decisions based simply on common sense or on what he thought was best, but he submitted everything to the Lord and His will. When he mentions how Epaphroditus got well from his illness, he doesn't say, "Thank goodness he got better!" but rather, "*God* had mercy on him, and not on him only, but also on me." When he instructs the church to welcome Epaphroditus, he tells them to "receive him *in the Lord* with all joy." Clearly, the Lord was the focal point of Paul's life and ministry.

Timothy's focus was also on the Lord. Paul states that, unlike many others, Timothy was not seeking after his own interests instead of those of Jesus Christ (2:21). Timothy served with Paul in the furtherance of the gospel (2:22). Christ and the gospel were at the center of Timothy's life.

Epaphroditus also was a faithful servant whose focus was on the things of Christ. He had pushed himself almost to the point of death to bring the gift to Paul from the Philippian church. Maybe he grew ill on the six-week journey and pushed himself almost beyond his limits in an effort to get to the apostle's side. Or, perhaps after arriving he contracted some illness, but he kept pushing himself in his service to Paul in the cause of the gospel. His longing and concern for the church back in Philippi also reveal his servant's heart for the things of Christ.

Paul calls Epaphroditus a "minister to my need" and states that he had completed by his presence what the Philippians could not do in their absence in service to Paul (2:25, 30). The word translated "minister" and "service" comes from a Greek word from which we get our word "liturgy." In secular Greek, the word was used of a man who, out of love for his city and the gods, would finance a great drama or outfit a battleship. It has the flavor of sacred service, or worship. Every servant of Jesus Christ does what he does, whether giving or helping or speaking, as an offering to the Lord Jesus. A servant's heart is centered on the Lord Jesus Christ and His work.

This focus on Christ and His work should not just be true of those who earn their living from the gospel. Every Christian, however you earn your living, should live every day in fellowship with the Lord, in submission to His will, in obedience to His Word, available to do His work. Christian servants will be eager to talk about the great truths of the Bible with fellow Christians. They will be ready to tell lost people about the Savior and His work on the cross. They watch for opportunities to please Him by helpful deeds toward others. Three attitudes mark servants who are focused on the Lord Jesus Christ:

(1) *They are willing to be sent anywhere.* It wouldn't have been easy for Timothy to leave the side of his beloved father in the faith in order to go to Philippi, but he was willing to go if that was God's will. It hadn't been easy for Epaphroditus to leave the comforts of home and journey to Rome, but he had done it. Now, it also would be difficult for him to leave Paul and return home, but he was willing to go where the Lord wanted him.

Have you told the Lord, "I'm willing to go anywhere You want me to go"? I remember as a teenager being hesitant to do that, because I was afraid He might say, "Go to Africa as a missionary," and I didn't want to do that! But then I reasoned, "God is a loving Father who knows what is best for me. If it's best for me to serve Him in Africa, I'd be stupid to stay in the United States." So I surrendered to Him on that matter. Then, after seminary, an opportunity came up to pastor a church in northeastern Indiana. I can think of few places in this country I'd rather not be more than northeastern Indiana! But Marla and I knelt down and reaffirmed our submission to His will. The packet of material from that church never arrived in the mail, and the Lord soon opened up the church in the mountains of Southern California, where I served for 15 years.

(2) *They are willing to serve anyone.* Timothy served Paul, but he was willing to go and serve the Philippian church. Epaphroditus served the Philippian church, but he was willing to go and serve Paul. He reminds me of Philip, who was being used by God to reach great multitudes in Samaria, but who was willing to go to a deserted road where the Lord used him to

reach the Ethiopian eunuch (Acts 8:5-8, 26-40). A servant of Christ isn't out to make a name for himself by speaking to large crowds only. He's available to his Lord to serve anyone the Lord directs him to serve.

(3) *They are willing to sacrifice anything.* Timothy had given up his own interests to become a servant of Christ. Epaphroditus almost lost his life in his service for the Lord. To the Ephesian elders, Paul said of his own ministry, "I do not consider my life of any account as dear to myself, in order that I may finish my course, and the ministry which I received from the Lord Jesus, to testify solemnly of the gospel of the grace of God" (Acts 20:24). Have you told the Lord, "I'll give up everything--my desires, my ambitions, my comforts, my time, my money--to serve You"?

I have emphasized this point at length, that a servant's heart is centered on the things of Jesus Christ, because if you have any other motive or reason for Christian service, you will eventually burn out or bomb out. You'll get angry and be hurt because of the way people treat you; you'll be frustrated and grow weary of the hardships you have to endure; you'll quit in disgust or disappointment--if you're serving for any reason other than love for the Lord Jesus who gave Himself for your sins. A servant's heart must be constantly captivated with Christ.

B. A servant's heart puts others ahead of himself for the sake of Christ.

The Apostle Paul was in prison facing possible execution. Timothy was his right hand man, a faithful man who had served with Paul as a child serving his father (2:22). It would have been understandable if Paul, thinking of his circumstances, had said, "I can't spare Timothy at this time. He must stay here with me." But, instead, he was willing to send Timothy for the sake of the Philippian church. The Philippians had been willing to serve Paul by giving monetarily and by sending Epaphroditus, who himself had been willing to serve to the brink of death on Paul's behalf.

Of Timothy, Paul says, "I have no one else of kindred spirit who will genuinely be concerned for your welfare. For they all seek after their own interests, not those of Christ Jesus" (2:20, 21). These are hard words to understand, because you would think that out of all the faithful Christians in Rome (Paul wrote Romans 16 about five years prior to this, where he greets many faithful believ- ers in Rome), he could have found some who were not living for themselves! And, what about Luke, Titus, Aristarchus, Trophimus, and Epaphroditus? Paul must have meant that of those available to him at that time as messengers, Timothy was the only one he knew of who would genuinely seek after the interests of others instead of their own.

There are at least three ways you can tell if you're putting oth- ers ahead of yourself:

(1) *You will have heartfelt love*--These verses are oozing with Paul's heartfelt love for Timothy, Epaphroditus, and for the Philippians. Also notice how Epaphroditus longed for the Philippians and was distressed (the word is used of Jesus' distress in the garden) because they had heard that he was sick (2:26). There are some super-spiritual Christians who try to remove all emotion from the Christian life. They think that spiritual maturity means being stoical, not showing any grief or anxiety or tenderness or tears. But Paul here says how if Epaphroditus would have died, he would have been overwhelmed with grief at the loss of this dear servant of God. Paul knew Romans 8:28--he wrote the verse! He also knew Philippians 4:6-7, about not being anxious. Yet he didn't chide Epaphroditus because he was distressed over how the Philippian church felt about his sickness (2:26). Paul wasn't afraid to be human and to express his deep feelings for others.

(2) *You will show genuine concern*--This spills over with heartfelt love, but here I am especially focusing on Timothy's genuine concern for these people, that he was not seeking his own interests, but the welfare of the church (2:20-21). Sad to say, many who serve the Lord, including some in full-time ministry, do it with mixed motives. They're out for the strokes others can give them. They like being in the limelight. They're manipulative in using people for their own advancement or gain.

I knew a pastor in California who was outwardly very friendly. He seemed loving and caring. But when you got to know him you could see that he had an inordinate need to be liked. He would tell people what he thought they wanted to hear so they would like him, even though sometimes it was not the truth. He was really seeking his own interests, not the welfare of the church.

(3) *You can work cooperatively with others*--Timothy served with Paul like a child his father (2:22). Paul and Epaphroditus worked together

harmoniously in the gospel cause. To do that, you've got to die to self and put others ahead of yourself for the sake of the work. Some people are not team players, unless they are the boss. Even though Paul was clearly the leader among these men, and was about 25 years older than Timothy (we don't know how old Epaphroditus was), he didn't lord it over them. He humbly calls Epaphroditus his brother, fellow worker, and fellow soldier. He deflects any glory from himself and lifts up these two faithful servants.

So we must cultivate a servant's heart, centered on the things of Jesus Christ, putting others ahead of ourselves for the sake of the gospel.

2. We must endure a servant's hardships.

Serving Christ is not easy. The term fellow soldier implies warfare. It brings us under the withering attacks of the enemy, who wants to hinder the cause of Christ. Just as soldiers must go through boot camp so that they can learn to endure the hardships they will encounter on the battlefield, so the Lord's servants must be tested. Paul mentions Timothy's "proven worth" (2:22). The word means "approved by testing." It is the same word used in Romans 5:3, 4, where Paul says that tribulation brings about perseverance and perseverance brings proven character. A product that has been approved by testing is a reliable product. Either the manufacturer or a consumer advocate has submitted the product to severe conditions to see if it holds up. You can know that the product won't give out just when you need it most. Timothy had endured enough testing that Paul knew he was faithful. Testing or hardship in Christian service can come from many sources:

A. The hardship of persecution both from without and within.

Paul was in prison due to persecution from without. But also he was under attack from those who preached the gospel from envy and selfish ambition (1:15, 17). Perhaps they are the ones he refers to in 2:21. They claimed to be serving Christ, but in reality they were serving themselves. Alexander Maclaren wrote, "Many a professing Christian life has a veneer of godliness nailed thinly over a solid bulk of selfishness" (*Expositions of Holy Scripture* [Baker], "Philippians," p. 284). Paul knew the keen disappointment of professing Christians who were not faithful because they were living for themselves. It's often more difficult to bear the attacks from those within the flock than from those outside, because you expect the world to be against you, but not fellow Christians.

B. The hardship of the work itself.

In 2 Corinthians 11:23-29, Paul catalogues the hardships he experienced as a servant of Christ: persecutions, physical hardships, dangers that brought him to the brink of death, and, on top of everything else, intense concern for all the churches. In our text, he mentions his concern for the Philippian church (2:28). He mentions Epaphroditus' risking his life (it's a gambling term, "to throw the dice"), as well as his concern about the church. So the work of the gospel involves both physical and emotional hardships that can wear us down. We must be prepared for hardships in serving the Lord and rely on His sustaining grace, not on our own strength or resources.

I would encourage you to read the biographies of the great saints who have gone before us. One of the best is Ruth Tucker's *From Jerusalem to Irian Jaya* [Zondervan], which is a biographical history of the missions movement. It will move you to tears as you read of the incredible hardships that God's people have gone through to take the gospel to the unreached parts of the earth. In the early years of missionary work in Africa, only one out of four missionaries survived the first term of service (p. 155)! They were plagued by disease, by hostile people, by tribal warfare, by government hindrances. Yet they kept going. Our hardships are nothing in comparison with theirs!

Why go through such hardship? If we cultivate a servant's heart and endure a servant's hardship, ...

3. We will receive a servant's honor.

We don't seek the honor for ourselves, but for our Lord who alone is worthy. But He promises, "Those who honor Me I will honor" (1 Sam. 2:30). He will reward every faithful servant with the crown of righteousness (2 Tim. 4:8). Any hardship we suffer now in serving Christ will be well worth it when we see His face and hear from Him, "Well done, good and faithful slave; you were faithful with a few things, I will put you in charge of many things, enter into the joy of your master" (Matt. 25:21).

Paul here honors Timothy by sending him as his own representative. He honors Epaphroditus by his commendation and tells the church to "hold men like him in high regard" (2:29). As Calvin points out, the devil is intent on undermining the authority of godly pastors, and so the church must hold such men in high regard (*Calvin's Commentaries* [Baker], "Philippians," p. 84).

Conclusion

Did you notice how these seemingly mundane words about the travel schedules of these men illustrate what Paul has been saying throughout chapter 2? He has told us that we should do nothing from selfishness or empty conceit, but with humility of mind to regard others more highly than we do ourselves; not looking out for our own interests, but for the interests of others (2:3-4). Then he gave us the great example of our Lord, who laid aside His rights, took on the form of a servant, and became obedient to death on the cross. Therefore, God highly exalted Him (2:5-11). Jesus had a servant's heart; He endured a servant's hardships; He received a servant's honor. That's the pattern for all who serve Him. Let's all strive to become imitators of Timothy and Epaphroditus; but not only of them, but of the Apostle Paul; and, beyond him, of our Lord Jesus Himself. There should be only one entrance to the church: the servant's entrance!

Application Questions

1. Interact with the comment, "A non-serving Christian is a contradiction in terms." How are you serving Christ?

2. Must every Christian be willing to be sent anywhere? Is the missionary calling something every Christian must consider?

3. What's the difference between genuine concern for others, which is good, and worry, which is wrong?

4. How do we draw the line between accepting the criticism of other Christians versus ignoring it as being wrongly motivated?

Finally, my brethren, rejoice in the Lord. To write the same things again is no trouble to me, and it is a safeguard for you. Beware of the dogs, beware of the evil workers, beware of the false circumcision; for we are the true circumcision, who worship in the Spirit of God and glory in Christ Jesus and put no confidence in the flesh,

† Philippians 3:1-3

TRUE VERSUS COUNTERFEIT CHRISTIANITY
Philippians 3:1-3

About 20 years ago a survey of 7,000 Protestant youths from many denominations asked whether they agreed with the following statements: "The way to be accepted by God is to try sincerely to live a good life." More than 60 percent agreed.

"God is satisfied if a person lives the best life he can." Almost 70 percent agreed. (Reported by Paul Brand & Philip Yancey, *Fearfully & Wonderfully Made* [Zondervan], p. 108.)

I have found that many church-going people, like these young people, are confused on the most important question in life: "How can I be right with God?" Many think that sincerity is a big factor. If you're sincere, God will let you into heaven even if you're a bit fuzzy on the truth. But that's like saying that a man who swallows deadly poison, sincerely thinking that it is medicine, will get better. All the sincerity in the world is fatal if it is not in line with the truth.

Many also think that human effort plays a big role. If you try your best, even though you aren't perfect, God will say, "I'll let you into heaven because you tried so hard." If that is what the Bible teaches, then it is so. But if it is contrary to what the Bible teaches, then trying your best to get into heaven is like trying your best to broad jump across the Grand Canyon. You're not going to make it!

Have you ever been stuck with a counterfeit bill? You thought it was legal tender, but when you took it somewhere and offered it as money, the teller or clerk said, "I'm sorry, but this is counterfeit money. It's no good." The Bible teaches that Satan is a master counterfeiter, trying to pass off on unsuspecting people a version of Christianity that looks pretty good, but it is not going to be accepted by the bank of heaven. It's traumatic to get stuck with a counterfeit bill; it would be far more traumatic to stand before God someday and hear Him declare that your Christianity is counterfeit!

In Philippians 3:1-3, the apostle Paul contrasts true and counterfeit

Christianity. To understand this section of Philippians, you must know a bit of history. Soon after the gospel began to spread among the Gentiles, some Jewish men who claimed also to believe in Christ began teaching the Gentile converts that they could not be saved unless they also were circumcised according to the law of Moses (see Acts 15:1). They did not deny that a person must believe in the Lord Jesus Christ, but they added to faith in Christ the keeping of the Jewish law, especially circumcision, as necessary for salvation.

The issue was debated and resolved in Jerusalem at a council of the church leaders where it was decided that Gentiles do not have to become Jews or be circumcised to be saved; but that every person, Jew or Gentile, is saved by grace through faith in Christ alone (Acts 15:1-29). But that decision did not cause Satan to give up his efforts to pervert the truth of the gospel. He continued to work through a group of men known as Judaizers who followed Paul on his missionary journeys, infiltrating the new churches and teaching their subtle error, that faith in Christ was not sufficient if a person did not also keep the Law, especially circumcision. Paul wrote Galatians to refute this error. He contends there that these men were preaching a false gospel and he calls down damnation on those who so pervert the true gospel (Gal. 1:6-9). The Judaizers are the men Paul is warning the Philippian church about in our text. The three terms in 3:2, "dogs, evil workers, and false circumcision," all refer to one group, the Judaizers, who were promoting a counterfeit Christianity.

While the Judaizers no longer exist under that name, the core of their teaching is still quite prevalent. Thus our text is extremely important in helping us to discern what true Christianity is and to reject any counterfeit version. Paul is teaching that ...

To be true Christians we must put off all confidence in human merit and trust in Christ alone for salvation.

True Christianity relies totally on the person and work of Christ; counterfeit Christianity adds to this reliance on human worth or works. Concerning counterfeit Christianity, Paul warns,

1. Beware of counterfeit Christianity which adds human merit to the person and work of Christ!

The severity of Paul's warning is underscored by his threefold repetition: *"Beware ... beware ... beware ...!"* Counterfeit Christianity is a strong danger for all of us because we're all prone to pride and self-reliance. We all want to take for ourselves at least some of the credit for our salvation. We'll be generous and grant that most of the credit goes to the Lord, but we still want to reserve a bit of the honor for ourselves. People will say, "I was saved by my own free will," which implies, "I was smart enough or good enough to make the right choice." But the Bible knocks our pride out from under us by clearly stating that our salvation does not depend on our will, but on God's sovereign mercy (Rom. 9:16). Or, people will say, "Christ died for me because I was worthy." But Scripture is clear that He died for us when we were unworthy sinners (Rom. 5:8).

Counterfeit Christianity glories in the flesh, which means, human worth or merit. The names Paul calls these false teachers reveal three common forms such human merit takes:

A. Counterfeit Christianity takes pride in racial or ethnic status, as if it put us in right standing with God.

Paul sarcastically calls these Judaizers "dogs." He is taking a slur that the Jews used against the Gentiles and turning back against these false teachers. It referred to the packs of wild dogs that used to raid the garbage and eat anything they could find. Since the Gentiles were not concerned about clean and unclean foods, or about purifying themselves according to the Jewish rituals, the Jews viewed them as unclean dogs. Just beneath the surface was ethnic pride, as if being a Jew by birth made one right with God.

Much of the strife in the world today stems from racial or religious pride. The Catholic-Protestant violence in Ireland, the ethnic cleansing in Bosnia, the Arab-Jewish conflicts in the Holy Land, Iraq's persecution of the Kurds, the recent civil war in Rwanda, the racial tension in South Africa, and many more conflicts are due to people mistakenly thinking that their racial status puts them in God's favor. Here in America, many of the white supremacy groups justify their ethnic pride and hatred of blacks and

Jews on a mistaken understanding of the Bible.

Scripture is clear that while God chose the nation Israel as His people and still has a special purpose for the Jews, He is no respecter of persons when it comes to granting salvation through Jesus Christ (Acts 10:34-47). As Paul writes in Romans 10:12, 13, "For there is no distinction between Jew and Greek; for the same Lord is Lord of all, abounding in riches for all who call upon Him; for 'Whoever will call upon the name of the Lord will be saved.'"

B. Counterfeit Christianity takes pride in human works as if they put us in right standing with God.

Paul calls these men, who prided themselves on their good works, "evil workers." They thought they were obeying God's law. Outwardly they were good, moral people, zealous for religious activities. But their religious works were evil in God's sight, because they took pride in their own achievements and trusted in their good deeds as the means of making themselves right before God. Such trust in human works brings glory to man and nullifies what Christ did for us on the cross.

The Bible is clear that while we are saved by grace through faith apart from any works, genuine saving faith always results in a life of good works (Eph. 2:8-10; Titus 2:11-14; 3:4-8; James 2:14-26). But the order of faith and works is essential! No human efforts can commend us to God. A true Christian never glories in his good works, but glories in Christ alone, as we will see.

C. Counterfeit Christianity takes pride in religious rituals as if they put us in right standing with God.

Paul calls these men "the false circumcision," which is a play on words. In Greek, circumcision is *peritome*; Paul calls these men *katatome*, which means "mutilators." Just as the pagan priests of Baal in Elijah's day cut themselves in a religious frenzy, so these false teachers were mutilating people through their emphasis on circumcision. They wrongly thought that the ritual of removing the male foreskin somehow gained them favor with God. But as Paul argues in Romans 4, even Abraham, to whom God first gave the rite of circumcision, was not made right with God through circumcision, but through faith.

Today there are many professing Christians who mistakenly think that religious rituals such as baptism or communion or attending church services or going through prescribed liturgies will get them into heaven. But, as Jesus told the religious Nicodemus, "... unless one is born again, he cannot see the kingdom of God" (John 3:3).

Thus Paul is strongly warning us to beware of trusting in any form of human goodness, human worth, human merit, or good works as the basis of our standing with God. Salvation is clearly shown in Scripture to be due to God's choice, not due to our being worth it, "that no man should boast before God" (see 1 Cor. 1:27-31).

These verses also show us that it is the job of faithful pastors to warn the flock of such dangerous teachings. We live in a day marked by tolerance and positive thinking. Many Christians say, "Why attack those who teach error? Just preach the positives." I have often been criticized because I preach against popular errors that have flooded into the church, such as the self-esteem teaching that runs counter to the heart of the gospel. There is also a strong movement toward unity, where doctrine is viewed as divisive and against love. Anyone who points out doctrinal error is labeled a "heresy hunter" who is against unity. But notice that even though Paul is exhorting the Philippian church to unity, it is not a unity devoid of doctrinal truth. If you didn't need pastors to warn you of such subtle errors, verses like these would not be in the Bible.

2. Embrace true Christianity, which relies totally on the person and work of Jesus Christ for salvation.

Note that Paul is reminding the Philippians of something they already knew (3:1). When he says "Finally," he isn't necessarily being like some preachers, who say that half way through their sermon! It can mean simply that he is turning to a new section. Although scholars differ on it, I believe that by "the same things" Paul is referring to his emphasis on rejoicing. He has mentioned "rejoicing" (1:18 [2x], 2:17 [2x], 18 [2x], 28) and "joy" (1:4, 25; 2:2, 29) eleven times already in chapters one and two! But, he's going to remind them again, because it is such an important, central part of the genuine Christian life. He will hit it again in 4:4. It is no trouble to him to hammer on it, and it is a safeguard against the subtle danger of trusting in human merit. Rejoicing in the Lord is the great antidote to rejoicing in self-reliance or achievement. It takes our focus off ourselves, it humbles our pride, and it fills us with great hope to rejoice in the Lord.

A. True Christianity is summed up by, "Rejoice in the Lord."

I understand "rejoice in the Lord" (3:1) to be a summary of true Christianity, while the three phrases in 3:3, "worship in the Spirit of God," "glory in Christ Jesus," and "put no confidence in the flesh" are simply other ways of saying the same thing. Test yourself by this measure: True Christians rejoice in the Lord.

What does this mean? It means that *the Lord Jesus Christ is everything to a true Christian*. Christ, and Christ alone, is our salvation. Without Him, we would be lost and without hope. In Him we are saved and have hope! As Paul puts it (1 Cor. 1:30-31), "But by His doing you are in Christ Jesus, who became to us wisdom from God, and righteousness and sanctification, and redemption, that, just as it is written, 'Let him who boasts, boast in the Lord.'"

Also he wrote (Col. 2:10-11), "In Him you have been made complete, and He is the head over all rule and authority; and in Him you were also circumcised with a circumcision made without hands, in the removal of the body of the flesh by the circumcision of Christ." This is what Paul is referring to when he calls true Christians "the circumcision" (Phil. 3:3). It is a spiritual, inner work performed on us by Christ. So when Paul tells us to rejoice in the Lord, he means that the Lord is everything to us and we are in Him. So we are to focus our thoughts on Him and what He has graciously done for us through the cross. We will be filled with joy in the Holy Spirit as we daily walk with our eyes on the Lord Jesus and what He is to us.

"Rejoice in the Lord" also means that *true Christianity is not just a matter of the head, but also of the heart*. It involves and is built on sound doctrine which is grasped by the intellect. Our minds must appropriate the great truths of who Christ is and what He did for us on the cross and what He has promised to those who believe in Him. But, if it stops there, you are not a true Christian. A true Christian is marked by what Jonathan Edwards called "religious affections." His emotions or heart is affected, so that he rejoices in the inner person as he thinks on the blessedness of what Jesus is to him.

A Christian leader and seminary professor, who has been in ministry for over 20 years, told me that his wife, due to her "dysfunctional" upbringing, had never felt God's love and that she did not understand His grace. In spite of all the teaching and training to which she had been exposed, he said that when she heard me preach on God's grace and love, it just went right past her. He attributed this to the fact that her father had been a cold, unemotional, unloving man. I shocked him and made him angry when I responded, "If your wife has never *felt* God's love in Christ and has never been moved by the great truth that Christ died for her sin, she isn't saved." True Christianity is not merely a matter of subscribing to the great doctrinal truths of the Bible, although it is built on that. It is a matter of God changing our hearts, so that we rejoice in the Lord. This summarizes true Christianity. But, also,

B. True Christianity is marked by "worship in the Spirit of God."

Jesus said, "God is spirit, and those who worship Him must worship in spirit and truth" (John 4:24). True worship is the inner sense of awe, gratitude, and love for God that stems from an understanding of who God is and who we are in His presence. The false teachers were making worship a matter of outward ritual. Paul is saying that true Christians are marked by inner worship prompted by the indwelling Holy Spirit. The Spirit works submission in our hearts so that we bow before God, caught up in love and praise, giving all glory to Him for His great salvation!

C. True Christianity is marked by "glorying in Christ Jesus."

The King James Version inaccurately translates, "rejoice in Christ Jesus." The word is "boast" or "glory." Paul is basing this on Jeremiah 9:23-24: "Thus says the Lord, 'Let not a wise man boast of his wisdom, and let not the mighty man boast of his might, let not a rich man boast of his riches; but let him who boasts boast of this, that he understands and knows

Me, that I am the Lord who exercises lovingkindness, justice, and righteousness on earth; for I delight in these things,' declares the Lord."

Have you ever been around a boaster? He goes around telling everyone how wonderful he is, how smart he is, how much he knows. Christians should go around telling people how wonderful Christ is, how great He is, how merciful, how kind, how powerful, how awesome, how righteous, etc. Boasting in ourselves is sinful pride; boasting in the Lord deflates our pride and gives all the glory to Him. True Christians confess, "The only thing I'm great at is being a great sinner; but Christ Jesus is a great Savior!"

D. True Christianity is marked by "no confidence in the flesh."

Counterfeit Christianity builds a person's self-esteem: "You're great, you're worthy, you're somebody!" True Christianity humbles all pride and confidence in self. As Jeremiah 17:5, 7, 8 puts it, "Cursed is the man who trusts in mankind and makes flesh his strength, and whose heart turns away from the Lord.... Blessed is the man who trusts in the Lord and whose trust is in the Lord. For he will be like a tree planted by the water, that extends its roots by a stream and will not fear when the heat comes; but its leaves will be green, and it will not be anxious in a year of drought nor cease to yield fruit."

Conclusion

Why do people ignore strong warnings? I guess they think that somehow it doesn't apply to them or that it isn't to be taken seriously. On our vacation, we went to the Columbian icefields in Jasper National Park in Canada. You can walk to the edge of one of the glaciers, but there are signs in several languages warning of the extreme danger of walking onto the glaciers. The signs even explain why it is dangerous: there are hidden crevasses, covered by recent snowfalls, where you can easily fall to your death. A ranger told us that a year to the day before we were there, a man had gone about 60 feet out onto the glacier and had fallen through the snow into a crevasse where he died before rescuers could free him. Yet in spite of the clear warnings, dozens of people were wandering hundreds of yards out onto the glacier!

Paul warns us, "Beware of counterfeit Christianity!" You could fall into it if you disregard his warning! Just as you would examine a suspect bill to see whether it is true or counterfeit, so you should examine your heart: True Christians put off all confidence in human merit and trust completely in Christ Jesus for salvation. They rejoice in Him and all that He is to them. Beware of any false substitutes!

Application Questions

1. Some argue that to preach the lordship of Jesus in salvation is to add works (submission) to faith. Why is this a false charge?

2. Why is human depravity (= inability to seek God; Rom. 3:10-18) an essential factor in the true gospel?

3. How does "rejoicing in the Lord" sum up true Christianity?

4. In what ways does counterfeit Christianity look like the real thing? In what ways is it essentially different?

...although I myself might have confidence even in the flesh. If anyone else has a mind to put confidence in the flesh, I far more: circumcised the eighth day, of the nation of Israel, of the tribe of Benjamin, a Hebrew of Hebrews; as to the Law, a Pharisee; as to zeal, a persecutor of the church; as to the righteousness which is in the Law, found blameless. But whatever things were gain to me, those things I have counted as loss for the sake of Christ. More than that, I count all things to be loss in view of the surpassing value of knowing Christ Jesus my Lord, for whom I have suffered the loss of all things, and count them but rubbish so that I may gain Christ, and may be found in Him, not having a righteousness of my own derived from the Law, but that which is through faith in Christ, the righteousness which comes from God on the basis of faith,

† Philippians 3:4-9

THE LOSSES AND GAINS OF TRUE CHRISTIANITY
Philippians 3:4-9

At the end of World War I, General Pershing sent word to the troops in Europe announcing a victory parade through the streets of Paris. There were two requirements for the soldiers to qualify to march in the parade: They had to have a good record; and, they had to be at least 186 centimeters tall. Word came to one company of American soldiers and the excitement built about how great it would be to march in that victory parade. Being Americans, no one knew for sure just how tall 186 centimeters was. But the men began comparing themselves, lining up back to back to see who was the tallest. The taller men in the company were ribbing the shorter ones, "Too bad for you, Shorty! We'll think of you when we're in Paris!"

Then the officer came to find out if there were any candidates for the parade. He put the mark on the wall at 186 centimeters. Some men took one look at the mark and walked away, realizing that they weren't even close. Others tried, but fell short by a small amount. Finally, the tallest man in the troop stood up to the mark and squared his shoulders. But he discovered that he was a quarter of an inch shy of the mark (6' 1/2"). When those men compared themselves with themselves, some thought they were tall enough to qualify. But when the standard came, it proved that none qualified.

It is commonly thought that the way to get into heaven is by being a good person. People who believe that compare themselves with others and think, "I'm good enough because I'm better than my no good neighbor who drinks beer and watches sports on TV every Sunday. I usually go to church; I don't get drunk (at least not on Sunday); I don't gamble (sure, I buy an occasional lottery ticket, but I don't gamble as much as he does). I don't hit my wife (we yell a lot, but I've never hit her!). I pay my taxes (well, at least most of what I owe; nobody declares everything!)." That's the way people justify themselves and convince themselves that they're going to get to heaven. They compare themselves with others and figure that they're in the top half that's going to make it.

How good does a person have to be to get into heaven? Jesus made it clear in the Sermon on the Mount: "Therefore you are to be perfect, as your heavenly Father is perfect" (Matt. 5:48). In that sermon, Jesus hit at the Pharisees, who thought that they were good enough to qualify for heaven. They had never murdered anyone. But Jesus said that if we've been angry with our brother, we have broken God's law and are guilty enough to go into the fiery hell (Matt. 5:22). The Pharisees prided themselves on never committing adultery. Jesus said that to lust after a woman in our heart is to break that commandment (Matt. 5:28). The absolute righteousness of God, not just in our outward behavior, but in our thoughts, is the standard we must live up to if we want to get to heaven by our good works.

God's Ten Commandments are like a ten-link chain that holds a boat to a dock. It only takes one broken link to cause the boat to be swept away by the current and dashed to pieces by the waterfall just down stream. Some, who are pretty good people outwardly, may look at someone who has broken every link in the chain and think, "I'm better than he is." But one broken link is just as effective as ten broken links in plunging that boat to destruction. That's why Paul concludes in his argument in Romans 3:23, "for all have sinned and fall short of the glory of God." Or, as he puts it in Galatians 2:16, "by the works of the Law shall no flesh be justified."

In spite of the repeated clear teaching of God's Word, the error persists that everyone who by human standards is a decent person, will get into heaven on the basis of his good deeds. At the root of that persistent heresy is pride, which is what keeps most people from Christ and the gospel. As we saw in the last chapter, Paul was plagued by a group of false teachers, called Judaizers, who infected the churches he founded with a subtle error that appealed to pride. They did not deny that a person must trust in Jesus Christ for salvation. But they added works, especially the Jewish rite of circumcision, to faith in Christ as an essential requirement for salvation. Paul strongly warns the Philippians to beware of this subtle, but damnable, error (3:2).

In our text, he goes on to argue that if ever there was a person who could be right with God on the basis of keeping the Jewish law, it was himself. He had the credentials by birth; he had the track record by experience. But on the Damascus Road he came to realize that all those things he was counting on for right standing with God were worse than worthless. He threw them all on the trash heap and laid hold of Christ through faith. In warning us against this counterfeit Christianity, which still persists today, that mixes faith in Christ with faith in good works, Paul shows that ...

True Christians count all human merit as loss in order to gain Christ through faith.

The picture here is a ledger sheet of your life. Before Christ, you entered on the asset side a number of things that you thought were gains that would qualify you for heaven. But, if you've truly met Jesus Christ, you had to take all those things and move them to the debit side of the ledger:

1. True Christianity means writing off all human merit as loss.

You cannot cling to the notion of your own goodness and be a true Christian. True Christianity requires that we see the utter worthlessness of the best of our worth or works when it comes to commending us to God so that we give up all trust in such things (Isa. 64:6). And, while not all conversions are as sudden and dramatic as Paul's was, every person who is truly converted will have the same radical change of focus that Paul experienced. You will recognize that there is no place for human goodness of any kind as justifying evidence in the court of heaven. If you are trusting in anything you are or anything you have done for eternal life, you abandon it and throw yourself completely on the mercy of God through the cross of Christ.

A. We must write off all inherited and acquired merit as loss.

Paul is challenging the Judaizers to a showdown, saying that he can match and excel any human goodness they want to glory in as the basis for right standing with God. He is proving that he did not change directions because somehow he couldn't come up with the necessary credentials for the good works route to God. His list (3:4-6) contains four inherited and three acquired qualities which he formerly trusted in for right standing with

God, but which he had written off as loss rather than gain.

Of the inherited qualities, he begins with circumcision, since that was what the Judaizers put at the top of the list. Paul lets them know that he wasn't circumcised as an adult convert, but in accordance with Jewish law, he was circumcised on the eighth day. He was a blood-born citizen of the covenant nation of Israel, specifically of the tribe of Benjamin, in whose territory was the holy city Jerusalem, the tribe that provided the first king and later remained with the tribe of Judah in the southern kingdom when the northern tribes broke away. "A Hebrew of Hebrews" points both to his lineage and language, that he spoke the native tongue.

In addition to these qualities, Paul had worked hard to acquire a number of things which he thought would commend him to God. He had become a Pharisee, the strictest sect of Judaism. They sought to obey the Law in the most scrupulous manner possible, down to tithing even their table spices (Matt. 23:23). Also, as a Pharisee Paul was zealous to persecute the Christians, whom he viewed as rejecting the Mosaic Law. As to the righteousness which is in the Law, that is, outward obedience, you couldn't have found any violation with Paul.

Let's bring these inherited and acquired qualities into our cultural framework. I've asked some people, "Are you a Christian?" and they've replied, "Of course, what do you think I am, a Hindu?" They thought that because they were American and America is predominately Christian, therefore they are Christian. If you think that because you were born in a "Christian" nation or family, you're therefore a Christian, you must write that plus off as a loss if you want to gain Christ by faith. Others think that because they were baptized, either as an infant or later, they are Christians. Others put faith in their church attendance or membership. Some trust in the fact that their doctrine is orthodox or that they have served faithfully in the church. The most common idea of all is that because I've always tried my best to live a good life, that will get me into heaven.

Please note that Paul was sincere, totally committed, zealous, faithful, outwardly righteous, and yet utterly wrong and headed straight for hell! He was using the wrong measuring stick, comparing himself with others and trusting in his own good deeds and dedication as the basis for his eternal destiny. But when he saw the blinding glory of the righteous Lord Jesus Christ, he was undone. He had to write off everything he had been trusting in as a total loss. I like the way Bishop Lightfoot brings out the nuance of the Greek text of verse 7: "All such things which I used to count up as distinct items with a miserly greed and reckon to my credit-- these I have massed together under one general head as loss" (*Saint Paul's Epistle to the Philippians* [Zondervan], p. 148).

In verse 8 Paul not only calls his former credits a loss, but garbage. He may be playing off his calling the Judaizers dogs (3:2), meaning, "Let the dogs who eat garbage go after all my former deeds that I thought were good." You must take every item of human goodness and merit and throw them in the garbage if you want to gain the righteousness of God through Jesus Christ.

B. We must continue to write off all human merit as loss as we walk with Christ.

Verse 7 looks at what Paul did starting at his conversion (the Greek perfect tense means a completed action with ongoing results); verse 8 emphasizes the ongoing aspect of it (present tense), that every time Paul felt any pride in human merit, in his dedication, in his many labors, in his persecutions, or anything that he had done, he would sit down with his ledger and move that item from the gain to the loss column.

Because we all struggle with pride, it can sneak up on us in many ways. We can take pride in our moral purity, in our faithfulness, in our devotional life, in our doctrinal correctness, in thinking that we are somehow better than other Christians. We must constantly put self to death by counting whatever we think is gain due to our efforts as loss so that we can more fully apprehend Christ as all in all. True Christians count all human merit as loss.

2. True Christianity means gaining the Lord Jesus Christ as our only basis for acceptance with God.

Paul expresses the same idea over and over here so that we don't miss it: he counted all things as loss "for the sake of Christ" (3:7); "in view of the surpassing value of knowing Christ Jesus my Lord" (3:8); "that I may gain Christ" (3:8); that I "may be found in Christ" (3:9); "that I may know Him" (3:10, which we'll look at in the next chapter). Salvation centers in the person of Jesus Christ. If you have Him, you have it all. If you don't have Him, you don't have anything in terms of gaining heaven. What does it mean to gain Christ?

A. Gaining the Lord Jesus Christ means coming to a per- sonal knowledge of Him.

Note, "Christ Jesus *my* Lord" (3:8). There are no group or family plans! Just because He is your parents' Savior does not mean He is yours. Every true Christian can say with Paul that He is "Christ Jesus *my* Lord." And while growing to know Him is a lifelong quest (as we'll see in the next chapter), it begins at the point of salvation when He becomes *to you* "Christ Jesus *my* Lord." If you have not personally come to know Jesus Christ as the one who died for *your* sins and was raised up so that you could be right with God (Rom. 4:25), you are lost.

B. Gaining the Lord Jesus Christ means a positional identification with all that He is.

When we personally come to know Christ as Savior and Lord we are *placed in Christ*, so that all that is true of Him becomes true of us. In Him we are blessed with every spiritual blessing in the heavenly places (Eph. 1:3; see also vv. 4, 6, 7, 9, 11, 13; 2:4-6). At the instant we abandon trust in our own good works and put our trust in the person and work of Jesus Christ, we are placed in Him. God the Father views every believer through the merits of His Son. This standing or position before God is given to us through faith in what Christ did for us on the cross.

A dad took his son and some of his son's friends to the carnival. He bought a roll of tickets to the rides. He was standing at the turnstile where he handed a ticket to his son, to his son's friend behind him, to the next boy, etc. Then a boy whom the dad didn't recognize came along and held out his hand. The dad yanked back the ticket and said, "Who are you?" The boy said, "I know your son." So the dad gave him a ticket, too. God treats everyone who truly knows His Son the same as He treats His Son.

Part of that position we inherit in Christ is a righteousness that is not of our own, derived from keeping the law, but the righteousness which comes from God on the basis of faith (3:9). There are two ways to go about qualifying yourself for heaven, but only one will work. The way that never works is to try what Paul tried before his conversion, to attain a righteousness of your own by attempting to keep God's law. It is an attempt to commend yourself to God by your own good deeds. The reason it cannot work is that it is always at best an external righteousness. It cannot deal with the corruption that is in every fallen, rebellious heart. It can never come close to keeping the spiritual nature of God's law which is that we must love God with all our being and love our neighbor as we love ourselves.

The other way, the only way to be right with God, is to receive the righteousness that comes from God through faith. We can never attain to God's perfect righteousness. Because of His great mercy, God sent His Son Jesus who perfectly fulfilled the law of God both in its requirements and in its penalty on sin, which is death. The astounding offer of the gospel is that apart from human works, God takes your sin and puts it on Jesus and He takes His righteousness and puts it on you. This transaction takes place the instant you believe in Christ as your Savior and Lord.

If it all happens at that instant, then why does it sound as if its a process? Paul says that he continues counting all his former merits as garbage so that he might gain Christ and be found in Him, which suggests he is looking toward the day of Christ in the future. How so? F. F. Bruce explains that though Paul was already in Christ, "his ambition to be found in him on that great day can be realized only if he is continuously and progressively living in union with him during this mortal existence, and to this end Paul gladly jettisons everything else, including his formerly prized righteous- ness that comes from the law" (*New International Biblical Commentary* [Hendrikson Publishers], pp. 114-115). In other words, those who are in Christ by faith must continue to walk as they received Christ Jesus the Lord, not depending on their own works as the basis of their standing with God, but on the finished work of Christ. On the day of judgment, human works will be revealed as worthless; righteousness from God by faith will stand.

3. True Christianity means gaining Christ and all that is in Him through faith in Him.

Faith is not something we must work up; it is simply the hand that takes what God freely offers. Salvation does not depend on our faith, but on Christ and His faithfulness. Faith does not save us or make us righteous; Christ saves us and God declares us righteous based on what Christ did on the cross. Faith is simply receiving what God has promised. It looks to God, not to itself, and not to any human merit or works. Even faith is the gift of God, so that we cannot boast in it (Eph. 2:8-9; Phil. 1:29).

Conclusion

In the 1730's in England, a young man named George Whitefield desperately wanted to be right before God. As a student at Oxford, he was part of the Holy Club, along with John and Charles Wesley. The members of that club rose early every day for lengthy devotions. They disciplined themselves so as not to waste a minute of the day. They wrote a diary every night in which they examined and condemned themselves for any fault during that day. They fasted each Wednesday and Friday and set aside Saturday as a sabbath to prepare for the Lord's Day. They took communion each Sunday. They tried to persuade others to attend church and to refrain from evil. They visited the prisons and gave money to help the inmates and to provide for the education of their children. Whitefield nearly ruined his health by going out in cold weather and lying prostrate before God for hours, crying out for deliverance from sin and Satan. For seven weeks he was sick in bed, confessing his sins and spending hours praying and reading his Greek New Testament. Yet, by his own admission, he was not saved, because he was trusting in all these things to save him.

Finally, "in a sense of utter desperation, in rejection of all self-trust, he cast his soul on the mercy of God through Jesus Christ, and a ray of faith, granted him from above, assured him he would not be cast out" (Arnold Dallimore, *George Whitefield* [Cornerstone Books], 1:77; see pp. 60-77 for full account). The burden of his sins was lifted, he was filled with joy, and he went on to become the great evangelist used of God in the First Great Awakening.

Thankfully we do not all have to go through the agony of soul that George Whitefield went through. But we must all come to the same place he did, where we throw overboard as worthless all trust in human merit and cling to the Lord Jesus Christ as our only basis for acceptance with God. If we lose all our pride and self-trust in exchange for Christ and His merit, we gain everything!

Application Questions

1. Why is trusting in Christ plus our own good works not to trust in Christ at all?

2. Some argue that to preach submission to Christ as Lord for salvation is to add works to faith. Why is this fallacious?

3. How would you counsel a person who said, "I'd like to believe in Christ, but I just don't have faith"?

4. If Paul was already "in Christ," why does he make it sound as if it is an objective yet to be gained?

...that I may know Him and the power of His resurrection and the fellowship of His sufferings, being conformed to His death; in order that I may attain to the resurrection from the dead.

† Philippians 3:10-11

KNOWING CHRIST AND BEING LIKE HIM
Philippians 3:10-11

Someone has wisely pointed out, "One of the most dangerous forms of human error is forgetting what one is trying to achieve" (Paul Nitze, in *Reader's Digest* [7/92], p. 137). That is especially true in the Christian life. It's easy to get sidetracked. We need to be clear and focused at all times on what it is we're after.

What is the goal of the Christian life? If we forget it, we're not likely to achieve it. It can be stated in several forms, but in our text, the apostle Paul nicely sums up what we're supposed to be aiming at:

The goal of the Christian life is to know Christ and to be like Him.

That's it, isn't it! Christianity is definitely *not* a religion of rules and rituals that we must work at keeping in order to climb the ladder to heaven. Rather, it is a personal, growing relationship with the risen, living Lord Jesus Christ that results in our growing conformity to Him. Our goal is to know Him and to become like Him.

1. The goal of the Christian life is to know Christ.

Jesus said the same thing when He prayed, "And this is eternal life, that they may know You, the only true God, and Jesus Christ whom You have sent" (John 17:3). Christianity is primarily a growing relationship with the infinite God who has revealed Himself through the Lord Jesus Christ.

As with all relationships, it begins with an initial meeting or introduction. In Paul's case, it was not a planned or polite introduction, at least from his point of view! He wasn't seeking after Christ, inquiring as to how he could become a Christian. Far from it! "Breathing threats and murder," he was on his way to Damascus to arrest men and women who were followers of Jesus, when suddenly a light from heaven flashed around him. He fell to the ground and heard a voice saying, "Saul, Saul, why are you persecuting Me?" He answered, "Who are You, Lord?" The Lord said,

"I am Jesus whom you are persecuting" (see Acts 9:1-6). So Paul met the risen Lord Jesus Christ.

If we went around the room and asked husbands and wives to tell how they met their mate, we would hear many different stories. Some met each other as teenagers; others were further along in life. Some were looking for a mate at the time they met their partner; others weren't looking at all. Some met but things didn't develop between them for many months or even years. Others met and things took off like a rocket. For some it was love at first sight; for others, a long friendship led to romance and marriage. But for everyone, you began a personal relationship with your mate and because of it your life took a new direction that it never would have taken if you had not met.

It's the same with your relationship with Jesus Christ. Your introduction to the Lord Jesus may have been far different than Paul's. You may have met Christ as a young child, reared in a Christian home. Or, you may have met Him later in life. It may have been a traumatic situation, where in a moment of crisis you called out to Him and were saved. It may have been less dramatic, so that you can't even recall the exact time or place. But one thing is certain: *If you are truly a Christian, you know Jesus Christ personally.* You don't just know *about* Him; you *know Him.* You can say with Paul that He is "Christ Jesus *my* Lord."

You can know a lot about someone without knowing the person himself. I know about Billy Graham because I've read his biography and I've seen him preach on TV and in person. I've read some books he has written. I know a bit about his wife and her upbringing as a missionary kid in China. But I do not know Billy Graham because I've never been introduced to him and we do not have a personal relationship.

Becoming a Christian requires that you know some things about Jesus Christ. You need to know who He claimed to be, eternal God in human flesh. You must know some of the things He did and taught. You need to understand that He died on the cross for your sins, and that He was raised bodily from the dead. But beyond these facts, you need to know Christ personally. That relationship begins at the moment you recognize that your sins have separated you from God and that you need a Savior. You also realize that you cannot save yourself from God's judgment through your efforts or good works. Letting go of all human merit, you call upon the Lord to be merciful to you based on the merits of the death of His Son Jesus. Your object of trust for commending yourself to God shifts from self to Christ. You are saved. You have met Jesus Christ personally.

Like any relationship, once you've met, you must *cultivate that relationship*. If you meet the girl of your dreams, but then never see her again, you won't have a relationship with her. You must spend time together, getting to know one another through conversation and shared experiences. You learn about her history, her family, her likes and dislikes, her hopes for the future, etc. If you do something to offend her, you ask her forgiveness and learn to work through difficulties in a harmonious way.

It's the same in a personal relationship with Christ. It requires cultivation and that requires time. It never ceases to amaze me how a young man and a young woman can be extremely busy, but when they meet and things click between them, suddenly they can find many hours every week to be together. What were they doing to fill all those hours before? Whatever it was, it gets shoved aside so that they can pursue this new relationship.

Do you often make time to spend with the Lord? It's sure easy for that first love to cool off, and time between you and the Lord gets squeezed out with other things. Or, it becomes your duty to have a quiet time, so you get out your Bible, grimace, and swallow a chapter a day to keep the devil away. But there wasn't any love in it. You weren't seeking to know Christ in a more intimate way. You weren't opening your heart to Him, so that He could confront you and cleanse you and make you more like Himself. There's no closeness, no intimacy.

We cannot know the Triune God except as He has chosen to reveal Himself to us. He is infinite and altogether apart from us. We can never come to know Him through philosophy or speculation. We can't know Him through our own imagination or feelings. We can't know Him through the ideas or experiences of others. We can only know Him as He has chosen to reveal Himself. That revelation comes through His written Word which tells us of the eternal living Word, the Lord Jesus Christ (see Heb. 1:1-3).

Thus we come to know God through Jesus Christ, and we come to know Him through His Word which tells us of Him. The Old Testament points ahead to Christ; the New Testament tells us of His life, His death for our sins, and His resurrection and present reign in heaven. It also tells us of His coming again and future kingdom. It expounds on His teaching and reveals His will for His people. We can never know Him fully because He is infinite and we are finite. But we can know Him definitely as Savior and Lord and we can and must spend our lives focused on that great goal, "to know Him." But it won't happen if you aren't committed to becoming a man or woman of the Word.

But, there's a word of caution here. It's possible to gain knowledge *about* Christ through studying His Word, and yet not grow to *know Christ Himself* through His Word. In fact, you can read and study your Bible all your life and never get to know Jesus in an intimate way! In John 14:21, Jesus tells us how we can get to know Him: "He who has My commandments and keeps them, he it is who loves Me; and he who loves Me shall be loved by My Father, and I will love him, and will disclose Myself to him." If you don't know the Word, you neither have nor keep Jesus' commandments. But it's possible to have them through knowledge, but not keep them. If you want Jesus to reveal Himself to you, He says that you must both *have* and *keep* His commandments. So the goal of Bible study is always growing *obedience* so that we can get to know the Lord Jesus better. This leads to the second part of our goal as Christians:

2. The goal of the Christian life is to be like Christ.

When you met your future mate, fell in love and got married, your life was permanently changed. You would never be the same again. It is the same, only much more so, when you meet Jesus as Savior and Lord. He marks you for life, and the more time you spend growing to know Him, the more you are different. The rest of verses 10 & 11 shows the components and direction of the change that goes along with knowing Christ.

A. To be like Christ requires knowing the power of His resurrection.

Paul came to know the power of the resurrected Lord when he was struck down on the Damascus Road. Even though not all conversions are as dramatic as Paul's was, all conversions do require the same mighty power of the risen Lord Jesus Christ, because they all require God to raise the sinner from spiritual death to spiritual life (Eph. 2:4-6). Other Scriptures compare conversion to opening the eyes of the blind so that they can turn from darkness to light; and, to delivering captives from Satan's domain to God's kingdom (Acts 26:18; Col. 1:13). These are not things that can be accomplished through human persuasion or through a self-improvement program. They require the same mighty power of God that raised Jesus from the dead.

That same resurrection power is necessary to sustain the believer as he walks in victory over sin. Paul prays for the Ephesians (1:19-20) that they would know "what is the surpassing greatness of His power toward us who believe [which is] in accordance with the strength of His might which He brought about in Christ, when He raised Him from the dead ...." He prays for these same Christians (Eph. 3:16-17) that God "would grant you, according to the riches of His glory, to be strengthened with power through His Spirit in the inner man; so that Christ may dwell in your hearts through faith."

In Romans 8:11 he explains, "But if the Spirit of Him who raised Jesus from the dead dwells in you, He who raised Christ Jesus from the dead will also give life to your mortal bodies through His Spirit who indwells you." He means that the Holy Spirit, whose power was necessary to defeat Satan by raising Jesus from the dead, indwells every believer to give us power over indwelling sin. We experience this power as we walk moment by moment yielded to and in dependence on the indwelling Holy Spirit. If we live defeated lives, it's safe to say that we are not living in dependence on the Holy Spirit (Gal. 5:16). We must learn to live experientially in power of Christ's resurrection.

B. To be like Christ requires knowing the fellowship of His sufferings.

Our Savior came to suffer for our sins on the cross. His entire ministry was marked by misunderstanding, opposition, betrayal, and death. While we can never enter into His sufferings in the same way that He suffered on the cross, there is a sense in which we can never be like Him if we do not go through suffering and learn to entrust our souls to a faithful Creator in doing what is right (1 Pet. 4:19; see also 1 Pet. 2:21-23; 4:13;

Rom. 8:17-25; 2 Cor. 1:5).

Hebrews 5:8 makes the startling statement that "Jesus learned obedience through the things He suffered." It does not mean that Jesus was disobedient and had to learn to be obedient through suffering. It means that He had never experienced the test of obedience until He suffered. His suffering for our sins on the cross was the ultimate test of His submission to the will of the Father. If we are to be like Him, we must also learn to obey God through suffering.

Unlike Jesus, we have the powerful force of indwelling sin to contend with. God uses suffering to burn off the dross and purify us. But, we have to cooperate with Him by humbling ourselves under His mighty hand when we go through trials, trusting His sovereignty over our suffering, and casting all our cares on Him (1 Pet. 5:6-11).

Fellowship points to closeness or intimacy. Though few of us American Christians know it, those who suffer because of their faith in Christ know a special intimacy with Him. When Shadrach, Meshach, and Abed-Nego were thrown into the fiery furnace for refusing to bow before Nebuchadnezzar's idol, he looked and saw not three men, but four, walking in the fire (Dan. 3:25). I believe the fourth was Jesus Christ who stood with them in their hour of trial. They knew the fellowship of His sufferings.

Paul knew this fellowship. When he was preaching in corrupt Corinth, he was afraid. The Lord appeared to him in a vision and said, "Do not be afraid any longer, but go on speaking and do not be silent; for I am with you, and no man will attack you in order to harm you, for I have many people in this city" (Acts 18:9-10).

Although I know nothing when it comes to suffering for the sake of Christ, I had a small taste of it once when I was under attack because of taking a stand for God's truth. One night as I was getting into bed, feeling somewhat discouraged, I was suddenly impressed with the reference, Acts 18:9-10. I was vaguely familiar with the text, but I had not been reading in Acts lately to remind me of it. I opened my Bible and read those words that directly applied to my situation. And I was flooded with joy at being able to enter, just a little bit, into the fellowship of His sufferings.

C. To be like Christ requires being conformed to His death.

This phrase is related to "the fellowship of His sufferings" and grows out of it. But it also has another dimension, which Paul describes in many other places, that of dying to sin and self through the cross of Christ. When we trust in Christ, we are placed "in Christ," which means that we are identified with Him in His death and resurrection. But, we have to live experientially what is true of us positionally. In Galatians 2:20 Paul states, "I have been crucified with Christ; and it is no longer I who live, but Christ lives in me; and the life which I now live in the flesh I live by faith in the Son of God, who loved me, and delivered Himself up for me." In Colossians 3:5, just after explaining how we have died and been raised up with Christ (3:1-4), he exhorts us to "put to death" the members of our bodies with regard to various sins (also Rom. 6:1-11, compare Rom. 8:13).

This is what Jesus meant when He said that whoever follows Him must deny self and take up his cross daily (Luke 9:23). Jesus always lived by denying temptations to live in His own power or for His own ends. He lived only to do the Father's will. To the degree that we learn to die to self and sin by being conformed to His death, to the same degree we grow to be like Him.

D. To be like Christ will be realized in the resurrection from the dead.

Philippians 3:11 is literally, "if somehow I may attain to the out-resurrection from among the dead ones." The word "out-resurrection" occurs here only. There are two possible interpretations, and it is difficult to decide between them. Paul may be expressing his hope that he will fully realize what it means in this life to experience what he has just stated, namely, the resurrection life of Christ being lived out fully through him. In favor of this view is the preceding and following context, where Paul says that he has not yet attained it, but presses on. The uncertainty ("if somehow") points to Paul's humility and recognition of the weakness of his flesh. The problem with this view is, if Paul had not attained to this experience after 25 years as a Christian, who can? And, it's an unusual use of the word resurrection.

The other view is that Paul is referring to the future resurrection of the righteous at the return of Christ, when our mortal bodies will be transformed into the likeness of Christ's resurrection body, free from all sin. We will then share in His glory throughout eternity. "If somehow" would then not reflect uncertainty, since Paul is absolutely certain about the future resurrection (1 Cor. 15), but rather the manner in which he would attain it, whether he may still be alive when Christ returned. The problems with this view are that it doesn't seem to fit the context quite as well as the other view and the uncertainty doesn't fit with Paul's certainty about the future resurrection. The strengths of the view are that the word "out-resurrection" most likely refers to the future resurrection, and is intensified to distinguish it from the normal word in verse 10; and, if it refers to the future resurrection, then verses 9-11 refer to the believer's justification (v. 9), sanctification (v. 10), and glorification (v. 11). So, it's hard to pick!

But whatever this verse means, other verses make it clear that the process of sanctification will be completed. We will be like Him, totally apart from sin, sharing in His glory throughout eternity (Rom. 8:17-21, 30; 9:23)! John applies this wonderful truth, "Everyone who has this hope fixed on Him purifies himself, just as He is pure" (1 John 3:2, 3).

Conclusion

So that's our goal, to know Jesus Christ and to become more and more like Him. Is that *your* goal? If it is, you should have thought about it this past week. Have you ever noticed that when you buy a new car, you suddenly see that make of car everywhere? This summer, we bought a Sears luggage carrier to go on top of our car for vacation. We started seeing those things everywhere. We've gone on many vacations and never seen how many of those are on the road until this year. If you will set before yourself each week this goal, *to know Christ and be like Him,* you will see opportunities all over the place to apply it. You will have temptations where you need to rely on the *power of His resurrection.* You will face trials where you come to know the *fellowship of His sufferings.* You will encounter irritations where you must learn to be more *conformed to His death.* View it all as an opportunity to know Christ and to remind you that it is preparing you for that great day when He comes and you will be raised up in glory with Him for all eternity. That's our goal!

Application Questions

1. How can we rekindle and maintain our first love for Jesus?

2. How can a defeated Christian learn experientially Christ's resurrection power over temptation and sin?

3. Why is a godly response to suffering so crucial for Christian growth (see 1 Pet. 5:6-11)?

4. Some say that since we are already crucified with Christ, we do not need to put ourselves to death regarding sin. Why is this not biblically balanced (see Rom. 8:13; Col. 3:1-5)?

Not that I have already obtained it or have already become perfect, but I press on so that I may lay hold of that for which also I was laid hold of by Christ Jesus. Brethren, I do not regard myself as having laid hold of it yet; but one thing I do: forgetting what lies behind and reaching forward to what lies ahead, I press on toward the goal for the prize of the upward call of God in Christ Jesus. Let us therefore, as many as are perfect, have this attitude; and if in anything you have a different attitude, God will reveal that also to you; however, let us keep living by that same standard to which we have attained.

† Philippians 3:12-16

THE CHRISTIAN GROWTH PROCESS
Philippians 3:12-16

For many years I have jogged, but I've never won a race. There are at least three reasons I've never won: (1) I've only entered one race so far in my life. You don't win races if you don't enter them. (2) I don't have the attitude it takes to win. Winners are a determined bunch. I don't have that kind of mind-set. (3) I don't put into my running the kind of determined effort required to win. Winners don't just jog for exercise; they're into it all the way. They read magazines about running; they set goals for themselves; they train and push themselves toward those goals. But I don't work at it as they do.

Several times in the New Testament the Christian life is pictured as a race (1 Cor. 9:24-27; 2 Tim. 4:7; Heb. 12:1). In our text the apostle Paul uses that analogy to describe his own spiritual experience. In so doing, he gives us some basic principles for spiritual growth or, to use the athletic analogy, how to get into shape spiritually so that we can run to win the race set before us.

In the last chapter, we saw the goal of the Christian life (3:10-11): To know Jesus Christ and to be like Him. Christianity is a developing personal relationship with the living Lord Jesus. In 3:12-16 Paul shows us how to reach this goal through the process of Christian growth:

To grow as a Christian you've got to be in the race, have the proper attitude, and give it the proper effort.

1. To grow as a Christian you've got to be in the race.

This may sound perfectly obvious, but in reality there are a lot of people trying to run in a race they've never entered. They're trying to grow as Christians by living a good life and doing what Christians are supposed to do, but they've never truly become Christians in the first place. As we saw in 3:4-6, Paul himself thought that he was doing everything he needed to do in order to be pleasing unto God. He was sincere; he was dedicated; he was zealous and energetic. But there was one major problem: he was not genuinely converted to Jesus Christ.

179

Because it's such an important principle and because so many people think that being sincere and trying hard is the way to be right with God, Paul repeats it again in verse 12. He is speaking here of his effort in the Christian race, but he clarifies again that behind his effort is the foundational fact that he was first apprehended by Jesus Christ: "I press on in order that I may lay hold of that for which also I was laid hold of by Christ Jesus."

The word "lay hold" is an intensified word that means to apprehend or seize something after a pursuit. It is used of a demon seizing a boy and throwing him to the ground (Mark 9:18). If a policeman chased a robber and apprehended him, he would have a firm grip on the man, so as not to let him get away. Paul says that the reason he runs in this race is because Christ Jesus chased him down, seized him, and put him in the race. On his part, Paul was headed for Damascus to persecute Christians. But the Lord seized Paul and turned him around so that he began serving Jesus.

The same idea is reflected in verse 14, "the upward call of God in Christ Jesus." God's call almost always refers to His effectual calling of His elect unto salvation (Rom. 9:11; 1 Cor. 1:24, 26). We're saved because God called us to salvation. To use the sports analogy, it's as if a coach calls a player to himself and says, "I want you to go into the game." The player is in the game because the coach has called him into the game. He gives it his best effort to please the coach who called him to play.

If you have not been laid hold of by Christ, you're not in the race. The Christian life begins not with the weakness of a human decision to follow God, but with God's powerful, effectual calling you and laying hold of your life. This means that no Christian is his own person; you belong to Jesus Christ who bought you. The reason you're in the race is because Christ grabbed you and said, "I want you to run for Me." Because He laid hold of you, you give it all you've got. It's the same balance we saw in 2:12-13, that because our salvation comes from God who both wills and works in us, therefore we must work it out.

Thus Christian growth is a process that stems from the definite awareness of being apprehended by Christ Jesus. To grow as a Christian, you've got to be in the race because Christ laid hold of your life. This is foundational to all else.

2. To grow as a Christian, you've got to have the proper attitude.

Any athlete will tell you that attitude is often the difference between victory and defeat. A team that lacks in raw talent can sometimes defeat a team with much more ability because they have the right attitude going into the game. Attitude is crucial in the spiritual life as well. The Greek word translated "to think" or "be minded" (in 3:15, "have this attitude") is used 10 times in Philippians out of 26 New Testament uses. Since the theme of Philippians is joy, there is a definite correlation between attitude and joy. Two strands of Paul's attitude come through in these verses: He views Christian growth as a lifelong process, so he has a long-haul attitude; and, he views Christian growth as the kind of thing where you never can say, "I've arrived," so you have to keep moving ahead.

A. The long-haul attitude: Christian growth is a lifelong process.

Paul had been converted for at least 25 years when he wrote Philippians. There is no question that he is one of the outstanding believers of all times. Yet over and over he reveals his mind-set, that he was still in the process: "Not that I have already obtained it" (3:12), meaning, "I have not yet come to know Christ and the power of His resurrection and the fellowship of His sufferings and conformity to His death in a complete and total way." "I do not regard myself as having laid hold if it yet" (3:13). Twice he says, "I press on" (3:12, 14); the word literally means to pursue, and by way of extension, to persecute (Paul uses it of himself in this way in 3:6). He's still "reaching forward" (3:13) as a runner stretches toward the finish line. He's been at it for 25 years, but he doesn't view himself as having arrived!

The Christian life isn't a 100 yard dash; it's a lifelong marathon. You need the mentality of a long-distance runner if you're going to make it. You may have been a Christian for 40 or 50 years, but you can't start thinking, "I don't need to grow any more" and stop running. Long distance runners have to complete the entire course; they can't decide after many miles that they've run far enough.

This attitude of viewing Christian growth as a lifelong process is crucial for at least two reasons. First, we all have the human tendency to *want quick fixes and easy answers to difficult problems*. I believe that many get into the charismatic movement because it appeals to this desire for easy answers: "Do you have major problems? What you need is the baptism of the Holy Spirit. Let us pray over you in tongues, you'll have an emotional experience and speak in tongues yourself, and you'll be delivered once and for all from all these tough problems you're struggling with." They emphasize instant, miraculous deliverance from any problem. I wish it was that easy!

Another form of this teaching is that you need to just "let go and let God." If you struggle against sin or wrestle with stubborn emotional problems, you're told that it's because you're in the flesh. The implication is that life in the Spirit is effortless and easy once you've discovered the secret of "the exchanged life."

But both of these views go against the clear teaching of Scripture, that the spiritual life is a continual battle against the world, the flesh, and the devil. We are instructed to discipline ourselves for the purpose of godliness (1 Tim. 4:7), which also is an athletic metaphor. There is no quick, easy, instantaneous way to get in top physical conditioning. You have to work at it every day, and the day you stop is the day you start going downhill. Olympic champions who retire do not stay in shape the rest of their lives because of their former training. They have to keep working out all their lives. It is the same spiritually.

The second reason it's important to maintain this attitude, that Christian growth is a lifelong process, is that it *enables us to be gracious and patient with one another.* If you view Christian growth as an instant experience where you're delivered once and for all from all problems, then if you've got problems, obviously it's because you haven't had this experience. So, get with it! Stop having your problems! This view makes us impatient and intolerant toward people who are struggling.

But if we remember that growth is lifelong and that even Paul admits that he hasn't arrived after 25 years, we can bear with one another and be gracious to those who are still struggling with problems even after many years of being Christians. The analogy of how we grow as humans is helpful and applicable to us as children of God. It takes years for children to grow to maturity. You don't expect more of them than they're capable of at their stage in life. You expect babies to dirty their diapers and to burp in your face and to cry in the middle of the night. If your teenager is still dirtying his diapers and burping in your face and waking you up with his crying in the night, you've got a problem! If a brother or sister is growing, we need to be patient and gracious, realizing that it is a lifelong process. We need this long-haul attitude. Spiritually, the important thing to ask yourself is, "Am I actively involved in the growth process?"

B. The "not-having-arrived" attitude: Christian growth requires always moving ahead.

If anyone could think he had arrived, it would have been Paul. But he always kept in mind that he wasn't there yet. He didn't want to rest on his laurels or to start coasting. Remember, this is a man who had had numerous visions of the Lord. He had been caught up into heaven and had seen things that no other living person had seen. He had written some of the most profound theology ever penned. But his attitude was, "I need to keep moving ahead." You see this even in his final days, when he was in the dungeon in Rome, and he wrote to Timothy asking him to bring his coat, and then he adds, "and the books, especially the parchments" (2 Tim. 4:13). He was facing execution, but he wanted his books so he could keep growing!

In verse 13, notice that "*I do*" is in italics, meaning that it is not in the original. The brevity of Paul's phrase in Greek makes it more emphatic: "But one thing!" Paul's single attitude of always moving ahead has three ramifications: Forgetting the past, reaching forward to the future, and pressing on in the present.

(1) *An attitude of moving ahead from the past: Leave it there!* "Forgetting what lies behind." Again, the picture is of a runner who does not make the mistake of looking over his shoulder. His eyes are fixed on the goal. If he made mistakes earlier in the race, he doesn't kick himself by replaying them in his mind. If he did well, he doesn't gloat about it. He leaves the past behind and keeps moving on toward the finish line.

Many Christians today are being told that to experience healing from their difficult pasts, they need to delve into their pasts and relive the hurtful things that happened to them. This approach has come into the church from the world, not from the Word. It would be wrong to say that verse 13 is all that the Bible says about the past. Even earlier in the chapter, Paul has mentioned his own past life in Judaism. It can be helpful to reflect on what happened to us in the past in order to understand where we're at in the present and where we need to grow. There is a biblical case for self-examination, which means evaluating things that have happened in the past, both good and bad, as a means of growing now.

But our text shows that there needs to be a balance. Paul means here that we should not be controlled by the past. Someone has used the analogy of a car's rear view mirror. You don't drive by looking in the mirror. You drive by looking ahead out of the windshield. But it's helpful to take occasional glances in your mirror and use the information to make decisions about how to drive safely in the present and future. But if you spend too much time looking in your mirror, you'll probably crash because you're not paying attention to the present. In the same way, we need to take periodic glances backward, but we also need to put the past (good and bad) behind us, accept God's grace and enabling for the present, and move on with what He is calling us to do now.

(2) An attitude of moving ahead toward the future: Aim for the goal! "Reaching forward to what lies ahead" (3:13). Paul uses a term describing a runner who stretches and strains every muscle as he runs toward the finish line. "The upward call of God" is His call to salvation which culminates when we stand before Him to give an account and receive rewards for how we've run the race. Will our work stand the test and receive His "Well done" because we did it out of love for Him and for His glory? Or, will it be burned up and we be saved, but as through fire (1 Cor. 3:14-15)? Everything we do--how we conduct ourselves in our families and in public; how we spend our time and money; how we serve the Lord--should all be done with the mind-set, "I'm going to stand before the Lord and give an account someday; I want to be pleasing unto Him."

(3) An attitude of moving ahead in the present: Keep moving! "I press on toward the goal" (3:13-14). Paul had a holy dissatisfaction with where he was at, so he kept pressing on. Yesterday's blessings or experiences wouldn't do for today. He walked daily with the Lord, always wanting more, always learning, always growing, never treading water or coasting.

In 3:12 Paul says that he is not perfect, but in 3:15 he implies that he and some of his readers are perfect. He isn't contradicting himself within four verses. In 3:12, he means that absolute perfection is not attainable in this life. In 3:15, he uses the word in relative terms to mean "mature." We can become mature, and the mature Christian will share Paul's view that he is setting forth here, that we haven't arrived, but that we can and must keep growing.

But Paul recognizes that some will not share his attitude because they are not mature. To those who disagree with him, Paul says, "Stay teachable and God will show you where you need to grow" (see 3:15). He adds verse 16 so that no one will mistake him to mean that you can just kick back and not work at growing. He means that wherever you're at, you need to keep living in obedience to the light God has shown you and keep seeking Him for more. If God has dealt with some sin in your life, don't slip back into it again. If He has cleaned out a dirty closet of your life, don't start throwing junk in there again.

If you want to grow in the Lord, it's essential that you maintain a teachable heart. A teachable heart is humble, because it admits, "I may be wrong or lacking in understanding; I may need to repent and change." A teachable heart is submissive, ready to respond to new light God gives from His Word. A person with a teachable heart is not a know-it-all, refusing to learn from other Christians. With that kind of teachable heart, keep moving in the present.

3. To grow as a Christian, you've got to give it the proper effort.

We need the balance of God's Word here. Some say, "God is sovereign and we don't need to do anything." Others say, "It's all up to us." Scripture says, "God is at work in you, so you work!" It's both/and, not either/or. Some say that any effort on your part shows that you're in the flesh. If that's so, Paul was fleshly, because it's clear here that he was pressing on, he was reaching forward to the goal as a runner giving it his all. The Christian life is an active cooperation with the sovereign God.

Paul's "one thing" (3:13) implies focused concentration and effort, that he sets aside distractions and works at keeping his mind on the goal of knowing Christ and becoming more like Him. A runner in a race can't afford to admire the scenery or look at the people on the sidelines. An Olympic champion is not a person of many interests, who dabbles at his sport when it's convenient. Every day he gets up and puts his mind on the goal, to win the gold. Everything else--his social life, his schedule, his diet-- takes subservience to that overarching goal.

The question each of us needs to answer is, "Do I devote myself to knowing Christ and being like Him in the same way an athlete devotes himself to winning his event? Does knowing Christ and growing in Him consume me, or do I just dabble at it when it's convenient?" If you want to grow, you've got to put your full effort into it--not just occasionally, but all the time.

Conclusion

Dr. Howard Hendricks, in the video series we just watched on Sunday evenings, tells about an elderly Christian woman he knew who would come into a social gathering, where everyone was chit-chatting about nothing significant, and say, "Tell me, Howie, what are the five best books you've read this past year?" Even though she was up in years, she was still actively growing in the Lord. When she died in her nineties, her daughter discovered on her desk that the night before she died in her sleep, she had written out her personal goals for the next five years! Like Paul in prison, right up to the end she wanted to be growing! I heard about a mountain climber whose epitaph was, "He died climbing." That ought to be true of every Christian.

If you want grow as a Christian, make sure you're *in the race*-- that Christ has laid hold of your life and saved you from sin. Make sure you have the *right attitude*--that you haven't arrived, but you're in the lifelong process of moving ahead. And, give it the *proper effort*--focusing on the goal of being like Christ, and doing everything in light of that high calling.

Application Questions

1. How can a person know that Christ has laid hold of him? What are some signs of true conversion?

2. How can a Christian know how much (if any) to delve into the past? Do we need to work through "repressed" memories, etc.? Support your answer biblically.

3. Should every Christian have clearly defined written goals? Do you suppose Paul did? How can goals help? Can they hinder?

4. How can we determine what is God's part and what is our part in the Christian life?

Brethren, join in following my example, and observe those who walk according to the pattern you have in us. For many walk, of whom I often told you, and now tell you even weeping, that they are enemies of the cross of Christ, whose end is destruction, whose god is their appetite, and whose glory is in their shame, who set their minds on earthly things. For our citizenship is in heaven, from which also we eagerly wait for a Savior, the Lord Jesus Christ; who will transform the body of our humble state into conformity with the body of His glory, by the exertion of the power that He has even to subject all things to Himself. Therefore, my beloved brethren whom I long to see, my joy and crown, in this way stand firm in the Lord, my beloved.

† Philippians 3:17-4:1

THE RIGHT AND WRONG WAY TO LIVE
Philippians 3:17-4:1

Imagine two young men in their early twenties. Both are of comparable intelligence and natural ability. They live only 20 miles apart. But their circumstances are very different. The first young man lives in a comfortable apartment, drives a decent car, has many fine clothes in his closet, eats well, and is pursuing the career for which he has just been educated in college. The second young man lives in a dirt-floored shanty, has no car, has only one ragged change of clothes, eats a minimal diet, has no hope for an education, and tries to find manual labor jobs to make ends meet.

What's the difference between these two young men? Citizenship! The first young man lives in San Diego, California, and is a United States citizen. The second young man lives in Tijuana, Mexico and is a citizen of that country. The way these men live is greatly affected by their respective citizenships. If the young man from Mexico could somehow move north, acquire his U.S. citizenship, and get an education and a better paying job, his life would change dramatically.

In Philippians 3:17-4:1 (4:1 ought to be the concluding verse of chapter 3), Paul uses this analogy of citizenship to show that as citizens of heaven, we should live differently than those who are citizens of this earth. In Philippians 3:1-11, Paul uses the analogy of an *accountant* to show that the human effort and merit he formerly was counting on for right standing with God he had written off as loss so that he could gain Christ as his righteousness. In 3:12-16 he uses the analogy of an *athlete* to show that the Christian life is a marathon race in which we must keep pressing on toward the goal, the purpose for which Christ first laid hold of us. Now (3:17-4:1) he uses the analogy of an *alien* to show that ...

Christians must live as citizens of heaven, not as citizens of this earth.

As we saw in the first chapter, this analogy would have especially

189

related to the Philippians. Philippi was a Roman colony, some 800 miles east of Rome, surrounded by territory subject to Rome but whose residents lacked Roman citizenship. But those in Philippi had legal status as Roman citizens, so that the city was an outpost of Roman life. It was governed by Roman law. They practiced Roman customs. A Roman could go to Philippi and feel right at home, just as a British citizen in the last century could have gone to India, Hong Kong, Australia, or New Zealand and felt quite comfortable because those places were British colonies.

To these Christians who lived in a city that took pride in its Roman citizenship, Paul is saying, "You have a higher citizenship than that of Rome. You are citizens of heaven. Just as your Roman citizenship greatly affects the way you live, even more so your heavenly citizenship should affect how you live. Don't fall into the trap of living as those around you." Apparently there were some, even in the church, who professed to be Christians, but whose lives revealed that they were not true citizens of heaven. So Paul warns the flock of this danger and urges them to stand firm in the Lord.

The word "walk" (3:17 & 18) reveals two different ways of life, one right, the other wrong. First we'll look at the way we're *not* supposed to live, and then at how we *are* to live.

1. Christians must not live as citizens of this earth (3:18-19).

In our day, if you warn the church about false teachers, you are labeled as an alarmist or heresy hunter. Instead, we're encouraged to focus on the positive and not worry about doctrinal error. But the apostle Paul repeatedly ("often told you") warned the Philippians about these promoters of a false version of Christianity. One of the primary tasks of elders is to guard the flock from wolves who come in sheep's clothing (Acts 20:28-31; Matt. 7:15; Titus 1:9-16).

Who were these dangerous false teachers (in Phil. 3:18-19)? We know that Paul was talking about people who circulated among the churches professing to be Christians, not about pagans or outsiders. Paul would not have been so deeply disturbed as to warn them often with tears about such licentious behavior among the heathen, since he knew that heathens live for sensual pleasure and the things of this earth. Paul was upset because these people made claim of being Christian, but didn't live as

Christians, thus causing great confusion both in the church and outside. We don't know whether they had actually infiltrated the church at Philippi or if it was just a serious danger for which the church needed to be on guard, but probably the latter.

Many commentators think that this group was the Judaizers, whom Paul has already warned against earlier in this chapter. The problem with this view is, the people in 3:18-19 seem more inclined to loose, licentious living than to the legalistic, ascetic practices of the Judaizers. It seems clear that Paul is warning about people who turned the grace of God into licentiousness, taking their freedom from the Jewish law off the deep end into supposed freedom from God's moral law. Of course, legalists often just have a thin veneer of morality papered over a heart that is full of sensuality and indulgence (see Matt. 23:25-28; Col. 2:20-3:5; Gal. 5:2-24). So perhaps the Judaizers, like some TV preachers in our recent history, made a profession of living according to God's Word, but actually lived a double life. Whoever they were, Paul gives us three distinguishing marks that show us how we, as citizens of God's kingdom, are not to live:

A. Citizens of this earth are enemies of the cross of Christ.

The cross of Christ is the central principle of the gospel and of the Christian life. "For the word of the cross is to those who are perishing foolishness, but to us who are being saved it is the power of God" (1 Cor. 1:18). The cross humbles human pride, because it shows us that our good works are not able to make us right with a holy God. It shows us that we cannot save ourselves from God's righteous judgment. It shows that we cannot even help God out, because we are not saved by our merit, but only by the worthiness of the Lord Jesus and His shed blood. To come to the cross for salvation means that we must abandon all hope in our ability to commend ourselves to God and we must trust completely in the merits of the Lord Jesus Christ.

Enemies of the cross diminish its value by emphasizing human worth or merit in addition to what Christ did on the cross. They lift up fallen man and bring down the holy God, thus shortening the "mighty gulf that God did span at Calvary." One prominent enemy of the cross says, "If Christ died for me, I must be of infinite value in God's sight" (Robert

191

Schuller, *Self-Esteem: The New Reformation* [Word], p. 74). This man redefines our sinfulness. He says, "... our rebellion is a reaction, not our nature. By nature we are fearful, not bad. Original sin is not a mean streak; it is a nontrusting inclination" (p. 67). He explains that the core of original sin "could be considered an innate inability to adequately value ourselves. Label it a 'negative self-image,' but do not say that the central core of the human soul is wickedness" (*ibid.*). He goes on to say, "To be born again means that we must be changed from a negative to a positive self-image--from inferiority to self-esteem, from fear to love, from doubt to trust" (p. 68). He even has the audacity to twist the Lord's Prayer, claiming that we can now pray, "Our Father in heaven, honorable is *our* name" (p. 69, emphasis his)!

The amazing thing is that this man is welcomed into evangelical circles as being completely orthodox. On the book jacket is a glowing endorsement from the president of a major evangelical seminary, as well as a recommendation from a prominent Southern Baptist preacher who tells us that the theology is traditional! Test all theology and self-help books by this: Does it diminish or elevate the cross of the Lord Jesus Christ? The cross means death to our pride.

B. Citizens of this earth are heading for eternal punishment.

"Whose end is destruction" (3:19). Paul is referring to eternal punishment, not to some temporal judgment. Destruction does not mean annihilation, that these sinners are wiped out by God so that they cease to exist. The uniform teaching of Scripture is that those who reject God's mercy at the cross will be cast into the lake of fire where they will endure eternal punishment (John 3:16; Rev. 20:10, 15). Thus destruction means eternal ruin or loss. While this is not an easy or pleasant teaching, it is the clear teaching of the Lord Jesus (Mark 9:42-48). If you struggle with this, I encourage you to read Jonathan Edwards' sermon, "The Justice of God in the Damnation of Sinners" (*The Works of Jonathan Edwards* [Banner of Truth], 1:668-679), where he argues that sin against God is a violation of infinite obligations and therefore is an infinitely heinous crime, deserving of infinite punishment.

C. Citizens of this earth live for the things of this earth.

Their "god is their appetite" (3:19), which means that they live for
selfish and sensual pleasures, rather than denying self in order to live for
Christ. The Bible does not promote asceticism, the self-imposed denial of
all pleasure as a means of purifying oneself and getting right with God.
Rather, it teaches that God has richly supplied us with all things to enjoy (1
Tim. 6:17). But if we remove God from the center as the chief object of our
joy and replace it with some earthly pleasure, we are guilty of idolatry.

These false teachers gloried "in their shame" (3:19). They boasted
in their supposed "freedom," when in reality they were slaves to their lusts.
Many well-known Christians today glory in things they should be ashamed
of, writing books and appearing on TV talk shows to tell titillating stories
about their sinful "addictions."

Further, they "set their minds on earthly things" (3:19). One form
this takes in our day is our emphasis on how Christ can make you happy in
the here and now. He can give you peace, joy, and a happy marriage. He
can solve all your problems. So people come to Jesus and find out that they
have trials and persecutions, as the Bible clearly promises, so they bail out.
Obviously, we all have earthly things that consume our time and energy:
jobs, bills to pay, houses to maintain, family problems, health problems, etc.
But the point is, the true Christian does not put earthly comfort and
happiness at the center of his life. We should put Christ and our hope of
being with Him in heaven at the center, and that enables us to deal properly
with the earthly problems we all encounter. Setting our minds on Christ and
the things above is the key to dealing with sin and relational problems (Col.
3:1-17).

So, Paul's point is that as citizens of heaven, Christians are not to
live as citizens of this earth, who are enemies of the cross of Christ, who are
headed for eternal destruction, who live for the things of this earth.
Remember, these people were in the church, making a profession of
knowing Christ, but they were not truly converted to Christ.

Two practical applications before we move on: *(1) Don't be turned
from the truth of the gospel because of the presence of hypocrites in the church.* Just
because there are counterfeit dollar bills doesn't mean that you give up
earning and spending money. There are counterfeits because the real thing

is worth imitating. Satan has always made sure that there are counterfeit Christians who talk as if they're true believers, but whose lives belie that fact. But the existence of hypocrites does not deny the reality of the truth. Even true Christians will disappoint you, because as we saw in the last chapter, they're all in process, which means, they still sin. But Christianity centers on the person of Jesus Christ, not on Christians.

(2) *Deeds are a more certain evidence of what people truly are than their words.* Jesus said that we can spot false prophets, wolves in sheep's clothing, by their fruit or deeds (Matt. 7:15-20). Paul warned of those who "profess to know God, but by their deeds they deny Him, being detestable and disobedient, and worthless for any good deed" (Titus 1:16). Again, this does not mean that believers are sinless. But, if a true believer sins, he will make it right by confessing that sin, asking forgiveness, and seeking to rectify the problem. Look at the walk, not the words.

Enough about the wrong way to live. Let's focus on the right way to live:

2. Christians must live as citizens of heaven (3:17, 20-21; 4:1).

Just as being a citizen of Rome meant that you lived differently than those lacking such a privilege, so being a citizen of heaven means that you live distinctly, representing your native land in this alien land where you are temporarily staying. Three things distinguish the citizens of heaven:

A. Citizens of heaven follow godly examples.

"Join in following my example, and observe those who walk according to the pattern you have in us" (3:17). Paul is not being egotistical. It is a false humility that denies the truth by saying, "Well, I'm really not worth imitating." Paul knew that he lived with integrity before God. He also just admitted that he was still in the process of coming to know Christ and the power of His resurrection (3:12-14), so he is not implying that he is sinlessly perfect. But his life was an example of how believers should live. He also adds that there were others, probably referring to Timothy, Epaphroditus, and men like them who walked with God. Such men show us in practical ways how we should walk with God, how we should deal with relationships, etc.

194

The most helpful source for spiritual growth for me, apart from studying the Bible, has been reading the biographies of men of God. The summer of 1970 was a turning point in my walk with God because of reading *George Muller of Bristol*, by A. T. Pierson. That book showed me in human form a man who lived by faith, prayer, and obedience to the Word. Since then I've been helped immensely to read the lives of John Calvin, Martin Luther, Jonathan Edwards, Adoniram Judson, C. H. Spurgeon, Hudson Taylor, Martyn Lloyd-Jones, Francis Schaeffer, and many others. I have an article in print on this as well as a bibliography if you're interested.

B. Citizens of heaven eagerly wait for the coming of the Lord Jesus Christ.

The bodily return of Jesus Christ in power and glory is one of the most frequently emphasized truths in the New Testament. It is mentioned in every book of the New Testament except Galatians, which deals with a particular doctrinal matter, and the short books of Philemon and 2 & 3 John. While there may be debate over the particulars, there is no debate over the certainty of His bodily return. Just as He promised that He came the first time to die for our sins and kept His word, so He promised to return.

When He comes, it will be in power to rule and reign. Two things will happen. First, He will transform our "lowly bodies," which are subject to disease and death and prone toward sin, into conformity to His resurrection body. This will involve not only an outward, physical transformation, in which we receive bodies not subject to disease and death; but also an inward, spiritual transformation, in which we are delivered finally and forever from all sin. If you wonder how God will do it, Paul simply states that it is by the exertion of the power that He has even to subject all things to Himself.

That's the second thing that will happen when Jesus comes: He will subject all things to Himself. If you are not willingly subject to Him, you will be forced into subjection to Him. His enemies will bow before Him. He will reign as King of kings and Lord of lords. Because of this, you should make certain that you are in submission to the Lord Jesus Christ now, so that He comes as your Savior, not as your Judge. It's safe to say that the extent to which we wait for His coming now reveals the condition of our hearts before Him. Citizens of heaven long for His appearing.

C. Citizens of heaven stand firm in the Lord in light of His coming.

As mentioned, 4:1 is really the conclusion of chapter 3. "Therefore" means, in light of this truth of His coming, stand firm in the Lord. Notice Paul's tender heart for these people, whom he calls "my beloved brethren," "my joy and my crown," and again, "my beloved." He longs to see them, and especially to see them standing firm in the Lord, not swayed by these false teachers. Remember, Christianity is knowing Christ Himself, and being found in Him. He is our wisdom, our righteousness, our sanctification, and our redemption (1 Cor. 1:30). He is our all in all (Col. 3:11). He is our sufficiency for every need, our refuge, our rock in times of trouble. Stand firm *in the Lord*!

Conclusion

Are you a citizen of heaven right now? You can only become such through birth, the new birth. Just as you could not do anything to bring about your physical birth, so you can do nothing to effect your spiritual birth. It must come from the Lord. Just as He is powerful to raise the dead and subject all things to Himself when He comes again, so He is powerful now to raise the dead spiritually and impart new life to all who call upon Him. He can even now take your rebellious heart and bring it into submission to Him through His mighty power. Scripture promises, "Whoever will call upon the name of the Lord will be saved" (Rom. 10:13). Cry out to Him for the new birth.

Our text is especially a warning to those who profess to be Christians, but who really are living as citizens of this earth, living for self and pleasure, with no view to the coming of our Lord. I can think of nothing more tragic than to profess to be a Christian, to be involved in serving Christ, and to stand before Him one day and say, "Lord, Lord, did we not prophesy in Your name, and in Your name cast out demons, and in Your name perform many miracles?" only to hear the horrifying words, "I never knew you; depart from Me, you who practice lawlessness." (Matt. 7:22-23). Make sure your citizenship is truly in heaven. Then live as a citizen of heaven, not as a citizen of this earth.

Application Questions

1. Can a professing Christian who is living in sin have assurance of salvation? Use Scripture to defend your answer.

2. Is it wrong to present the gospel by emphasizing the temporal benefits over and above the eternal?

3. How can a Christian who honestly is caught up with the things of this life gain a deeper love for the Lord's return?

4. Many confuse grace with sloppy living and obedience with legalism. Why is this wrong (see Titus 2:11-14)?

I urge Euodia and I urge Syntyche to live in harmony in the Lord. Indeed, true companion, I ask you also to help these women who have shared my struggle in the cause of the gospel, together with Clement also and the rest of my fellow workers, whose names are in the book of life.

† Philippians 4:2-3

GETTING ALONG WITH ONE ANOTHER
Philippians 4:2-3
(Also, Matt. 5:23-24; 18:15-17; Acts 15:36-41; Gal. 6:1)

There's a story about six men who were stranded on a deserted island. Two were Jewish, two were Catholic, and two were Baptists. The two Jews got together and founded the Temple Immanuel. The two Catholics established the Church of the Holy Name. The two Baptists formed two Baptist churches and got into a squabble over who got to use the name, "First Baptist"!

If you've never had the "wonderful" experience of having a conflict with someone in the church or having your feelings hurt by another Christian, either you're a new believer or you've never gotten involved in serving. I can guarantee that if you get involved, you will have a conflict with another Christian, probably sooner than later. I don't say that to discourage you from getting involved, but rather to help you think realistically and to be prepared for the inevitable.

We all tend to think idealistically that since we're all Christians, living by the Bible, filled with the Holy Spirit, obeying the command to love one another, that there won't be any conflicts among us. Such idealism is not realistic, whether in a church or in a Christian family. To quote again the ditty:

> To dwell above with the saints we love, O that will be glory;
> But to dwell below with the saints we know, that's a different story!

As we've seen, the first church at Philippi was made up of people from diverse backgrounds. There was the mature, probably widowed, business woman from Asia, Lydia, with a Jewish background. There was the career military man, the jailer, with a pagan background. And, probably there was the slave girl from the occult background. It is the glory of the church to be composed of different racial and cultural groups. But that also sets the stage for conflict. Two women in the Philippian church, of whom we know nothing except what is written here, were having a conflict. By looking at what Paul writes here and at a few other verses on the same topic, we can learn how to get along with one another. It's of vital importance that we do so, not only so that we can be at peace, but for the sake of the gospel.

Christians must work at resolving conflicts so that the church can focus on the work of the gospel.

1. Resolving conflicts is work.

It's never easy. It's always easier to avoid it. We all have a tendency to shrink from confrontation. We feel anxious about how the other person will take it. We're not sure if it will escalate the conflict to try to deal with it. Because of these factors, the most common way people deal with conflict with another church member is to leave and find another church. In New Testament times they didn't have that option, since there was only one church per city. It would be better if we couldn't just hop to another church, because we take the easy way out and miss the growth and the testimony that can come through working things out in a biblical manner. But we need to recognize that it is work and commit ourselves to at least attempt to work through the problems before we consider separating.

2. Resolving conflicts is first the job of those involved in the conflict.

Paul repeats the verb with each woman: "I urge Euodia and I urge Syntyche to think the same in the Lord" (literal translation). In Matthew 18:15, Jesus says, "If your brother sins [many manuscripts add, "against you"], go and reprove him in private; if he listens to you, you have won your brother." In Matthew 5:23-24, the situation is reversed in that your brother has something against you. Yet in both situations it is incumbent on you to take the initiative to go to your brother.

Many relational problems in churches would be quickly resolved if we would follow this simple guideline, to take the initiative in going to the other person to try to clear up the problem between us. One common mistake (or, sin!) is for the one who feels wronged to talk to many others about the person who wronged him rather than going directly to the person. It is fine to go to a mature spiritual leader who can be trusted to keep confidences in order to gain their wisdom on how to approach the person who wronged you. But it is not okay to talk to several others! This is gossip or slander and just compounds the problem. When you go or, if you can, before you go, ...

(1) Identify the true problem or source of the conflict. We don't know what the root problem was between Euodia and Syntyche. Most problems between Christians can be grouped under several heads: A personal wrong (someone sinned against you or did something to offend you); a personality clash (the person just "rubs you the wrong way"); a methodology difference (you don't agree with how they're doing something); a doctrinal difference; or, (most commonly) some combination of the above.

I've often found that Christians tend to label problems as doctrinal differences because it sounds spiritual and makes me look right: "I'm defending THE TRUTH!" But often the doctrinal difference is just a covering for a personal problem or sin (which doesn't make me look so good!). Also, it's possible to hold correct doctrine in an insensitive, proud manner that results in relational conflict. You can be right doctrinally, yet sinning in the way you use your correct view to think you're better than your brother. Or, you use it to put him down for being wrong rather than gently to correct him and build him up.

We have to be careful not to compromise the truth, but also to be sensitive and gentle in how we try to lead others to the truth (2 Tim. 2:24-26). We need to evaluate the magnitude of the doctrine in question. If it's essential, so that the other person will be in heresy or will suffer greatly in his walk with the Lord if he doesn't correct it soon, we need to be more strong than if it is not so serious. Timing is important. Sometimes a person will say something that I know is wrong doctrinally, but either I don't have a strong enough relationship or I sense it isn't the right time to offer correction. We must be patient (1 Thess. 5:14).

It's embarrassing to admit, but quite often some degree of self-love is at the root of my problem with someone else. I don't mean a lack of self-love (as is erroneously taught, "you must love yourself to love your neighbor"), but rather that I love myself more than I love my neighbor. So I need to humble myself and be open to what God wants to teach me through the conflict situation. Maybe I need to learn more about the Scriptures. I may need to judge myself and grow in humility or sensitivity to others. Quite often, I failed to communicate properly (both in what I said or didn't say, or how I said it; and in what I heard or didn't hear), and so I need to grow there. So first, identify the true source of the conflict.

(2) Remind yourself of the goal. "Be of the same mind in the Lord," is the same phrase Paul used in 2:2, "being of the same mind, maintaining the same love, united in spirit, intent on one purpose." As we saw there, Paul does not mean that we all are supposed to think exactly the same about every issue. Nor are we supposed to set aside essential truth for the sake of unity. Rather, he means that we must have our minds geared toward Christian love, seeking the highest good for one another; and, that we must be growing to experience what we possess--the mind of Christ, revealed to us in His Word (1 Cor. 2:16).

Note Ephesians 4:3 & 13: There are two types of Christian unity. There is the *unity of the Spirit* (4:3), created by the Holy Spirit when He baptizes all true believers into the one body of Christ. This is a reality we must be diligent to *preserve*. Then there is *the unity of the faith* (4:13), which we are to *attain to*. We attain unto it as we grow to understand Scripture (in part, through the ministry of preaching, 4:11-12) and to know the Lord Jesus Christ in a deeper way.

Our goal in any relational conflict is not to win or to put the other person in his place. Our goal is to honor Christ by growing in maturity and by helping our brother or sister grow in maturity through the resolution of the conflict in line with biblical truth. So we need to ask prayerfully: What does God want to teach me in this situation? What does He want to teach the other person? What does He want to accomplish in the larger picture of His church in this community? The honor of Christ and the testimony of the gospel should be at the forefront as we seek to resolve any conflict.

(3) Go to the other person in a spirit of gentleness and humility, seeking to restore the relationship. If the other person has sinned, you don't go to blast him or give him a piece of your mind. You check yourself, making sure that you are spiritual (i.e., in submission to the Holy Spirit, Gal. 6:1) and that your motive is to restore the person, not blow him away. You "look to yourself lest you, too, be tempted." This means that you recognize that you, too, are a sinner. Deal with any anger or bitterness that you may feel. Spend time in prayer, waiting on God for the right attitude, timing, and place. Think through the proper wording that will be winsome and not communicate arrogance or self-righteousness. Your manner and attitude

must be gentle, not abrasive or caustic. Don't go in an accusing spirit, trying to convince him of how wrong he was. When you go, it's good to ask questions first, to make sure that you understand the situation.

I heard a brother share how he was supposed to stop and pick up some chairs to bring to an evangelistic Bible study at someone's home. He had a lot on his mind that day and completely forgot. When he got there and the host found out that he forgot, the host said, "It figures." He didn't say anything at the time, but those words really stung him. So later he went to the host and asked, "When I forgot the chairs and you said, 'It figures,' what did you mean?" The host explained that it didn't have anything to do with him, but it was just that it had been one of those days where nothing had gone right. By asking for clarification, it cleared up what could have been a strained relationship.

So the first thing in any conflict is for those involved to get together in a spirit of love, in submission to God, and seek to work it out. If that fails,

3. Resolving conflicts sometimes requires the help of an outside party.

Paul calls on his "true comrade" ("loyal yokefellow," NIV) to help these women. Commentators make many suggestions as to who this might have been, but the bottom line is, nobody knows. Some think that the man's name was Syzygus (the Greek for "comrade"). In favor of this view is that a proper name makes more sense in the midst of all these other names. Also, it would be a play on words, much as in Philemon 10, 11, where Paul tells Philemon that his runaway slave, Onesimus (whose name meant "useful") was formerly useless to him, but now, as a Christian, was useful both to Paul and to Philemon. Here, "Yokefellow," whose name points to someone who brings two people together, should be true to his name and help these women. The major objection to this view is that this name has not been found in any Greek literature of the time.

Others have suggested that Paul meant Epaphroditus, the bearer of the letter, who did not need to be named (since Paul told him personally to do this), but who is mentioned here so that the church knew he was acting under Paul's direction. But, whoever it was, we can learn that it often is helpful for an outside party to help resolve a conflict. Not just "yokefellow," but also Paul was involved in trying to help these women get things worked out. We can learn several things about such a mediator:

(1) The outside party should be a mature, committed Christian. The title, "true comrade," shows that Paul considered whoever this was as a mature Christian who was committed to the work of the gospel. The same principle is stated in Galatians 6:1, "you who are spiritual," that is, spiritually mature.

(2) The outside party should be objective. Paul's objectivity is hinted at in his double use of the verb, "I urge ... I urge." He doesn't take sides or imply that one person is right and the other is wrong. The outside party needs to hear both sides before he makes any judgments about who is most at fault. Proverbs 18:17 states, "The first to plead his case seems just, until another comes and examines him." If there's clearly a sin or doctrinal error on the part of one side, it's relatively easy to bring resolution, assuming that the erring party is repentant and teachable.

Speaking from experience, it gets sticky when both sides are saying contradictory things and neither party will admit to lying. When that happens, about all you can do is put the past out of the way and deal with the wrong attitudes and words that you perceive in the present. But you need to be as objective toward both sides as you can be.

(3) The outside party should be open, direct, and truthful. Can you imagine how these two women felt when this letter was read in the assembly? Here they are, known in church history for one thing, the quarrel they had! But Paul didn't beat around the bush. He named names. In several other places he corrects people by name or directly names his source of information: "Say to Archippus, 'Take heed to the ministry which you have received in the Lord, that you may fulfill it'" (Col. 4:17). "For I have been informed concerning you, my brethren, by Chloe's people, that there are quarrels among you" (1 Cor. 1:11). (See also 1 Tim. 1:20; 2 Tim. 2:17; 4:10, 14). Sometimes we are so careful to tiptoe around so as not to offend anyone that we end up being vague and confusing. Paul didn't drop hints. He was direct, specific, and truthful.

(4) The outside party should be affirming and positive where possible. Paul didn't scold or berate these women. He affirms them by mentioning how they had shared in his struggle in the cause of the gospel, along with Clement and others not named (we know nothing more about Clement).

He acknowledges that the names of all these dear people are known to God, written in the book of life, that book in heaven that contains the names of all of God's elect (see Exod. 32:32; Ps. 69:28; Dan. 12:1; Luke 10:20; Rev. 3:5; 13:8; 17:8; 20:12, 15; 21:27).

Paul affirms these women by referring to them as fellow workers with himself. This does not mean that they had the same ministry role that Paul had. He makes it clear in other Scriptures that women are not allowed to teach or exercise authority over men in the church (1 Tim. 2:11-15; see also, 1 Cor. 11:3-16; 14:34-35). He was gifted as an apostle and preacher of the gospel. These women had other gifts. But each Christian is gifted by God and is vital to the cause of Christ. We should lift up the giftedness and ministry of each person and not make anyone feel despised or belittled, even if they are a part of a conflict. We should affirm each person and express appreciation for their ministry.

Recognizing and affirming differing gifts is a key to conflict resolution, especially in the work of the gospel. I believe that if Paul and Barnabas had stopped long enough to affirm their differing gifts, while they still may have parted, they could have parted more amicably. Paul was gifted as a pioneer missionary, ready to endure hardship and forge into unreached territory. Barnabas was gifted as an encourager, one who picked up hurting or broken people and nurtured them back to health and usefulness in the Lord's work. Both gifts are needed. Paul was right: It would have been a mistake to take Mark back to the front lines after his failure. Barnabas was also right: Mark deserved another chance. He needed to be restored.

In any conflict resolution, we need to keep in mind that our overall goal isn't just to have peace. Peace is nice and we all feel better when everyone is getting along. But there's a greater goal:

4. Resolving conflicts is necessary so that the church can focus on the work of the gospel.

When Paul says that these women have shared his struggle in the gospel, the word he uses means to be on the same team in an athletic contest. Team members have to work together; if they start fighting each other, the other team will make easy work of them. Lord Nelson once came on deck and found two of his officers quarreling. He whirled them about, pointed to the enemy ships, and exclaimed, "Gentlemen, *there* are your enemies!" We need to remember that the enemy is out there, the prince of darkness, who wants nothing more than to divide God's people into quarreling factions so that lost people do not hear the good news that Christ the Savior has come. Quarreling church members are not witnessing church members.

Often conflicts come in the context of working together in ministry. Workers with different gifts and personalities have opposing views of how to go about the work. While every effort should be made to resolve the differences and while there should be reconciliation on a personal level, sometimes you end up spending too much time trying to bring about harmony. At that point, as with Paul and Barnabas, it's better to agree to go your separate ways and get on with the work. But if it comes to that, we must never bad-mouth the other person. Paul was always affirming toward Barnabas and Mark. We need to remember that we're on the same team with everyone who is proclaiming the gospel. Their name as well as mine is in that book of life, which means that we'll all be spending eternity together. The enemy is out there. We need to focus on the work of the gospel.

Conclusion

I want us all to ask ourselves two questions: *(1) Am I at odds with anyone else in this church?* If so, I need to work at getting the problem resolved. The answer isn't just to pick up and move to another church. It may be hard work, it may require some painful self-confrontation, it may require the help of an outside party. But you need to resolve it. "If possible, so far as it depends on you, be at peace with all men" (Rom. 12:18). This includes family members!

(2) Am I involved in the work of the gospel? You say, "I'm not gifted in evangelism!" It doesn't matter. If you know Christ, you're on the team, and there are no bench warmers on His team. God has gifted you to do something toward the cause of the gospel. Euodia, Syntyche, Clement, and all the others who aren't named were not seminary graduates, with "Reverend" before their names. They were just people in Philippi who had met Jesus as Savior and Lord. That qualified them as team members and fellow workers with Paul in the cause of the gospel. If you know Christ as Savior, you're on the same team! Get off the bench and into the game!

Application Questions

1. What doctrines are significant enough to divide over? How much doctrinal unity if required to work effectively together?

2. What is the most difficult aspect about going to someone who has wronged you? Is it always required, or do some problems just work themselves out over time if left alone?

3. Does the Bible support particular methods, or is one method as good as another as long as it works?

4. Are denominations sinful divisions? Should we drop all denominational distinctives and meet together as one church?

Rejoice in the Lord always; again I will say, rejoice!

† Philippians 4:4

THE CHOICE TO REJOICE
Philippians 4:4

Everyone wants joy in life. On the surface, Paul's words, "Rejoice in the Lord always; again I will say, rejoice!" are some of the simplest in Scripture to read and understand. But when you scratch beneath the surface, they raise a pile of questions: Is it *really* possible to rejoice *always*? What does this mean? Am I supposed to go around with a perpetual smile on my face? Is it a sin to feel depressed or sad? Am I supposed to deny pain or sorrow? How can you command a feeling, anyway? Are these the words of a bubbly, incurable optimist, or what? Just reading the verse might get some people depressed, because they despair of ever being able to do it!

We need to recognize that what Paul commands here is not just a cheerful disposition, which many have by nature, but rather something that requires supernatural power--it is joy *in the Lord*. And, while we may never perfectly attain such joy in this troubled world, Paul repeats the command for emphasis, as if to say, "It *is* possible, so don't shrug off what I am saying." His emphatic words show us ...

Abiding joy in the Lord should be the aim of every Christian.

First, I want to define what Paul means when he commands us to rejoice in the Lord always; and then we'll look at how we can obey such a command. Scripture must be our authoritative and sufficient source, not human wisdom or psychology.

WHAT DOES "REJOICE IN THE LORD ALWAYS" MEAN?

1. To rejoice in the Lord always does not mean that we will never feel depressed or sad.

The Bible is realistic and balanced. We must look at the totality of Scripture rather than taking a verse like this as if it were all that is written on the subject. It's interesting that the shortest verse in the Greek New Testament is, "Rejoice always" (1 Thess. 5:16). The shortest verse in the English New Testament is, "Jesus wept" (John 11:35). They are not contradictory! Our Savior could weep and yet have the fullness of joy, even as He faced the cross (John 15:11). Paul commands us to weep with those who weep (Rom. 12;15), and yet to rejoice always. The Bible says that godly people are marked both by mourning (over sin, Matt. 5:4; James 4:9; 5:1) and yet by irrepressible joy. Scripture acknowledges that discipline and trials are not joyful at the moment, but that afterward they yield the peaceful fruit of righteousness if we submit to God (Heb. 12:11; John 16:20-22).

Thus we would misapply Paul's words if we took him to mean that a Christian should deny or never feel sadness or grief. The Psalms are helpful in this regard. The psalmist often is overwhelmed with despair or sadness, and he readily acknowledges his feelings to God. He never puts on a happy face and denies the intensity of his troubles. But in the process of crying out to God for help and refocusing his thoughts on the Lord and His great mercies, by the end of the psalm his mood has changed, even though his circumstances are no different. So the psalmist often experiences a flood of God's joy even in the midst of tremendous pain. Thus to rejoice in the Lord always does not mean that we deny our feelings or that we stoically endure our trials by ignoring how much we hurt.

2. To rejoice in the Lord always is not primarily a matter of feeling, but of obedience.

Philippians 4:4 is a commandment, repeated twice for emphasis, so that we will not shrug it off. It is a command that we must deliberately *choose to obey*, especially when we're in difficult circumstances. It has to do with our attitude which depends on our mental focus which depends on our choice. The choice to rejoice often must go deliberately against how we feel. When we go through trials, when we're treated unfairly, when we're disappointed by people or circumstances, we are faced with a decision: Will we obey this command to rejoice in the Lord or will we allow ourselves to be swept along by our feelings?

I just wish that Paul had been more realistic and had said, "Rejoice most of the time"! But if he had said that, most of us would have justified ourselves by thinking, "I usually do rejoice." But we wouldn't have had to confront our grumbling and complaining when things don't seem to go our way; our lack of trust in God in the midst of trials; our anger when we're treated unfairly; our disappointment when people let us down or, to be honest, when we feel that God has let us down.

We see this choice to rejoice illustrated in Paul's life in this very epistle. He has been incarcerated for well over two years and is facing possible execution because the Jews in Jerusalem falsely accused him of bringing Gentiles into the temple and of stirring up rebellion against the Jewish people and their Law (Acts 21:28). Though he should have been released, the Roman governor kept him in custody because he was hoping to receive a bribe from Paul and because he wanted to do the Jews a favor (Acts 24:26, 27). The next governor also should have released him, but he, too, was playing politics with the Jews (Acts 25:9).

Not only that, but on the way to Rome Paul had gone through a shipwreck at sea. Once he arrived, many of the pastors in Rome were not only distancing themselves from Paul the prisoner, but were preaching out of envy, selfish ambition, and strife (Phil. 1:15, 17). Paul had good reason to be angry and depressed at the treatment he had received over the past few years. You would think that he would have been in need of the Philippians writing to cheer him up. But instead, this short letter to them is filled with joy (15 x). As Paul's words in 1:18 show, his joy was not an automatic feeling, but rather a deliberate choice: "... in this I rejoice, yes, and I will rejoice."

3. To rejoice in the Lord always is an attitude of contentment and hope that transcends circumstances.

Though our hearts may be heavy with sorrow or grief because of trials, beneath the surface is the abiding confidence that our God is sovereign and that our lives are in His hand, so that not even the hairs of our heads fall to the ground without His knowledge. Paul had learned to be content in every situation (Phil. 4:11- 13). "Every situation" for Paul included some severe trials, in some cases where he despaired even of life. But this, he writes was "in order that we should not trust in ourselves, but in God who raises the dead;" then he adds, "He on whom we have set our hope" (2 Cor. 1:8-10).

This joy in the Lord which we must aim for is not a superficial happiness based on circumstances or on the absence of trials, but rather is a solid, abiding contentment and hope that is as steady and certain as our faithful God who has given us His promises in His Word. Our Lord Jesus knew that joy even as He faced the cross (John 15:11; 17:13). The apostles knew that joy when they were flogged for preaching the gospel, and they went on their way "rejoicing that they had been considered worthy to suffer shame for His name" (Acts 5:41). Paul and Silas knew that joy when they were unjustly thrown in the Philippian jail, their backs torn open, their feet in the stocks, as they sang hymns of praise to God (Acts 16:25). Many martyrs, like John Hus, knew that joy. He died singing praises in the flames as his enemies gloated.

God intends for every believer to know this same joy in the Lord, especially in difficult times. Joy is a fruit of the Holy Spirit and the Bible is filled with commands, such as our text, to rejoice (Ps. 5:11; 33:1; 64:10). It's a matter of obedience, not of temperament. If we're constantly depressed and weighed down with care, we're not attractive advertisements for our Lord Jesus Christ. We can't be effective leaders in the church or godly examples to our families if we are dominated by depression. So we must work at developing this abiding joy in the Lord. How?

HOW CAN WE "REJOICE IN THE LORD ALWAYS"?

I preface my remarks by saying that if you struggle with frequent depression, you should get a medical checkup, since it can be due to physiological causes. Also, you may need personal counsel from a mature Christian who can help you apply Scripture to your situation. Avoid anyone who mingles the Bible with psychology. The joy Paul is exhorting us to is decidedly not the kind of joy the world offers through psychological insights. Almost 50 years ago, Martyn Lloyd-Jones commented on this verse, "... there is perhaps no greater travesty of the gospel of Jesus Christ than psychological teaching which presents itself in Christian terms" (*The Life of Peace* [Baker], p. 146). It is joy *in the Lord*, joy that comes from the very life and power of God operating in the believer, not through some supposed insights into your unconscious mind or how your parents treated you.

The world's latest prescription for overcoming depression is Prozac or other anti-depressant drugs. For sake of time I refer you to what I wrote in my booklet, "Christians and Psychology: Some Common Questions Answered." I'm not totally opposed to the careful use of such drugs, but I do urge caution. And, even if such drugs help restore normalcy, each person must still learn to deal with sinful thoughts and habits. In almost every case, a depressed person has certain unbiblical thought and behavior patterns that contribute to the depression. Psychology has nothing to offer Christians in this regard. Every believer must learn to apply the biblical principles I am going to enumerate.

1. Make sure that you are in a right relationship with God through saving faith in the Lord Jesus Christ.

As we saw in chapter 3, where Paul first exhorts us to rejoice in the Lord (3:1), many who claim to be Christians are not relying only upon Christ and His shed blood for salvation, but rather are trusting in themselves (3:2, 4-6). Paul explains how he had to come to the point of counting everything of himself to be a total loss so that he could be found in Christ, not having a righteousness of his own derived from keeping the Law, but rather that which comes from God through faith in Christ. Martyn Lloyd-Jones observed, "There are many people who never know the joy of the Lord because they have failed to see themselves as miserable sinners. The only way to be happy in Christ is to be desperately unhappy without him" (ibid., p. 148).

2. Walk in submission to the sovereign Spirit of God.

In Galatians 5:16 Paul says, "Walk by the Spirit, and you will not carry out the desire of the flesh." He goes on to catalog some sins that characterize the flesh. There is a direct correlation between many of those sins and depression. Then Paul lists the fruit produced by the Holy Spirit: "Love, joy, peace, patience, kindness, goodness, faithfulness, gentleness, self-control" (Gal. 5:22-23). To walk by the Spirit means to live in moment-by-moment submission to the indwelling Holy Spirit, saying no to self and yes to the Lord. It means to trust in the sufficiency and power of the Spirit because you distrust your own ability (see Prov. 3:5). As we learn to walk by the Spirit, the fruit of the Spirit, including joy, will grow in our lives.

The words "walk" and "fruit" imply a process, not something instantaneous. If you have spent your life walking in the flesh, it may take some time before you experience steady joy in the Lord. Also, walking in the Spirit is a deliberate process that involves putting self to death and submitting to the sovereign God. This means confronting your anger, because anger usually stems from not submitting to God's sovereign dealings in your life. A crucified self doesn't shake its fist in God's face, saying, "I don't like what You did to me when I was a child (or, what You're doing to me right now)!" Anger and depression often go together (Gen. 4:6-7; Jonah 4:1-4). So if you want God's abiding joy, you've got to walk in submission to His sovereign Spirit.

3. View your trials through the lens of Scripture.

Paul was going through some pretty intense trials and could easily have become depressed. Instead, he had abundant joy because he viewed his trials in light of God's Word. He submitted to God's sovereignty over his imprisonment (1:12-14), over the preachers who were trying to cause him distress in his imprisonment (1:17), and even over his possible impending execution (1:20). He was living for the gospel, to proclaim Christ in every way (Phil. 1:18). He knew that when he died, he would be with Christ for eternity, so he could write, "For to me, to live is Christ, and to die is gain" (1:21).

Many Christians get depressed because they do not understand God's purpose in trials or they do not mentally deal with their trials in the light of God's Word. Often it can start with a simple disappointment-- something you hoped would happen didn't happen. Someone you were counting on let you down. A situation you were hoping and praying for did not come about. If you don't consciously yield your disappointment to the Lord and thank Him by faith, trusting in His sovereign love, you can slip into depression. Satan often comes to you in a moment of disappointment and tempts you to doubt God's loving care. Peter tells us to humble ourselves under God's mighty hand, casting our cares on Him, and to resist the devil, firm in our faith, in such times of trial (1 Pet. 5:5-11).

4. Deal properly with relational conflicts.

The verses before and after verse 4 deal with proper relationships. If we have wronged others and have not done all we can to make it right, we will not have joy in the Lord. If we humble ourselves and go to our brother or sister and ask their forgiveness, we will be flooded with God's joy. It's no accident that love precedes joy in the list of the fruit of the Spirit.

214

5. Sing praises to God.

I have not validated it, but I've heard that the most frequent command in the Bible is, "Sing!" You may be thinking, "Singing is the last thing I feel like doing when I'm depressed." Well, where did you ever get the idea that the Christian life is living by our feelings? God doesn't need to command us to do what we already feel like doing. It's no accident that the longest book in the Bible is a hymn book. When you've feeling down, turn to the Psalms and create your own tunes to the words. Put on some praise music, or get out a hymnal and get alone and begin to sing to the Lord. Jesus and the disciples sang a hymn (Ps. 118) as they went out to Gethsemane (Matt. 26:30). Paul and Silas sang in the Philippian jail (Acts 16:25). "The joy of the Lord is your strength" (Neh. 8:10).

6. Serve the Lord with gladness.

(See Ps. 100:2.) Quite often people who lack joy are not involved in serving Christ. As we've seen in Philippians, Paul had great joy even in facing execution because he was living for the gospel (1:12-20). Get your focus off yourself and your problems and on to what God wants you to do for the furtherance of the gospel. There is great joy in seeing others trust Christ as Savior (Luke 15:5-7, 9-10, 32; Acts 8:8; 15:3); and, in seeing them stand firm in the Lord (Phil. 2:2; 1 Thess. 2:19-20; 3:9; 3 John 4). A Christian woman once told me that she had been depressed every day of her life. She had been going to psychologists for years, to no avail. I finally asked her, "What's your ministry? God has gifted you to serve Him. How are you doing that?" She was dumbfounded. She said, "I've never thought about that." She was consumed with self. If you want joy, get your eyes off yourself and on to how God wants you to serve Him.

7. Focus your mind daily on the Lord and the things He has promised us in Christ.

This joy is *in the Lord* and we are *in Christ*! Daily meditate on the cross of Christ and all the riches that are ours through His death. Think on the fact that you are risen with Him, seated in the heavenlies, with every spiritual blessing in Christ (Eph. 1:3; Col. 3:1-4). Revel in His abundant grace that is greater than all our sins. Marvel at His sovereign grace that chose you before the foundation of the world in Him, that predestined you to adoption as His son or daughter (Eph. 1:4, 5) and that will "keep you from stumbling" and will "make you stand in the presence of His glory blameless with great joy" (Jude 24). The Philippian jailer went from being suicidal to rejoicing greatly because of his salvation (Acts 16:27, 34). How can you be depressed if you are focusing daily on the marvelous grace shown to you in Christ?

8. Live by faith, not by feelings.

The Christian life is a walk of faith, of trusting in things not seen, not of "getting in touch with your feelings." Peter wrote to Christians going through intense trials, "... though you have not seen Him, you love Him, and though you do not see Him now, but *believe in Him*, you *greatly rejoice* with joy inexpressible and full of glory" (1 Pet. 1:8). Or, as Paul wrote, "Now may the God of hope fill you with all joy and peace *in believing*, that you may abound in hope by the power of the Holy Spirit" (Rom. 15:13).

Conclusion

I wish I had time to develop this last point, to tell you of the joy that men and women of God have known in the midst of sorrow as they trusted in the Lord. Hudson Taylor, the great pioneer missionary to China, lost his beloved wife, Maria, after 12 years of marriage. They had been delighted with each other's love. Shortly after her death, he wrote to his mother in England,

> From my inmost soul I delight in the knowledge that God does or deliberately permits all things, and causes all things to work together for good to those who love Him.
>
> He and He only knew what my dear wife was to me. He knew how the light of my eyes and the joy of my heart were in her.... But He saw that it was good to take her; good indeed for her, and in His love He took her painlessly; and not less good for me who must henceforth toil and suffer alone—yet not alone, for God is nearer to me than ever. And now I have to tell Him all my sorrows and difficulties, as I used to tell dear Maria; and as she cannot join me in intercession, to rest in the knowledge of Jesus' intercession; to walk a little less by feeling, a little less by sight, a little more by faith.

To one of his mission leaders he wrote at that time,

> My eyes flow with tears of mingled joy and sorrow. When I think of my loss, my heart--nigh to breaking--rises in thankfulness to Him Who has spared her such sorrow and made her so unspeakably happy. My tears are more tears of joy than of grief. But most of all I joy in God through our Lord Jesus Christ--in His works, His ways, His providence, in Himself. (*Hudson Taylor and the China Inland Mission, the Growth of a Work of God* [The China Inland Mission], pp. 199-200, emphasis his.)

Do you know such abiding joy in the Lord? One of Taylor's favorite hymns was, "Jesus, I am resting, resting, in the joy of what Thou art; I am finding out the greatness of Thy loving heart." That same Jesus and that same joy is available to everyone who will rejoice in Him.

Application Questions

1. Where's the balance between not denying our feelings and yet not living by feelings, but by faith?

2. Discuss: Is depression a sin? Always? Never? Sometimes?

3. Agree/disagree: Every Christian can know God's abiding joy.

4. Agree/disagree: In almost every case of depression there is some unbiblical thought pattern or behavior.

Let your gentle spirit be known to all men. The Lord is near.

† Philippians 4:5

WHEN RIGHT IS WRONG
Philippians 4:5

We live in a day when everyone is pushing for their rights: civil rights, women's rights, consumer's rights, labor rights, gay rights, children's rights and every other minority group's rights. There is a backlash now against so-called affirmative action, because white males are claiming that their rights have been infringed upon.

Standing up for one's rights seems almost American. One of the flags from the American Revolution shows a snake with the motto, "Don't tread on me!" We go to great lengths to prove that we won't allow anyone to push us around. When Abraham Lincoln was a lawyer in Springfield, Illinois, a wealthy man asked him to take a lawsuit against a poor man who owed him $2.50. At first Lincoln hesitated to take the case, but on second thought he agreed--if the wealthy man would pay him a fee of $10 cash up front. The man quickly agreed and handed over the money. Lincoln went to the poor man and offered him $5 if he would settle the debt. So Lincoln got $5 for himself; the poor man made $2.50; and the rich man got his $2.50 debt settled at a cost of $10! But, he got his rights!

We're all prone to this mentality of demanding our rights because it stems from the love of self. At work, at home, and in the church, we're quick to react when we feel that we've been treated unfairly. When someone wrongs us, we defend ourselves and let others know how we were mistreated. We take courses in assertiveness training so that we can learn how to stand up for ourselves and get our way (as if we needed training in how to do that!). As a pastor, I've watched people go from job to job, or from marriage to marriage, or from church to church, each time claiming that they were in the right, but others wronged them. Even if you grant that they were right, they were wrong because they were not practicing what Paul commends in our text, the Christian virtue of forbearance. He is telling us that ...

Right is wrong when we insist on our rights and do not practice forbearance.

Martyn Lloyd-Jones points out (*The Life of Peace* [Baker], pp. 142-143) that in Philippians 4, Paul is implicitly speaking about the fruit of the Spirit (Gal. 5:22-23). In verses 2 and 3 we have an exhortation to love; in verse 4, to joy; verse 6 to peace; and here, in verse 5, to patience and, I would add, kindness, goodness, and gentleness, all rolled into the one word variously translated "forbearance" (NASB), "gentleness" (NIV , NKJV), "moderation" (KJV), "magnanimity" (NEB), and "unselfishness" (Amplified). In our study, we first need to answer the question, "What is the meaning of the Greek word translated 'forbearance'"? Then, Why do we need this quality? How do we develop it? And, finally, How do we practice it without getting trampled on in this dog-eat-dog world?

I. WHAT IS FORBEARANCE?

Webster (*Webster's Ninth New Collegiate Dictionary*) defines our English word, forbearance, as "a refraining from the enforcement of something (as a debt, right, or obligation) that is due." The Greek adjective (*epieikes*) occurs five times (1 Tim. 3:3; Titus 3:2; James 3:17; 1 Pet. 2:18, plus Phil. 4:5, as a substantive) and is often translated, "gentle." The noun occurs twice (Acts 24:4; 2 Cor. 10:1). But it means more than our word "gentle" conveys. Lightfoot calls it "the opposite to a spirit of contention and self-seeking" (J. B. Lightfoot, *St. Paul's Epistle to the Philippians* [Zondervan], p. 160). He cites Aristotle, who contrasts the forbearing person with one who is precise as to his rights, a person who sticks to the letter of the law to get his due. Calvin (*Calvin's Commentaries* [Baker]) takes it to mean that we are not to be easily angered when we are wronged or suffer inconveniences or injustice.

Archbishop Trench (*Synonyms of the New Testament* [Eerdmans], pp. 153-157) observes that the pattern for this quality is found in God, who goes back from the strictness of His rights against us, who allows for our imperfect righteousness, and does not exact from us the extreme penalties He has a right to exact. Trench points out that sometimes a legal right can become a moral wrong. The forbearing person goes back from the letter of right for the better preserving of the spirit of what is right. He is not harsh in demanding extreme penalties. He is softened by God's grace and deals with others in the same manner. The word has the nuance of leniency, of not being so overly strict that we demand our "pound of flesh," even if it is our due.

Building on Trench's observations, William Barclay (*New Testament Words* [Westminster], pp.95-96) says that the basic thing about this word is "that it goes back to God. If God stood on His rights, if God applied to us nothing but the rigid standards of law, where would we be?" Then he observes, "We live in a society where men insist on standing on their legal rights, where they will do only what they are compelled to do, and where they desire to make others do all that they can compel them to do. Again and again we have seen congregations torn by strife and reduced to tragic unhappiness because men and women, committees and courts stood on the letter of the law. When a congregation's governing body meets with a copy of its Church's book of laws prominently displayed on the chairman's table trouble is never far away."

Perhaps these two quarreling women, Euodia and Syntyche, were each standing on their rights. Paul is gently urging all parties involved to demonstrate forbearance. It is not a quality of the natural man, because selflessness is at the core of it. It means that we value the relationship above our rights, so we graciously back off and stop demanding our own way, even if we have a right to it. So we might modify Webster's definition and say that *biblical forbearance means graciously refraining from insisting on our rights because we put love for others ahead of love for ourselves.*

II. WHY DO WE NEED FORBEARANCE?

There are at least four reasons we need to develop this quality:

1. We need forbearance to be like Jesus Christ.

In 2 Corinthians 10:1, Paul says, "I ... urge you by the meekness and gentleness of Christ ...." The second word, "gentleness," is our word. The Corinthians were being bold and pushy, challenging Paul's apostolic authority. If necessary, he would come to them and flex his muscle and put the domineering, self-willed rebels in their place. But he does not want that kind of showdown, so he appeals to them to act in accordance with the meekness and forbearance of Christ, who did not assert His rights as the Son of God. If we want to be like our Lord, we must not fight for our every right, but rather, graciously yield our rights for the sake of others.

2. We need forbearance to have God's joy and peace.

The verses in Philippians 4 are not disjointed; there is a connection between having God's joy (4:4) and being forbearing people (4:5). Often our joy is disrupted by people who wrong us or irritate us. If we respond by saying, "He has no right to treat me that way! I have my pride! I have my rights! I'm not going to let him get away with that!"--if we go that route, we'll lose our joy in the Lord.

If we respond that way, it reveals something about us, namely, our selfishness! So we need to confront it and confess to the Lord our love of self. And then, just absorb the offense. The Lord is near, both in the sense that He knows what happened and is able to deal with the one who wronged you; and, that His coming is near, when He will right all wrongs. So trust in Him to deal with the other guy's selfishness and you deal with your own by yielding your rights out of love. If the wrong against you disrupts your relationship with the other person, you may need to follow the steps I outlined in the message on verses 2 and 3. But love covers a multitude of sins, and it's often better just to let it go. Don't let your hurt feelings that stem from your selfishness rob you of your joy in the Lord.

3. We need forbearance to get along with others.

"Let your forbearing spirit be known to *all men*." We need this quality in all our relationships--in the church, where we step on each others' toes. We need it in our families, in the irritations of daily life. We need it in the world, at work or at school, where unscrupulous, self-seeking people often try to take advantage of us. We will leave behind us a trail of broken or strained relationships if we do not learn to be forbearing people--to yield our rights, to be gentle and gracious, not demanding.

If we experience frequent relational problems, chances are that we are not practicing the golden rule, treating others as we want to be treated ourselves (Matt. 7:12). We all go easy on ourselves and we want others to treat us graciously. If I'm late for an appointment, I usually let myself off the hook with a good excuse--I got caught in heavy traffic, or I just had too much going on. Rarely do I get angry with myself for being late. Even if I don't have a good excuse, I shrug my shoulders and say, "Oh, well, I'm only human!" But do I give others the same grace when they're late for a meeting with me, or do I think, "How inconsiderate of them!" If I go easy on myself and allow myself to make mistakes, I need to do the same with others. That's forbearance.

To be forbearing means that we will not be easily offended because self is not on the throne. We won't take it personally if we're slighted. We'll be gracious and give others the benefit of the doubt. We won't jump to the conclusion that they deliberately wronged us. We'll try to be understanding and make things easier for the other person. Love "always protects, always trusts, always hopes, always perseveres" (1 Cor. 13:7, NIV). We need forbearance to get along with others.

4. We need forbearance to bear witness for Jesus Christ.

One of Paul's main concerns in Philippians is our witness. In his own situation, he wants Christ to be proclaimed in every way (1:18, 20). He wants us as the church to conduct ourselves "in a manner worthy of the gospel" (1:27). He tells us to do all things without grumbling or disputing, so that we will shine forth as lights in the world (2:14-16). As we saw in the last chapter, if we lack God's joy, especially in times of trials, we will not be effective witnesses of the power of the gospel. The same will be true if we are not forbearing people.

There is a cartoon strip in our local paper called "Crabby Road." The character is a grouchy, cantankerous, old woman who doesn't let anybody push her around and who makes life as miserable as she can for everyone else. Maybe people find it funny because it appeals to the flesh. Deep down inside, we all have a mean streak like that woman that says, "Who cares about others? I need to look out for myself! I'm going to fight for everything I deserve!" But if we live like that, we are not showing the spirit of our Savior to a lost world. And people who are like the cartoon woman are invariably lonely, alienated people because they do not practice biblical love.

Paul says, "Let your forbearing spirit *be known* to all men." In other words, "Go out of your way to show others that you are gracious, forgiving, patient, not easily offended, that you're quick to yield your rights and give preference to the other person." This quality is so unlike the world's way that we will stand out as distinct and have opportunities for witness.

III. HOW DO WE DEVELOP FORBEARANCE?

Paul tells us how to develop this quality by adding, "The Lord is near." He could mean two things, both of which are true: He could mean, since the Lord is always present, always a witness to our relationships, keeping that fact in mind will help us to put self to death and to show forbearance to those who act insensitively toward us. We should always act as we would if the Lord were standing there watching us. A number of verses in the Old Testament give assurance to God's people, especially when others oppress them, that the Lord is near (Ps. 34:18; 119:151; 145:18). He is near for us to take refuge in Him. He is near for us to call upon for strength to endure patiently any difficult person or situation we encounter. As Hebrews 13:5-6 assures us, since the Lord Himself has said, "I will never desert you, nor will I ever forsake you," we can confidently say, "The Lord is my helper, I will not be afraid. What shall man do to me?" Remembering the presence of the Lord will enable us to be forbearing.

Or, Paul could mean, since the Lord's coming is near, when He will make right all wrongs and will judge those who have selfishly taken advantage of you, entrust yourself to His care when you are wronged. Paul's reference just a few verses before to the Lord's coming (3:20-21) is the main support for this view. Scripture tells us never to take vengeance when we are wronged, because that prerogative belongs to the Lord alone (Rom. 12:19-20). If not in this life, we know that at the judgment the Lord will deal with the one who wronged us. Our duty is to be patient and forbearing, and to show grace to the person in the hope that he will repent and get right with God. If you don't need grace from the Lord, then I suppose you can be strict and demand full justice from those who wrong you. But if you need God's grace, then you need to show His grace to others through forbearance.

IV. HOW DO WE PRACTICE FORBEARANCE WITHOUT GETTING TRAMPLED ON OR WITHOUT COMPROMISING THE TRUTH?

By this time you're probably thinking, "If I practice forbearance, I'm going to get walked on! It's a dog-eat-dog world out there. You've got to stand up for your rights or everyone will take advantage of you. I live with (or work with) some aggressive, assertive people. How can I practice forbearance without getting run over?" Three things to keep in mind:

1. Remember that you are accountable first and foremost to the Lord, not to other people.

You are the Lord's servant or steward, and one day you will give an account to Him for how you spent your time, your money, and how you used the spiritual gifts He entrusted to you. You can't allow pushy people to determine your schedule or priorities. Jesus was forbearing, but He didn't allow others to dictate His ministry (Mark 1:35-39; John 7:1-10). Sometimes Paul stood up for his rights, but his motive was not self-love, but love for the gospel (Acts 16:35-40; 25:11). There are times when it is not loving to let an aggressive person continue walking all over you and everyone else. The loving thing is to confront the person and not allow them to dominate you. Check your motives!

2. Learn to discern the essential from the peripheral; don't bend on essentials; give room on peripherals.

Through a growing knowledge of God's Word, our only standard for truth, we must learn to discern what *doctrines* are essential to the faith and which are less crucial. What *methods* are so wrong biblically that they must be discarded, and which ones are tolerable, even though not perfect? What *behaviors* will shipwreck a person's faith, and which are, perhaps, not desirable, and you hope the per- son will grow out of them, but they aren't going to destroy the per- son at the moment? Your goal is to love the other person; biblical love always seeks the highest good of the one loved, namely, that the person grow to be like Christ. As we saw in Philippians 1:9, love must be coupled with discernment or it is not love at all.

One example: A Christian widow in her sixties in the church I pastored in California became engaged to an unbelieving man. One of our elders, who was very close to her, and whom she helped support in his ministry, told her how happy he and his wife were for her and wished her God's blessing. But he didn't confront her sin of becoming unequally yoked with an unbeliever! When I heard of what he had done, I was flabbergasted. He defended himself by saying that he was just being loving toward her. I suppose he could have said he was being forbearing. But I argued that he wasn't being loving at all, because biblical love doesn't let someone head for a cliff without warning them. Forbearance must always be tempered by love.

The same thing applies to doctrine. If a person is toying with teaching which denies the deity of Jesus Christ, it is not loving to be forbearing. It will destroy his faith if he goes down that road, and so we must strongly warn him. There are other errors that may not totally shipwreck his faith, but it will hinder his growth. But you don't need to come on quite as strongly. Forbearance, like love, must be coupled with biblical discernment.

3. Remember that growth is a life-long process.

If you have to deal with an irritating person, show them as much grace as God has shown you. If a guy is coming from a difficult background, it may take time for him to learn to be sensitive and loving to others. You've got to model love as you work with a difficult person, giving him room to grow. Remember, God didn't dump the whole load on you all at once. He is patient, tolerating our weaknesses, but still confronting us as we are able to bear it, moving us ahead in godliness. We have to show the same grace to others.

Conclusion

At the 1965 Wimbledon Tennis Finals, a linesman called "Fault" on a player's second serve. The player was sure that his serve had been within the line, so he protested to the umpire, but the umpire upheld the linesman's call. The server lost the point. But his opponent was also certain that the serve had been fair and that he should have lost the point. So when the next serve came over the net, he stood aside and let it go by, conceding the point (story in Leonard Griffith, *This is Living* [Abingdon], p. 120). He had "the right" to take the point, but he knew it would have been wrong. So he showed forbearance by graciously refraining from insisting on his rights.

Are you letting your forbearing spirit be known to your mate? Are you gracious and patient when he or she fails or falls short? What about with your kids? Some well-meaning Christian parents are so rigid and strict with their children that they provoke them to rebellion. We need to be as forbearing with our children as the Lord is with us. What about toward other believers? Do you give them room to grow and be different than you in peripheral matters, or do you insist that they agree with you or you cut them off? You can be right and yet be wrong if you fail to practice the Christian grace of forbearance.

Application Questions

1. How do we practice forbearance without getting sloppy about sin? How do we show grace and yet hold to godly standards?

2. How do we know when to absorb a wrong against us (or an irritation) and when to confront it?

3. Is it ever right for a Christian to be assertive and stand up for his rights? If so, when?

4. How do we determine whether a problem is essential or peripheral? Are there shades of gray in between?

Be anxious for nothing, but in everything by prayer and supplication with thanksgiving let your requests be made known to God. And the peace of God, which surpasses all comprehension, will guard your hearts and your minds in Christ Jesus.

† Philippians 4:6-7

THE ANSWER TO ANXIETY
Philippians 4:6-7

A family had put their Grandma on her first plane flight, but she hadn't been very confident about the experience of leaving the ground on this contraption. When they met her at the airport on her return, one of the family members kidded her by asking, "Well, did the plane hold you up okay?" She grudgingly replied, "Well, yes," and then quickly added, "But I never did put my full weight down on it!"

Many Christians are like that Grandma. The truth is, they're being sustained completely by God, but they're afraid to put their full weight down on Him. As a result, they're plagued by anxiety and aren't able to enjoy the flight.

Few of us are strangers to anxiety. It creeps in over big and little things, gnawing away at our insides. Someone graphically described anxiety as "a thin stream of fear trickling through the mind. If encouraged, it cuts a channel into which all other thoughts are drained" (Arthur Roche, *Reader's Digest* [6/88], p. 64). We now often hear phrases like being "stressed out," or having "a panic attack." Although I disagree with their psychological approach to the problem, the Christian psychiatrists, Frank Minirth and Paul Meier, say that anxiety is the most common mental disorder they encounter at their network of clinics across our country (*Worry-Free Living* [Thomas Nelson], p. 17).

We often feel anxious about our *finances*: How can we make this month's bills? How will I be able to fix my aging car if it breaks down? What if I lose my job? How will we put the kids through college? How can we meet our medical bills? How will we ever save enough for retirement? What if the economy fails?

We feel anxious about our *health*, especially as we grow older: What if I get cancer or Alzheimer's? What if I'm disabled or have to go into a nursing home? If we're younger, we may have these same anxieties concerning our aging parents.

We're anxious about our *children*: Will they turn out okay? Will they avoid drugs and sexual immorality? Will they be safe in this crime-ridden world? Will they be able to get into college and then get a decent-paying job? Will they marry a godly person and have a happy home? What kind of world will their children have to live in?

The lists could go on and on. Maybe you're getting anxious just listening to me give different reasons for anxiety! Sometimes we can't identify any specific reason for our anxiety, but it's there, nagging away at our insides. If we don't learn to deal with it properly, it can cause all sorts of health problems, which in turn feed our anxiety!

To those who follow Him, Jesus promised, "Peace I leave with you; My peace I give to you; not as the world gives, do I give to you. Let not your heart be troubled, nor let it be fearful" (John 14:27). He spoke those comforting words on the most difficult night He faced on this earth, the night before His crucifixion. Seven times in the New Testament our God is called either the God or Lord of peace. That peace can be the constant experience of every Christian, even in the midst of trials. In our text, Paul the prisoner tells us how:

To experience God's peace instead of anxiety, pray with thankfulness about every concern.

There are three key words in these verses that reveal the theme: Anxious; prayer; and, peace. Being *anxious* is the problem we are told to put off; *prayer* is the procedure we are told to practice; *peace* is the product we are promised by God.

1. We must put off anxiety which is sin.

"Be anxious for nothing." In the Sermon on the Mount, Jesus made it clear that anxiety stems from a lack of faith and from a wrong focus on the things of this world instead of on the kingdom of God (Matt. 6:25-34, especially verses 30 & 33). If we excuse our anxieties by saying, "Well, it's only human," or, "Anybody would feel anxious in this situation," we will not overcome it because we are not confronting the root cause of it, namely, our sin of not believing God and of not seeking first His kingdom and righteousness.

As I mentioned in the last chapter, our Christian witness to a lost world is one of Paul's main themes in Philippians. He wants Christians to have God's joy in every situation, not just so that they will be happy people, but so that they will be effective witnesses of Jesus Christ (see Phil. 2:14-18). In other words, we are to be seeking first God's kingdom, not our own happiness. If a non-Christian sees you as a believer weighed down with anxiety and care, he isn't going to be asking how he can have what you have! Anxiety and joy are mutually exclusive. So for the sake of our testimony of Jesus Christ, it is imperative that we learn to experience the peace of God, especially in the face of trials.

This means that when it comes to the matter of dealing with our anxiety, we must, at the outset, confront our motives for wanting to have peace. If our reason for wanting to be free from anxiety is so that we can live a peaceful, pleasant life, our focus is self-centered and therefore wrong. There are many people who come to Christ because they are anxious and they want the peace He offers. But if they do not confront the fact that they are living to please themselves rather than God, they will simply settle into a self-centered life where they "use God" for their own peace and comfort. Jesus said, "Whoever wishes to save his life shall lose it; but whoever loses his life for My sake and the gospel's shall save it" (Mark 8:35). The peace Christ offers is the by-product of enthroning Christ as Lord and living for His kingdom.

In the parable of the sower, Jesus warns (Luke 8:14) that the seed which fell among the thorns represents those who have heard the gospel, "and as they go on their way, they are choked with worries and riches and pleasures of this life, and bring no fruit to maturity." *Worries* is the noun related to the Greek verb *be anxious* in our text. The scary thing about Jesus' words is this: As I understand that parable, only one of the groups is truly saved, namely, those who bring forth fruit with perseverance. Those who profess to believe, but then get choked out by worries, riches, and pleasures, have never taken self off the throne of their lives and put Jesus and His kingdom on the throne. They are deceived into thinking that they are Christians, but the truth is, they are just living with the same focus the world has, namely, for personal pleasure and peace.

In relation to Philippians 4:6 this means that what we have here is not just a simple formula, "If you're anxious, try prayer; it works." Rather, it means, "If you're anxious, examine either your *lack of faith* in the living God, who has promised to supply the basic needs of His children." Or, "Examine your *focus*, whether you're living for Christ and His kingdom or for yourself." Whatever the root cause, anxiety is sin that must be confessed to God and put off.

Before we leave this point, let me clarify that Paul is not encouraging a careless, carefree, irresponsible attitude toward people or problems. I've seen Christians swing from anxiety to either apathy or inaction, claiming that they're obeying the command not to be anxious. But Christians should care deeply about people and their problems and should work hard to resolve problems. As members of the same body, we are to have mutual concern for one another (1 Cor. 12:25). Paul mentions the concern that he bears daily for all the churches (2 Cor. 11:28). He tells the Philippians that Timothy is genuinely concerned for their welfare (Phil. 2:20). In each of these verses, the word concern is the same as the Greek word for anxious, but clearly it is not sinful anxiety but proper concern. It is proper to be concerned about our future welfare to the extent that we take responsibility to plan and save for future needs (Prov. 6:6-11).

But proper concern turns to sinful anxiety when we lack faith in God's role as the Sovereign Lord and provider, and when we put self at the center instead of God's kingdom and righteousness. So the first step in dealing with anxiety is to examine whether it is due to lack of faith or to a wrong focus on self. Confess the sin to God and yield to Him.

2. We must practice prayer with thankfulness about every concern.

Paul mentions four Greek words for prayer which overlap in meaning and yet are helpful to distinguish: Prayer, supplication, thanksgiving, and requests.

Prayer--a general word for prayer, always used with reference to God, with the nuance of reverence. When Paul says to make our requests known "to God," the Greek word means "face to face with God," to come directly before Him. This means that when we pray, we must stop to remember that we are coming into the very presence of the holy God, where even the holy angels cover their faces and cry, "Holy, holy, holy is the Lord of hosts" (Isa. 6:3). Yes, He welcomes us into His presence as a father welcomes his children. Through our High Priest, the Lord Jesus, God invites us to draw near with confidence to the throne of grace to receive mercy and grace to help in time of need (Heb. 4:16). But we must remember that it is to the throne of the universe, to the Sovereign, Eternal

God that we come.

This means, of course, that we must always examine our hearts and confess and forsake all sin when we come to God in prayer. The psalmist says, "If I regard wickedness in my heart, the Lord will not hear" my prayers (Ps. 66:18). But we also have the assurance that if we confess our sins, the blood of Jesus is sufficient to cleanse us (1 John 1:7, 9).

Please notice that the believer is told to come directly to God in prayer. Christ is our mediator, our High Priest. The Holy Spirit who dwells in every believer prompts and moves us as we pray, interceding for us (Rom. 8:26-27). Thus prayer is a personal drawing near to the Triune God. But we should not pray to Mary or any of the so-called "saints." We do not need to go through any human priest. As believers, we all are priests before God, able to draw near directly to Him in effectual prayer.

Supplications--This word gives prominence to the sense of need and also looks at specific requests. Sometimes people ask, "Why pray, since God already knows what we need?" John Calvin has some of the most profound and practical words on prayer that I have ever read (*Institutes of the Christian Religion* [Eerdmans], ed. by John McNeill, III:XX). He points out that whatever we need and lack is to be found "in God and in our Lord Jesus Christ, in whom the Father willed all the fullness of his bounty to abide" (III:XX:1). It is through prayer "that we reach those riches which are laid up for us with the Heavenly Father" (III:XX:2). Prayer is not so much for God's sake as for ours. It shows us our total need for God Himself, and not just for certain temporal benefits. It casts us in dependence on Him, so that we will "seek, love, and serve Him, while we become accustomed in every need to flee to Him as to a sacred anchor." It purifies our desires, since we must bring them to God Himself. It prepares us to receive thankfully what He gives, being reminded that it comes from His hand. It helps us to meditate on His kindness as we delight in what He has given. It confirms to us our own weakness and God's great providence and faithfulness in meeting our needs (Calvin develops these points in III:XX:3).

This means that our supplications must be in line with God's will and purpose. In the Lord's Prayer, we learn that the first focus of our prayers should be on God's kingdom and righteousness, and only secondarily on our personal needs (Matt. 6:9-13).

Thanksgiving--When you're anxious, presumably you're in a situation that gives some cause for anxiety! At such times, thankfulness is not automatic or spontaneous. You have to do it deliberately by faith. Thanksgiving in a time of trials reflects three things:

(1) Remembrance of God's supply in the past. You think back over His faithfulness to you up to this point and realize that His mercies have sustained you. He has been with you in every trial. He never abandons or forsakes His children, even if we face persecution or death for His sake.

(2) Submission to God's sovereignty in the present. To thank God in the midst of a crisis or trial is to say, "Lord, I don't understand, but I submit to Your sovereign purpose in this situation. I trust that You know what You're doing and will work it together for good." We are not just to thank God when we feel like it, but also when we don't feel like it (1 Thess. 5:18).

(3) Trust in God's sufficiency for the future. A thankful heart rests upon the all-sufficient God, knowing that even though we don't see how He is going to do it, He will meet our every need as we cast ourselves on Him. I love Jeremiah 32:17, especially when I think about its context. Jeremiah was shut up in prison. Nebuchadnezzar was besieging Jerusalem which was about to fall (32:2). In that situation, the Lord told Jeremiah to do something that everyone would have thought was crazy, to buy a field from his uncle. Anybody knows you don't sink your money into real estate when a country is about to fall to a foreign tyrant. But God wanted to show His people that "houses and fields and vineyards shall again be bought in this land" (32:15). Then Jeremiah prays, "Ah Lord God! Behold, You have made the heavens and the earth by Your great power and by Your outstretched arm! Nothing is too difficult for You" (32:17). Jeremiah was trusting in God's sufficiency for the future.

When I first came to this church we had some difficult problems to resolve. We had a crucial meeting, where things could have gone either for my leadership or against me. I spent the day fasting and praying, but as I walked up the sidewalk from my car, I felt anxious. I was reciting Philippians 4:6 when the two little words, "with thanksgiving" jumped out at me, and the Lord reminded me that I had failed to give thanks for this difficult situation. I paused and said, "Thank You, Lord, even for these trials," and immediately I was flooded with His peace. He worked in that meeting in obvious ways.

Requests--This word overlaps with supplications, emphasizing the specific, definite nature of our petitions to the Lord. So often our prayers are so vague and general that we couldn't know whether God had answered them or not. This is the word used where Jesus tells us, "Ask, and it shall be given unto you; seek, and you shall find; knock, and it shall be opened unto you" (Matt. 7:7). He goes on to illustrate the point by saying that if a boy asks his father for a loaf of bread, the dad won't give him a stone. If he asks for a fish to eat, the dad won't give him a snake. Jesus concludes, "If you then, being evil, know how to give good gifts to your children, how much more shall your Father who is in heaven give what is good to those who ask Him!" (Matt. 7:11). Ask the Father, and if it's for your good, He will give it!

Sometimes we fail to ask because something seems too trivial or small to trouble God about. But if it's big enough to make me anxious, it's certainly big enough to ask God about. A woman once asked the British Bible teacher, G. Campbell Morgan, "Do you think we should pray about the little things in our lives, or just the big things?" He retorted, "Madam, can you think of *anything* in your life that is *big* to God?" So whenever you're anxious, come to God in reverent, humble, specific, thankful prayer. The result:

3. We are promised God's incomparable peace when we pray.

"The peace of God which surpasses all comprehension, shall guard your hearts and your minds in Christ Jesus" (Phil. 4:7). This is not some psychological peace gained through coping techniques. The Christian psychiatrists I mentioned earlier give all sorts of "common sense" and psychological methods (alongside the "spiritual") that you can use to alleviate your anxiety, including picking a phrase (any phrase will do, they say) and repeating it over and over (p. 110-111)! This is just thinly disguised Transcendental Meditation!

No, what Paul is talking about is the peace that comes from the God who is never subject to anxiety because He is the sovereign, omnipotent Creator and Lord of the universe. Nothing takes Him by surprise or makes Him bite His nails, wondering how it will turn out. This is the peace that Jesus promised, "not as the world gives." It is humanly not explainable. But, praise God, it is *real*, and every child of God has known it and has known that it comes from God alone, not from psychological insights.

Note that this peace stands guard like a sentry over our inner person, our hearts (the comprehensive term for our whole person) and minds (specifically, our thoughts which threaten to trouble us) *in Christ Jesus*. We are in intimate, permanent union with Him, and to get to us, anxiety must go through Christ Jesus! So what God promises isn't just a quick fix, where prayer is a technique that will bring you calm until you get through the crisis. Paul is talking about an ongoing, deepening, intimate relationship with the God of peace, where you seek to please Him with all your thoughts, words, and deeds. In a time of trial, you draw near to the God of peace, you focus on His grace to you in Christ Jesus, you pour out your heart to Him, and the result is, His peace stands guard over your heart and mind.

Conclusion

A little over a year ago, I learned that a woman who led the music ministry when I first began to pastor almost 20 years ago had been stricken with three malignant brain tumors. She and her husband are maybe ten years older than I am. I wrote to her and she wrote back and told how her husband, who has worked all his life in construction, now has such bad arthritis in his hip that he can no longer work. She said how the doctors had warned them to do anything they really wanted to do, because her time may be short. Her final paragraph said, "The peace the Lord gave me while I was in the hospital is far beyond understanding. Everything is in His control--especially the timing of our life. He said that His grace is sufficient and I found that to be so true. His strength is made perfect in weakness." She is now in the Lord's presence, free from this mortal body.

Do you know God's peace in the midst of situations that the world gets anxious about? If not, examine yourself: Is your faith in Him and your focus on His kingdom, rather than on selfish pursuits? Have you drawn near to God in reverent, specific, thankful prayer? You can put your full weight down on Him, and He will bear you up and give you His indescribable peace. It makes the flight so much more enjoyable!

Application Questions

1. How can we know when legitimate concern crosses the line into sinful anxiety?

2. Is it wrong for a Christian to take tranquilizers or sleeping pills to calm nervousness or anxiety? Is this any different than taking aspirin for a headache?

3. What is the difference between using prayer as a technique and prayer as a whole way of life?

4. Can God guide us in His will by withholding or granting His peace? Cite Scripture to support your answer.

Finally, brethren, whatever is true, whatever is honorable, whatever is right, whatever is pure, whatever is lovely, whatever is of good repute, if there is any excellence and if anything worthy of praise, dwell on these things.

† Philippians 4:8

THE CHRISTIAN'S THOUGHT LIFE
Philippians 4:8

Mark Twain wrote, "What a wee little part of a person's life are his acts and his words! His real life is led in his head, and is known to none but himself. All day long, the mill of his brain is grinding, and his thoughts, not those other things, are his history." (*Reader's Digest* [1/93], p. 155).

I would modify Twain by saying that our thought life forms the basis for and is largely revealed in our actions and words. But Twain's comments correctly affirm that our thought life composes a major part of who we really are. Jonathan Edwards put it this way: "The ideas and images in men's minds are the invisible powers that constantly govern them" (source unknown). Thus it is crucial for each of us to bring our thought life into submission to Jesus Christ by learning to think biblically about every aspect of life.

One of the most helpful things I have learned about the Christian life is that all sin begins in our thoughts, which the Bible often calls "the heart." Jesus said, "That which proceeds out of the man, that is what defiles the man. For from within, out of the heart of men, proceed the evil thoughts, fornications, thefts, murders, adulteries, deeds of coveting and wickedness, as well as deceit, sensuality, envy, slander, pride and foolishness. All these evil things proceed from within and defile the man" (Mark 7:20-23). No one commits these outward sins without first having committed them in his mind. If we want to grow in godliness, we must win the battle over sin on the thought level.

In Philippians 4:8 Paul exhorts us to develop a Christian thought life. His words should not be divorced from the context. Practicing verse 8 is essential if we want to develop and maintain healthy relationships (4:2-3, 5). A Christian thought life is also integral to a life of joy (4:4) and peace (4:6-7) in every situation. Since our thoughts form the basis for our behavior, a godly thought life is also essential for the obedience to which Paul exhorts us in verse 9. Clearly, Paul's thought life was at the heart of the contentment he had learned in every situation (4:10-12). So Paul is telling us the way to be whole people in our relationships with God, with one another, and within ourselves. But before we look specifically at what Paul is teaching and how to obey it, we need to think about:

I. WHAT PAUL IS NOT TEACHING: THE POWER OF POSITIVE THINKING.

I need to focus on this for a moment because the Christian world has been infiltrated with the false teaching of "positive thinking," popularized by Norman Vincent Peale and, with only slight variations, by Peale's protege, Robert Schuller. If you are at all familiar with the teachings of these men, you know that they are not Christian in any orthodox sense of the term, even though they both have been welcomed into evangelical circles. Through their influence, the idea has crept into the American church that it is wrong ever to be negative or critical. This has resulted in the loss of discernment.

A young woman once stopped attending the church I pastored in California because she said I was too negative. When I pressed her for specifics, she showed me my sermon outline from the previous week. Sure enough, I had to admit, my points were stated negatively rather than positively. But I pointed out to her that I had taken the points verbatim from the biblical text. But that didn't matter to her! And, of course, it didn't occur to her that she was being critical of my preaching, or that Paul and Jesus were often both critical and negative. She believed that we must always be positive.

The positive thinking heresy has further spread through the so-called "Positive Confession" heresy, also called the "Health and Wealth" or "Name it and Claim it" teaching, that whatever you confess positively by faith, God *must* do it. This heresy attributes power to faith itself, and says that even if you are sick, you must not give a negative confession by admitting it, but must claim your healing by affirming, "I am well!"

Also a number of purportedly Christian sales companies or successful salesmen have utilized a form of this error through a sales motivational teaching called "positive mental attitude." You're never supposed to entertain negative thoughts. You're supposed to use "positive self-talk," have faith in yourself, and visualize yourself as successful and wealthy so that it will become a reality.

All of these errors are based on the heresy of Science of Mind, taught by Ernest Holmes, the founder of the Church of Religious Science, that your mind can create reality, that through thinking positively, you can do anything or achieve any success you want. The variations mentioned above, though claiming to be Christian and appealing to Philippians 4:8 as support, are satanic in that they appeal to the flesh, promote self, and do not confront people with the need to be subject to the lordship of Christ. (Dave Hunt deals with many of these errors in his two books, *The Seduction of Christianity* and *Beyond Seduction* [both by Harvest House].) But, clearly, Paul is not teaching the power of positive thinking in Philippians 4:8.

II. WHAT PAUL IS TEACHING: THE CHRISTIAN'S THOUGHT LIFE SHOULD BE FOCUSED ON THE GREAT TRUTHS OF SCRIPTURE.

Even though Scripture is not specifically mentioned, it is assumed, because it is the only source for knowing what is true, honorable, right, pure, lovely, and of good repute. Let's look at the list:

1. Think on whatever is *true*.

The word means, "true as to fact ... it denotes the actuality of a thing" (G. Abbott-Smith, *A Manual Greek Lexicon of the New Testament* [Charles Scribner's Sons], p. 20). The "true" is that which corresponds to reality. God Himself is the only final test for truth. Since He is unchanging, the moral standards revealed in His Word, which stem from His holy nature, are also unchanging. They apply to every culture in every age. John 3:33 attests, "God is true" (see also, John 8:26; Rom. 3:4). As Paul writes to Titus, who was in Crete (the Cretans were notorious liars), "God ... cannot lie," and He made known His truth by "His word" (Titus 1:1-3). Jesus also claimed for Himself that He is true (John 7:18; also 5:31-32). Opposed to God and Christ, Satan is a liar and the father of lies (John 8:44). He is a deceiver, and he uses sin to deceive those ensnared by it (2 Cor. 11:3; Eph. 4:22; Heb. 3:13).

Since as fallen creatures we are prone to Satan's lies and deception, the only way we can know the truth and walk in it is to steep ourselves in God's Word. We should know the Word so well that we automatically run everything we encounter through the grid of God's Word. We live in a day that is geared toward emotions and strongly influenced by the supposed "virtue" of tolerance. Our culture assumes that love means being tolerant and accepting of everyone and everything, even if God's Word plainly declares that something is an abomination. If you go with the flow, you will be carried far from God's absolute standard of moral truth as revealed in His Word.

We also must resist the pragmatism of our culture, which determines the true by whatever works. If something works, which means, it brings you happiness (at least at the moment) or it accomplishes what you want, then it must be true. But God's Word doesn't always line up with what works. In fact, it's clear that sin often brings pleasure for a season; if it didn't we wouldn't be so enticed by it. Many of the "positive mental attitude" methods are effective in making you a successful sales person. But the question is, Are they biblical? We must test everything by God's Word, not by feelings or pragmatism.

2. Think on whatever is *honorable* (NIV = "noble").

The word means "that which inspires reverence or awe; dignified, worthy of respect." It is a character quality required in deacons and deaconesses (1 Tim. 3:8, 11). Elders should keep their children under control "with all dignity" (1 Tim. 3:4). All Christians should "lead a tranquil and quiet life in all godliness and dignity" (1 Tim. 2:2).

This means that Christians are to take life seriously. We are not to be silly goof-offs, who treat life as a perpetual joke. We live in light of eternity, keeping in mind the uncertainty of this short life and the reality of heaven and hell. This doesn't mean that we can't appreciate clean humor. But our overall tenor should communicate to a lost world that they must stand before a holy God someday soon. Think on these reverent themes.

3. Think on whatever is *right*.

This word is used of God Himself who is righteous (Rom. 3:26; 1 John 2:29; 3:7) and of Jesus Christ (Acts 3:14; 7:52; 22:14; 1 Pet. 3:18; 1 John 2:1). Thus we are to be righteous people, as John writes, "Little children, let no one deceive you; the one who practices righteousness is righteous, just as He is righteous; the one who practices sin is of the devil" (1 John 3:7-8). To think on what is right means to think on the holy nature of God, especially as revealed in the person of Jesus Christ, and to model our behavior after Him.

4. Think on whatever is *pure*.

The word refers to ceremonial purity, but also to the moral purity that is pictured by the ceremonial. It especially means keeping our bodies undefiled by abstaining from sexual sins (see 2 Cor. 11:2; 1 Tim. 5:22; Titus 2:5; James 3:17; 1 Pet. 3:2; 1 John 3:3). In Ephesians 5:3-5 Paul warns, "But do not let immorality or any impurity or greed even be named among you, as is proper among saints; and there must be no filthiness and silly talk, or coarse jesting, which are not fitting, but rather giving of thanks. For this you know with certainty, that no immoral or impure person or covetous man, who is an idolater, has an inheritance in the kingdom of Christ and God." As Christians, we must say no to our sexually impure culture and focus on moral purity.

5. Think on whatever is *lovely*.

This word occurs only here in the New Testament. It means what is pleasing, agreeable, and attractive. At times we all find ourselves attracted to that which is evil. But this word must be taken with the context, meaning that which is both pure and attractive. Jesus Christ is inherently attractive, and so we should think often on our lovely Savior, who gave Himself for us on the cross.

6. Think on whatever is *of good repute*.

This comes from a compound word meaning to speak well of something (our word "euphemism" comes from this Greek word). It refers to something that "deservedly enjoys a good reputation" (F. F. Bruce, *New International Biblical Commentary, Philippians* [Hendrickson], p. 146). As Paul says in 1 Corinthians 13, love believes the best about another person, it refuses to believe an evil report about a brother or sister until there is certain evidence to establish it.

After this list of six items, Paul changes the sentence structure, beginning the next two phrases with the word "if"; I take these final two qualities to sum up all the others plus anything Paul has omitted.

*To sum up, think on anything of virtue.

The word "excellence" (NASB, NIV) means moral virtue. Although it is common in Greek literature, this is the only time Paul uses the word. Peter uses it as a quality of God and thus as the first quality that we are to add to our faith (2 Pet. 1:3, 5). This means that as a new Christian, one of the first things you must do is to stop any behavior that is not in line with God's moral virtues as revealed in Scripture, such as the Ten Commandments, the Sermon on the Mount, and Paul's list of the deeds of the flesh (Gal. 5:19-21). To continue doing such things will hinder your growth in godliness. We must focus our minds on moral virtue.

To sum up, think on anything worthy of praise.

The word "praise" is used both of what is praiseworthy in God (Eph. 1:6, 12, 14; Phil. 1:11) and in people (Rom. 2:29; 13:3; 1 Cor. 4:5). Of course, every attribute and deed of God is praiseworthy, and so we should daily think about how great God is and on the marvelous works He has done, both in creation and in history. Toward other people, even toward those in the world, we should be gracious by focusing on their strong points and good qualities. Even though we all are depraved by nature, because of God's common grace even unbelieving people can be kind, caring, and loving. Ultimately those qualities, even in unbelievers, do not bring glory to the person, but to God. So we should be appreciative and affirming toward people rather than negative and critical.

Think on these things.

Paul means to reflect on these qualities that stem from God and should be characteristic of us as children of God. "Give them weight in your decisions" (Beare, cited by Bruce, p. 145). Allow them "to shape your conduct" (Ralph P. Martin, *Tyndale New Testament Commentaries, Philippians* [IVP/Eerdmans], p. 171). In other words, think on these things with a view to doing them.

III. HOW TO OBEY WHAT PAUL IS TEACHING: WE MUST CONTROL WHAT COMES INTO OUR MINDS.

Proverbs 4:23 says, "Watch over your heart with all diligence, for from it flow the springs of life." Patrick Buchanan has observed, "The food that enters the mind must be watched as closely as the food that enters the body" (*Reader's Digest* [11/89], p. 203). Frank Outlaw wrote, "Watch your thoughts, they become your words; watch your words, they become actions;

watch your actions, they become habits; watch your habits, they become character; watch your character, for it becomes your destiny" (*Reader's Digest* [date not known]). To obey what Paul is saying, we must exercise control over our thought life. This involves at least five things:

1. We need the mind of Christ through conversion.

Before a person knows Jesus Christ as Savior and Lord, he has a depraved mind (Rom. 1:28). He lives in the lusts of his flesh, indulging the desires of the flesh and of the mind (Eph. 2:3). God must supernaturally raise us from our state of being dead in our trespasses and sins (Eph. 2:1) and impart to us a new nature that is able to obey Him (Eph. 4:22-24). Paul says that "the mind set on the flesh is hostile toward God; for it does not subject itself to the law of God, for it is not even able to do so; and those who are in the flesh cannot please God. However, you are not in the flesh but in the Spirit, if indeed the Spirit of God dwells in you. But if anyone does not have the Spirit of Christ, he does not belong to Him" (Rom. 8:7-9). As he goes on to explain, the Holy Spirit gives us the power to put to death the deeds of the flesh and to live in obedience to God.

2. We must clean out and block out sources for sinful thoughts.

We cannot have a pure thought life without first ridding our- selves of things which defile us. It would be like trying to clean yourself while you're lying in a mud hole. The first step is to get out of the mud and get to a source of soap and water. If we allow things into our lives which promote sensuality, greed, sexual impurity, crude language, violence, hatred, love of self, or anything else not pleasing to God, we cannot grow in holiness.

I agree with Pastor Kent Hughes, who in his book, *Disciplines of a Godly Man* ([Crossway Books], p. 75) writes, "I am aware of the wise warnings against using words like 'all,' 'every,' and 'always' in what I say. Absolutizing one's pronouncements is dangerous. But I'm going to do it anyway. Here it is: *It is impossible for any Christian who spends the bulk of his evenings, month after month, week upon week, day in and day out watching the major TV networks or contemporary videos to have a Christian mind.* This is *always* true of *all* Christians in *every* situation!" (emphasis his). Amen!

It needs to be said: You *will not be a godly person* if you do not control the TV, videos, movies, music, magazines, books, and even the radio programs you take in. If something is polluting you or tempting you, get rid of it and make plans to avoid it!

3. Take in God's Word from every source.

Read it daily. If you're not a reader, listen to it on tape. You have no excuses for not saturating your mind with Scripture. As Kent Hughes also says, "You cannot be profoundly influenced by that which you do not know" (p. 77). I cannot encourage you enough to memorize verses that relate to problems you struggle with. Unless the Word is in your heart, God cannot use it when you are tempted (see Jesus' example in fending off temptation, Matt. 4:1-11). You do not need to read the newspaper every day, but you desperately need to read your Bible every day! It's like a daily shower--it cleanses off the dirt of the world (Eph. 5:26).

4. Expose your mind to the teaching and examples of the great Christians down through history.

Listen to and read sermons from godly men. The sermons and commentaries of John Calvin, Jonathan Edwards, Charles Spurgeon, J. C. Ryle, Martyn Lloyd-Jones, and other giants of the faith are available in print. Read the biographies of these and other godly men and women. With a few exceptions, avoid most of the modern Christian best sellers, and spend your time reading the works that have stood the test of time. These men walked with God, and they will feed your soul.

5. Listen to wholesome music, especially the great hymns of the faith.

I enjoy many of the praise choruses, especially those that are taken directly from Scripture. But also, some of the great hymns have a history of sustaining God's people down through the years, and they are doctrinally meaty. The Wesley's used hymns to teach theology to many who were illiterate. Get recordings of the great hymns and play them until you know them by heart. They will fill your mind with wholesome truth.

Conclusion

A number of years ago, the news media picked up the story of a woman known as "Garbage Mary." She lived in a smelly Chicago tenement amid mounds of garbage. She spent her time rummaging through trash cans. She would bum cigarettes off her neighbors. Police took her to a psychiatric hospital after she was stopped for questioning and found to be in a confused state of mind. When they went into her filthy apartment, they were astounded to find stock certificates and bank books indicating she was worth at least a million dollars. She was the daughter of a wealthy Illinois lawyer.

It's a pathetic story, but it pictures the lives of many professing Christians, who could be immersing their thought life in that which is true, dignified, right, pure, lovely, of good repute; that which is virtuous and worthy of praise. But instead, they surround themselves with moral filth, wallowing daily in raunchy TV programs, polluting their minds with the sordid stories of this condemned world, rather than focusing their thought life on the things of God and Christ.

An old Indian Christian was explaining to a missionary that the battle inside of him was like a black dog fighting a white dog. "Which dog wins?" asked the missionary. "The one I feed the most," replied the Indian. Paul says, "Feed your mind on the pure truth of God's Word."

Application Questions

1. Why are Peale's "Positive Thinking" and Schuller's "Possibility Thinking" fundamentally opposed to Scripture?

2. Some Christians argue that we need to be aware of what's going on in our culture through movies, TV, etc. Your response?

3. How should a Christian police officer apply Phil. 4:8 when he is daily confronted by moral filth in his job?

4. Someone may argue, "The Bible itself has stories of immorality, etc. What's the difference between reading it there and watching it on TV, movies, or video?" Your answer?

The things you have learned and received and heard and seen in me, practice these things, and the God of peace will be with you.

† Philippians 4:9

THE IMPORTANCE OF
CHRISTIAN CONDUCT
Philippians 4:9

A doctor from Texas owned a home in Mexico. He felt sorry for the poor people there, many of whom were often sick because they didn't pasteurize their milk. So he bought them a pasteurizing machine. The villagers built a special shed to house it in and made a big deal out of it when he finally brought it down and installed it. When the doctor returned a few months later, the leading man of the village greeted him, "Oh, doctor, good to see you! If we had known you were coming, we would have plugged in the pasteurizing machine."

Obviously, a pasteurizing machine doesn't do a bit of good if it isn't plugged in and used for its intended purpose. While we chuckle at the story, many Christians treat the Bible like those poor villagers were treating that machine. It occupies a central place on a coffee table in their home. They believe in all the good it can do. But they aren't plugging it in to deal with the very problems in their lives it is intended to solve. They are not applying Scripture to change their conduct.

They're like the gray-haired old lady, a long time church member, who shook hands with her pastor after the service one Sunday. "That was a wonderful sermon," she told him, "just wonderful! Everything you said applies to someone I know."

We all tend to think that attending church is a nice, safe thing to do. It feels good to sing and to fellowship with the nice people and to hear a message from God's Word. But James 1:22 warns us that if we hear God's Word but do not become doers of it, we deceive ourselves. Hearing the Bible and knowing the Bible without translating that knowledge into obedience is dangerous because we deceive ourselves. The Bible was not written to satisfy our curiosity or to fill our notebooks with charts on prophecy or theology. It was written to be translated into genuinely Christian conduct in our daily lives.

In Philippians 4:9, Paul exhorts us to follow his example by becoming doers of the Word. He shows us that;

Christian conduct is built on biblical content and is vital because it results in the very presence of the God of peace.

Verse 9 must not be separated from verse 8. Our thought life forms the basis for our behavior. If our conduct is simply outward conformity to the expectations of the Christian crowd, it is not genuine and will not stand up under pressure or temptation. Christian conduct must flow out of a Christian thought life, and as we saw in the last chapter, a Christian thought life is the result of genuine conversion, where God imparts to us a new nature that is able to please Him. Martyn Lloyd-Jones put it this way,

> ... the gospel is not something we add to our lives, it is rather, something which should entirely dominate them. ... The Christian life, therefore, is not merely a modification of the natural life, it is a new life, and Christians do not merely add something to their lives, they are people who have been changed at the centre, they are entirely different (*The Life of Peace* [Baker], p. 191).

Once we are converted through faith in Christ, we begin the process of sanctification, or growth in holiness, through the renewal of our minds through Scripture, and the corresponding changes in our conduct, so that we learn to please God with our lives. In verse 9, Paul shows us how this process works and why it is of vital importance, namely, that the sense of God's presence as the God of peace is linked with it. He mentions four components: (1) The intellectual--"What you have learned"; (2) The volitional-- "What you received"; (3) The behavioral--"What you have heard and seen, which you must practice"; (4) The emotional--"The God of peace shall be with you."

1. The intellectual component: The Christian faith has content that must be taught and learned.

The word "learned" implies that the Christian faith has content which must be taught by someone who understands it and mentally grasped by those he teaches. Of course, the Christian faith is much more than mere intellectual understanding, as we will see. And even on the intellectual level, Scripture teaches that "the god of this world [Satan] has blinded the minds of the unbelieving, that they might not see the light of the gospel of the glory of Christ, who is the image of God" (2 Cor. 4:4). Thus God must open the minds of unbelievers to respond to the gospel, as Paul goes on to say, "For God, who said, 'Light shall shine out of darkness,' is the One who has shone in our hearts to give the light of the knowledge of the glory of God in the face of Christ" (2 Cor. 4:6). God shines into our hearts to give us knowledge, and such *knowledge* is grasped with the mind.

We once visited a church where the pastor did not clearly communicate the content of the gospel, but when he gave the invitation at the end of the service, about a dozen people went forward. I said to Marla, "What in the world are they responding to?" It had to be a mostly emotional response to the mood and music rather than an intelligent response to the truth of the content of the gospel, because such truth had not been made clear. But Christian faith is not in a vague feeling. It is not faith in faith itself, as in the popular song, "I Believe." It is not faith in "God however you conceive Him to be."

This week at the Million Man March in Washington, D.C., Mayor Marion Barry, who spent time in jail for doing crack cocaine, thanked God for his recovery and told the crowd, "The vision for the Million Man March came directly from God himself. It was God-inspired.... Whether we call god Jesus Christ, Yahweh, Jehovah, Allah or just God, he's God. I know first hand God's power, God's grace and God's redemptive love" (*Arizona Daily Sun*, 10/16/95, p. 1). That is generic faith, but it is not biblical faith. Biblical faith is in the historical person of Jesus Christ as revealed in Scripture and in what He did for us in dying on the cross. Thus there is specific content, an intellectual element, to the gospel message.

Once a person has responded by faith to the person and work of Jesus Christ, he must go on to learn the great doctrines of the Christian faith. We live in a day that disparages doctrine. We think that it is some needless nicety for theologians and seminarians to banter about. But we need to remember that Paul didn't write the major doctrinal portions of his letters to theologians. He wrote Romans and Ephesians and the other great doctrinal sections to common people, many of them uneducated slaves, who had come to faith in Christ, to help them understand how to live in a manner pleasing to God.

Note the importance of teaching in Paul's ministry: In Acts 11:26,

Barnabas brought Paul (then called Saul) to Antioch, "And it came about that for an entire year they met with the church, and taught considerable numbers; ..." In Acts 17:2-3, Paul "reasoned with [the Jews] from the Scriptures, explaining and giving evidence that the Christ had to suffer and rise again from the dead, and saying, 'This Jesus whom I am proclaiming to you is the Christ.'" Paul's evangelistic efforts were not based on emotional appeals, but on a reasonable appeal to their minds.

We see the same thing in Acts 19:8-10, where Paul was in the synagogue in Ephesus for three months, "reasoning and persuading them about the kingdom of God." But when some became hardened and disobedient, he withdrew with the disciples, and continued to reason with them daily from the Word of God. In Acts 20:20, 27 he reminds the Ephesian elders how he "did not shrink from declaring to [them] anything that was profitable, and teaching [them] publicly and from house to house," how he "did not shrink from declaring to [them] the whole purpose of God."

In Colossians 1:28, Paul describes his ministry: "And we proclaim Him, admonishing every man and teaching every man with all wisdom, that we may present every man complete in Christ." In his pastoral letters to Timothy and Titus, Paul repeatedly emphasizes the theme of "sound doctrine." In the final chapter he wrote before his death, he exhorted Timothy with what must have been of utmost importance (2 Tim. 4:2-3), "Preach the word; be ready in season and out of season; reprove, rebuke, exhort, with great patience and instruction. For the time will come when they will not endure sound doctrine; ..."

Thus the Christian faith has content that must be learned and taught. The question is, *Are you studying and learning God's Word?* It doesn't happen without diligence and effort. I encourage you to apply yourself to learn the great truths of God's Word with a view to obedient application.

2. The volitional component: The content of the Christian faith must be responded to with our will.

Our text mentions "the things you have learned and *received*." The word means to take unto oneself, especially the traditions as delivered and handed down from Christ to the apostles. Here it has special reference to "the ethical and procedural guidelines for Christian living" (F. F. Bruce,

New International Bible Commentary, Philippians [[Hendrickson], p. 147). To receive the teaching concerning Christ, the gospel, and the moral and ethical demands which go along with it, means to submit our will to the lordship of Jesus Christ over every aspect of our lives, beginning with our thought life (4:8). In other words, the gospel always demands not just an intellectual response, but also a moral response, where we personally receive Christ as Savior and Lord.

I have found that invariably, people who claim to have intellectual problems that keep them from responding to the gospel in reality have moral problems that are the real reason for their not responding. Every person, from the Ph.D. at the university to the illiterate subsistence farmer in Mexico, has the same need, namely, that his sin has separated him from the Holy God. Thus he needs Christ as Savior. But, every person also has the same stubborn self-will that refuses to submit to Jesus as Lord. We all want to run our own lives without bowing before Jesus.

So if a person tells me that he can't believe in Christ because of intellectual problems, I will say, "Specifically, which problems?" He may name something, such as evolution or that he doesn't believe the Bible is God's Word. I respond, "If I can provide you with reasonable answers to that problem, will you then believe in Christ?" I've never yet had a person say, "Yes." Instead, he will say, "Well, there are other issues, too." I say, "Name them. Give me the list, and if I can provide reasonable answers to each problem on your list, then will you become a follower of Christ?" I'm trying to help the person see that the real issue isn't intellectual, it's moral. He doesn't want to give up sex with his girl friend or doing drugs or some other sin. But the content of the Christian faith must be received by submitting our will to Christ.

3. The behavioral component: The content of the Christian faith must be worked out in real life conduct.

Paul says, "The things you have ... *heard and seen in me, practice* these things; ..." Paul is not boasting in himself. He simply knew that his life had integrity. He did not teach one thing and live another. He did not act one way in public, but have a secret life of sin in private. You could follow him around 24 hours of the day, seven days a week, and see a man who walked with God, even in the trials he encountered. In fact, the Philippians had seen and heard about Paul and Silas singing hymns of praise and praying in the Philippian jail at midnight during his first visit to that city. You can't fake it when you have been wrongly denied justice, when your back is laid open and your feet are in the stocks in a smelly, rat-infested jail cell. Paul's Christian life was real in the crunch, and so he could honestly, without pride, call people to follow him as he followed Christ (see 1 Cor. 4:16; 11:1; Phil. 3:17; 1 Thess. 1:6; 2 Thess. 3:9; 2 Tim. 3:10).

His words point out the importance of having godly examples who show us not only by their words, but also by the way they conduct themselves in the home and in all their lives, how to live the Christian faith in the real world. Pastor John MacArthur correctly advises, "Never expose yourself to the ministry of someone whose lifestyle you can't respect" (*Anxiety Attacked* [Victor Books], p. 41). John Calvin said, "It would be better for the preacher to break his neck going into the pulpit than for him not to be the first to follow God."

It is not that Paul or any man, except Jesus, is sinless. But a man who teaches God's Word must live it with integrity. That's why an essential qualification for both elders and deacons is that they manage their own households well (1 Tim. 3:4-5, 12). If I am not living under the lordship of Christ with my wife and children, dealing with problems in a biblical manner, demonstrating the fruit of the Spirit in my relationships with them, then I need to get out of the ministry.

Those of us who have walked with the Lord for a few years need to be looking for younger men (or, women with women) we can spend time with to show them by the way we live how they should live as Christians in daily life. That may threaten you, because you can't fake it if a guy is watching you when difficult situations arise. Do you live Christ in those situations? Do you demonstrate godliness when you're provoked?

When I was in my early twenties, a brother in his early thirties, who was married with three young daughters, invited me to live with them for a short while. I spent three months with them, and while he and I couldn't spend as much time together as I had hoped for, because of his busy schedule, I still could see the reality of Christ in their family life.

Also, I have been helped tremendously by reading Christian biographies. I feel like I know many of the great saints who have gone before me because I have read their stories and I know how they dealt with the trials and tests that came into their lives. By reading their biographies, I learn how the content of the Christian faith takes on shoe leather, how it works out in daily conduct. I encourage you to read the biographies of the faithful saints who have gone before us.

When Paul says, "Practice these things," the word implies doing something repeatedly until it becomes a habit or way of life. At first, habits feel awkward and unnatural. Remember the first time you ever drove a car with a stick shift? It seemed like there were a million things to remember and do all at once. But once you get it down, so that it's a habit, you can hop in the car and drive off while discussing some fine point of theology with a friend, and you don't even think about what you're doing.

Habits can be either your friend or your foe. Godly habits work for you, since they determine your daily routine in ways that help you grow in holiness. In Luke 4:16 we read that Jesus came to Nazareth, where He had been brought up, and then it says, "and as was His *custom*, He entered the synagogue on the Sabbath ...." Jesus had a habit of spending the Sabbath with God's people, worshiping God. We should have the same habit every Lord's day. We should have the habit of reading God's Word and praying each day. We should have the habit of avoiding things that pollute our minds. Habits come from practicing these things over and over. At first, when you're changing from ungodly practices to pleasing God, it may seem awkward. Keep at it, practice it until it becomes your routine.

Thus, Christian conduct is built on the biblical content of the Christian faith. There is the *intellectual* component of the faith, which is grasped by the mind. There is the *volitional* component, yielding our will to receive God's truth personally. There is the behavioral component, learning to put the Christian faith into daily practice. Finally,

4. The emotional component: The result of Christian con- duct is the very presence of the God of peace with you.

In verse 7 we saw that specific, thankful *prayer* results in the *peace of God* guarding our hearts and minds. In verse 9 we see that the *practice* of Christian conduct results in the *God of peace* being with us. You may be wondering, "I thought that God is always with us. Why does Paul say something that's always true as if it were a special deal?" The answer is, because it is a special deal! Yes, God is always with the believer (Matt.

28:20; Heb. 13:5). But we do not always sense His presence, nor do we always know His presence with us as the God of *peace*. He is the God who is never troubled by the ups and downs of life, by the storms of circumstances that batter us around, because He is the eternal, sovereign, Almighty God who accomplishes His purpose (see Isa. 40).

Do you covet and seek for the presence of God, the God of peace, in your life? When Moses was faced with the awesome task of leading an entire nation out of bondage in Egypt through the barren Sinai desert, he prayed, "If Your presence does not go with us, do not lead us up from here. For how then can it be made known that I have found favor in Your sight, I and Your people? Is it not by Your going with us, so that we, I and Your people, may be distinguished from all the other people who are upon the face of the earth?" (Exod. 33:15-16). God responded by promising His presence. The presence of the God of peace with us is promised if we put our knowledge of the Christian faith into daily Christian conduct.

Conclusion

D. A. Carson writes (*Christianity Today* [6/29/79], p. 31),

> The supreme irony is that Christians hear best what the Spirit is saying to someone else. Speak to the fundamentalist about the truth, and he hears you, precisely because he doesn't need to; it is the person with fuzzy notions about the eternality of the truth who will not hear. Speak to the *genuinely* broad-minded ecumenist about love, and he hears you, precisely because he doesn't need to, but fundamentalists of a harsher variety will not.... The one who truly hears what the Spirit says to the churches will be the one who is receptive to the words of God that he least wishes to hear [emphasis his].

Elisabeth Elliot once overheard her young daughter singing to her cat, "Amazing grace, how sweet the sound, that saved a wretch like *you*!" We're all like that; the truth applies to the other guy! "If just my wife and kids would apply this to their lives, we'd have a happy family!" No, I need to apply the content of the Christian faith to *my* daily conduct. Then, the God of peace with be with me. Let's all practice being doers of the Word and not hearers only who deceive themselves!

Application Questions

1. Why is Bible knowledge without application dangerous?

2. Why does modern Christianity disparage doctrine? How can we overcome this?

3. Is most change in Christian conduct instantaneous deliverance or a slow struggle? Why?

4. On which of the four components (intellectual, volitional, behavioral, emotional) should our primary focus be? Why?

But I rejoiced in the Lord greatly, that now at last you have revived your concern for me; indeed, you were concerned before, but you lacked opportunity. Not that I speak from want, for I have learned to be content in whatever circumstances I am. I know how to get along with humble means, and I also know how to live in prosperity; in any and every circumstance I have learned the secret of being filled and going hungry, both of having abundance and suffering need. I can do all things through Him who strengthens me.

† Philippians 4:10-13

THE SECRET FOR CONTENTMENT
Philippians 4:10-13

An airline pilot was flying over the Tennessee mountains and pointed out a lake to his copilot. "See that little lake?" he said. "When I was a kid I used to sit in a rowboat down there, fishing. Every time a plane would fly overhead, I'd look up and wish I was flying it. Now I look down and wish I was in a rowboat, fishing."

Contentment can be an elusive pursuit. We go after what we think will make us happy only to find that it didn't work; in fact, we were happier before we started the quest. It's like the story of two teardrops floating down the river of life. One teardrop said to the other, "Who are you?" "I'm a teardrop from a girl who loved a man and lost him. Who are you?" "I'm a teardrop from the girl who got him."

The lack of contentment that marks our nation is reflected in many ways. We see it in our high rate of consumer debt. We aren't content to live within our means, so we go into debt to live just a bit better than we can afford, but then we suffer anxiety from the pressure of paying all our bills. Of course, the advertising industry tries to convince us that we can't possibly be happy unless we have their product, and we often take the bait, only to find that we own one more thing to break down or one more time consuming piece of equipment to add more pressure to an already overloaded schedule.

Our discontent is reflected in our high rate of mobility. People rarely stay at the same address for more than five years. We're always on the move, looking for a better house, a better job, a better place to live and raise a family, a better place to retire. Some of the moves are demanded by the need for decent jobs. But some of it is fueled by a gnawing discontent that we think will be satisfied when we find the right living situation. But we never quite get there.

Our discontent rears its head in our high divorce rate. We can't find happiness in our marriages, so we trade our mates in for a different model, only to find that the same problems reoccur.

Our lack of contentment is seen in our clamoring for our rights, all the while claiming that we have been victimized. If we can just get fair treatment, we think we'll be happy. We are suing one another at an astonishing rate, trying to get more money so we can have more things so that life will be more comfortable. We spend money that we can't afford on the lottery, hoping to win a big jackpot that will give us what we want in life. But even those who win large settlements in a lawsuit or a lottery jackpot are not much happier in the long run.

In Philippians 4:10-13, a man who sits in prison because of corrupt officials awaiting possible execution over false charges tells us how to find contentment. The answer lies buried in the midst of a thank-you note. The Philippian church had sent a financial gift to Paul the prisoner. He wants to express his heartfelt thanks, but at the same time he doesn't want to give the impression that the Lord was not sufficient for his every need. Even though he had been in a very difficult situation (4:14, "affliction"), he doesn't want his donors to think that he had been discontented before the gift arrived; but he does want them to know that their generosity was truly appreciated. So he combines his thanks with this valuable lesson on the secret for contentment. We'll look first at what contentment is as Paul describes it; and then at how we acquire it.

WHAT IS CONTENTMENT?

The word *content* (4:11) comes from a Greek word that means self-sufficient or independent. The Stoics elevated this word, the ability to be free from all want or needs, as the chief of all virtues. But the Stoic philosophy was marked by detachment from one's emotions and indifference to the vicissitudes of life. This clearly is not the sense in which Paul meant the word, since in 4:10 he shows that he rejoiced in the Lord greatly when he received the gift, not because of the money, but because it showed the Philippians' heartfelt love and concern for him. Paul was not detached from people nor from his feelings. He loved people dearly and was not afraid to show it. And, 4:13 clearly shows that Paul did not mean the word in the pagan sense of *self*-sufficiency, since he affirms that his sufficiency is in Christ.

Neither does contentment mean complacency. As Christians we can work to better our circumstances as we have opportunity. The Bible extols hard work and the rewards that come from it, as long as we are free from greed. Paul tells slaves not to give undue concern to gaining their freedom, but if they are able to do so, they should (1 Cor. 7:21). If you're single and feel lonely, there is nothing wrong with seeking a godly mate, as long as you're not so consumed with the quest that you lack the sound judgment that comes from waiting patiently on the Lord. If you're in an unpleasant job, there is nothing wrong with going back to school to train for a better job or from making a change to another job, as long as you do so in submission to the will of God.

So what does contentment mean? *It is an inner sense of rest or peace that comes from being right with God and knowing that He is in control of all that happens to us.* It means having our focus on the kingdom of God and serving Him, not on the love of money and things. If God grants us material comforts, we can thankfully enjoy them, knowing that it all comes from His loving hand. But, also, we seek to use it for His purpose by being generous. If He takes our riches, our joy remains steady, because we are fixed on Him (see 1 Tim. 6:6-10, 17-19). Contentment also means not being battered around by difficult circumstances or people, and not being wrongly seduced by prosperity, because our life is centered on a living relationship with the Lord Jesus Christ. So no matter what happens to us or what others do to us, we have the steady assurance that the Lord is for us and He will not forsake us.

HOW DO WE ACQUIRE CONTENTMENT?

The world goes about the quest for contentment in all the wrong ways, so we must studiously avoid its ways. Paul's words show ...

The secret for contentment in every situation is to focus on the Lord-- as Sovereign, as Savior, and as the Sufficient One.

He is the Sovereign One to whom I must submit; He is the Savior whom I must serve; He is the Sufficient One whom I must trust. If I know Him in these ways as Paul did, I will know contentment.

1. Contentment comes from focusing on the Lord as the Sovereign One to whom I must submit.

Paul mentions that the Philippians had revived their concern for him. The word was used of flowers blossoming again or of trees leafing out in the springtime. He is quick to add that they always had been concerned, but they lacked opportunity. We do not know what had prohibited their sending a gift sooner, whether it was a lack of funds, not having a reliable messenger to take the gift, not knowing about Paul's circumstances, or some other reason. But whatever the reason, Paul knew that God was in control, God knew his need, and God would supply or not supply as He saw fit. Paul was subject to the Sovereign God in this most practical area of his financial support.

I will develop this more in the next chapter, but I believe that Paul had a policy of not making his financial needs known to anyone except the Lord. Here he was in prison, unable to pursue his tent-making trade, and he was in a tight spot ("affliction" in 4:14 literally means "pressure"). He wrote a number of letters during this time to various churches and individuals (Ephesians, Philippians, Colossians, Philemon), and he asks for prayer in those letters. But never once does he mention his financial needs. Rather, he asks for prayer for boldness and faithfulness in his witness. He trusted in and submitted to the sovereignty of God to provide for his needs.

Sometimes God supplied abundantly, and so Paul had learned how to live in prosperity. Most of us would like to learn that lesson! But sometimes God withheld support, and so Paul had to learn to get along with humble means. At those times, he did not grumble or panic, but submitted to the sovereign hand of God, trusting that God knew what was best for him and that He always cared for His children (1 Pet. 5:6-7).

But notice, Paul *learned* to be content in all conditions. It didn't come naturally to him, and it wasn't an instantaneous transformation. It is a process, something that we learn from walking with God each day. Key to this process is understanding that everything, major and minor, is under God's sovereignty. He uses all our circumstances to train us in godliness if we submit to Him and trust Him. Our attitude in trials and our deliberate submission to His sovereignty in the trial is crucial.

George Muller proved the sovereign faithfulness of God in the matter of finances. He lived in 19th century Bristol, England, where he founded an orphanage. He and his wife had taken literally Jesus' command to give away all their possessions (Luke 14:33), so they had no personal resources. Also, he was firmly committed to the principle of not making his financial needs known to anyone, except to God in prayer. He was extremely careful not even to give hints about his own needs or the needs of the orphanage. The children never knew about any financial difficulties, nor did they ever lack good food, clothes, or warmth.

But there were times when Muller's faith was tried, when the Lord took them down to the wire before supplying the need. On February 8, 1842, they had enough food in all the orphan houses for that day's meals, but no money to buy the usual stock of bread or milk for the following morning, and two houses needed coal. Muller noted in his journal that if God did not send help before nine the next morning, His name would be dishonored.

The next morning Muller walked to the orphanage early to see how God would meet their need, only to discover that the need had already been met. A Christian businessman had walked about a half mile past the orphanages toward his place of work when the thought occurred to him that Muller's children might be in need. He decided not to retrace his steps then, but to drop off something that evening. But he couldn't go any further and felt constrained to go back. He gave a gift that met their need for the next two days (*George Muller: Delighted in God!* by Roger Steer [Harold Shaw Publishers], pp. 115-116). Muller knew many instances like that where God tried his faith.

If you are walking with God and you find yourself in a desperate situation, you can know that you are not there by chance. The sovereign God has put you there for your training in faith, that you might share His holiness. It may be a small crisis or a major, life-threatening crisis. Submit to and trust the Sovereign God and you will know the contentment that comes from Him.

2. Contentment comes from focusing on the Lord as the Savior whom I must serve.

The reason Paul knew that God would meet his basic needs was that Jesus had promised, "Seek first His kingdom and His righteousness; and all these things shall be added unto you" (Matt. 6:33). All these things refers to what you shall eat, what you shall drink, what you shall wear (6:25). Jesus was teaching that if we will put our focus on serving Him and growing in righteousness, God will take care of our basic material needs. In the context He is talking about how to be free from anxiety, or how to be content in our soul. Paul taught the same thing (see 1 Tim. 6:6-11). If our focus is on our Savior and on doing what He has called us to do for His kingdom, which includes growing in personal holiness, then we can be content with what He provides.

Please take note that He promises to supply our *needs*, not our *greed*. Most of us living in America have far, far more than our needs. We live in relative luxury, even if we live in a house that is too small or only have one car. Sometimes we need to remember that people in other countries squeeze ten family members into a one-room, dirt-floored shanty.

I read a story about a Jewish man in Hungary who went to his rabbi and complained, "Life is unbearable. There are nine of us living in one room. What can I do?" The rabbi answered, "Take your goat into the room with you." The man was incredulous, but the rabbi insisted, "Do as I say and come back in a week."

A week later the man returned looking more distraught than before. "We can't stand it," he told the rabbi. "The goat is filthy." The rabbi said, "Go home and let the goat out, and come back in a week." A week later the man returned, radiant, exclaiming, "Life is beautiful. We enjoy every minute of it now that there's no goat--only the nine of us." (*Reader's Digest* [12/81].) Perspective helps, doesn't it!

But the point is, if you live for yourself and your own pleasure, you will not know God's contentment. But if you follow Paul in living to serve the Savior, you will be content, whether you have little or much. Part of seeking first God's kingdom means serving Him with your money and possessions, which are not really yours, but His, entrusted to you as manager. We mistakenly think that we will be content when we accumulate enough money in the bank and enough possessions to make us secure. The truth is, you will know contentment when you give generously to the Lord's work, whether to world missions, to the local church, or to meeting the needs of the poor through Christian ministries. "Where your treasure is, your heart will be" (Matt. 6:21). If your treasure is in this world, your heart will be in this world, which isn't the most secure environment! If your treasure is in the kingdom of God, your heart will be there, and it is a secure, certain realm.

3. Contentment comes from focusing on the Lord as the Sufficient One whom I must trust.

Paul says that he had "learned the secret of being filled and going hungry, both of having abundance and suffering need" (4:12). That secret is stated in verse 13, "I can do all things in Him who continually infuses me with strength" (literal rendering). The all-sufficient, indwelling Christ was Paul's source of strength and contentment. Since Christ cannot be taken from the believer, we can lean on Him in every situation, no matter how trying.

Notice that there is a need to learn not only how to get along in times of need, but also how to live with abundance. In times of need, we're tempted to get our eyes off the Lord and grow worried. That's when we need a *trusting* heart. In times of abundance we're tempted to forget our need for the Lord and trust in our supplies rather than in Him. That's when we need a *thankful* heart that daily acknowledges gratitude for His provision. Thanking God for our daily bread, even when we've got enough in the bank for many days' bread, keeps us humbly trusting in Him in times of abundance.

By "all things," Paul means that he can do everything that God has called him to do in his service for His kingdom. He can obey God, he can live in holiness in thought, word, and deed. He can ask for the provisions needed to carry out the work and expect God to answer. If God has called you to get up in public and speak, He will give you the power to do it. If He has called you to serve behind the scenes, He will equip you with the endurance you need (1 Pet. 4:11). If He has called you to give large amounts to further His work, He will provide you with those funds. As Paul says (2 Cor. 9:8), "God is able to make all grace abound to you, that always having all sufficiency in everything, you may have an abundance for every good deed."

Notice the balance between God's part and our part. Some Christians put too much emphasis on "I can do all things," on the human responsibility. You end up burning out, because I cannot do all things in my own strength. Others put too much emphasis on "through Him who strengthens me." These folks sit around passively not doing anything, because they don't want to be accused of acting in the flesh. The correct biblical balance is that I do it, but I do it by constant dependence on the power of Christ who indwells me. As Paul expressed it (1 Cor. 15:10), "But by the grace of God I am what I am, and His grace toward me did not prove vain; but I labored even more than all of them, yet not I, but the grace of God with me." In Philippians 4:13, the verb is present tense, meaning, God's continual, day-by-day infusing me with strength as I serve Him.

The Greek preposition is "in," not "through." It points to that vital, personal union with Christ that we have seen repeatedly throughout Philippians. Paul is saying that because of his living relationship of union with the living, all-sufficient Christ, he can do whatever the Lord calls him to do for His kingdom.

This verse is one of many which affirm the sufficiency of Christ for the believer's every need. But this doctrine is under attack by the "Christian" psychology movement, which claims that Christ is sufficient for your "spiritual" needs (whatever that means!), but not for your emotional needs. But look at the list of the fruit of the Spirit (Gal. 5:22-23), look at the qualities of the godly person as described throughout the New Testament, and you'll find an emotionally stable person. You are not equipped for every good deed (2 Tim. 3:16-17) if you're an emotional wreck. The living Christ and His Word are powerful to strengthen you to serve Him, which includes emotional well-being. But the church today is selling out the joy of trusting in the all-sufficient Christ for a mess of worldly pottage that does not satisfy. Whatever your needs, learn to trust daily in the sufficient Savior and you will know His contentment in your soul.

Conclusion

Legend has it that a wealthy merchant during Paul's day had heard about the apostle and had become so fascinated that he determined to visit him. So when passing through Rome, he got in touch with Timothy and arranged an interview with Paul the prisoner. Stepping inside his cell, the merchant was surprised to find the apostle looking rather old and physically frail, but he felt at once the strength, the serenity, and the magnetism of this man who relied on Christ as his all in all. They talked for some time, and finally the merchant left. Outside the cell, he asked Timothy, "What's the secret of this man's power? I've never seen anything like it before." "Did you not guess?" replied Timothy. "Paul is in love." The merchant looked puzzled. "In love?" he asked. "Yes," said Timothy, "Paul is in love with Jesus Christ." The merchant looked even more bewildered. "Is that all?" he asked. Timothy smiled and replied, "That is *everything*." (Adapted from Leonard Griffith, *This is Living* [Abingdon], p. 149.)

That's the secret of contentment--to be captivated by Christ-- as the Sovereign to whom I submit; as the Savior whom I serve; as the Sufficient One whom I trust in every situation.

Application Questions

1. Where's the balance between being content and yet trying to better your situation or solve certain problems?

2. Someone says, "If God is sovereign over the tragedy that happened to me, then He is not good." What would you reply?

3. What does it mean practically to seek first God's kingdom and righteousness? Must we all become full-time missionaries?

4. Someone says, "We trust God and yet use modern medicine; why can't we trust God and use modern psychology?" Your answer?

Nevertheless, you have done well to share with me in my affliction. You yourselves also know, Philippians, that at the first preaching of the gospel, after I left Macedonia, no church shared with me in the matter of giving and receiving but you alone; for even in Thessalonica you sent a gift more than once for my needs. Not that I seek the gift itself, but I seek for the profit which increases to your account. But I have received everything in full and have an abundance; I am amply supplied, having received from Epaphroditus what you have sent, a fragrant aroma, an acceptable sacrifice, well-pleasing to God. And my God will supply all your needs according to His riches in glory in Christ Jesus. Now to our God and Father be the glory forever and ever. Amen.

† Philippians 4:14-20

FAITHFUL GIVING, FAITHFUL GOD
Philippians 4:14-20

Whenever I speak on the subject of giving, I'm aware that I'm dealing with a sensitive area where people are easily offended. "The church is always after my money," is the common complaint. I'm also reminded of the comment a preacher made, that when you throw a rock at a pack of dogs and one of them yelps, you know which one got hit. So before you yelp about this sermon, you'd better think about whether the Word of God may be hitting you where it hurts!

If you're visiting with us, you need to know that my usual method is to preach through a book of the Bible, and speak on what the text says. It's your lucky day--you just happened to come on a day when the text talks about giving money! The Bible speaks very plainly about money because our hearts and our wallets are tightly bound up together, and God is after our hearts. Jesus talked often about money: 16 of His 38 parables deal with how to handle money and possessions. In the Gospels, one out of ten verses (288 in all) deal directly with money. The Bible offers 500 verses on prayer, 500 verses on faith, but more than 2,000 verses on money and possessions (Howard L. Dayton, Jr., *Leadership*, Spring, 1981, p. 62).

I also want you to know that I do not know how much or how little anyone in this church gives. If you think I'm looking at you because you don't give very much, it's just your guilty conscience! If you fake it and smile back at me, I'll probably think you're a big giver! But it won't fool God. Also, you need to know that this year our giving is actually more than $4,000 over our budget, so I'm not addressing the subject because we're in a crunch. Our text is a "thank-you note" Paul wrote to the Philippians who had given sacrificially to meet his need. In it he gives us one of the most comforting promises in the Bible:

If we give faithfully to the Lord's work, He will supply all our needs.

In the context, it's a conditional promise; you can't divorce verse 19 from what goes before. It is to people who have given faithfully and generously that Paul says, "My God shall supply all your needs according to

His riches in glory in Christ Jesus." If we meet the condition--give faithfully, God will fulfill His part--supply all our needs. So what is faithful giving? There are many more principles than the ones found here, but these four we all must learn:

THE PRINCIPLES FOR FAITHFUL GIVING:

1. Faithful giving should be one of the first things we establish in our Christian walk.

Paul commends the Philippian church by reminding them of how, at the first preaching of the gospel, after he departed from their region (Macedonia), they shared with him in the matter of giving and receiving (4:15-16). At that point, they were the only church that took the initiative to send support to Paul. Even when he was still in Macedonia, at Thessalonica, more than once they sent gifts to him. Apparently those gifts were not enough to provide full support, because he reminds the Thessalonians how he worked with his hands to provide for his needs when he was with them (2 Thess. 3:7-9). But right from the start of their Christian experience, the Philippians had given.

Paul taught that it is proper for a man who labors in the gospel to receive his support from the gospel (1 Cor. 9:1-18; 1 Tim. 5:17-18). But for the sake of avoiding the charge that he was preaching for the money, Paul chose not to receive support from a new church where he was ministering while he was there. Instead, he supported himself by making tents. But if the funds came from another church outside the area, he would stop making tents and devote himself full time to the work of the ministry (compare Acts 18:1-11, 2 Cor. 11:7-12). As I mentioned in the last chapter, Paul never seemed to make his needs known, even as prayer requests, but trusted in the sovereign God to provide. When funds ran low, he would go back to work until God met the need.

But Paul must have taught the Philippians early on the importance of faithful giving to support those in Christian ministry, because soon after he left town, they sent gifts after him. They would have been just a few months old in the Lord, but they were already practicing faithful giving.

Jesus taught the same principle in Luke 16:10-13. After giving the parable of the unrighteous steward, which has to do with money, He said,

"He who is faithful in a very little thing is faithful also in much." He goes on to show that the "little thing" is our use of "unrighteous mammon," or money. If we are faithful in how we use our money to advance His kingdom, the Lord will then entrust "true riches" to us (16:11) which, in the context, are souls. If we want God to entrust us with souls, we begin by proving our faithfulness in what to us is a "big thing," but to God is a "little thing," the use of our money. That's His test. So financial faithfulness, which includes giving, but also how we manage all the material goods God has entrusted to us (earning, spending, saving), should be one of the first lessons we learn in our Christian walk.

One of the first lessons on giving should be that we learn to take the initiative in looking for faithful Christian workers who are focused on the glory of God and the work of the gospel (as Paul was) and support them without being pressured to give. It's a sad commentary on the American church that we live in relative luxury while faithful servants of the Lord are being held up from going to the field because of a lack of funds, or they have to return from the field to raise more support. Many American Christians are so used to the pressured appeals of TV preachers, that "if you don't give right now, this ministry will go off the air," that we overlook the faithful servants of the Lord who are not so forceful in their appeals for funds.

In our own church, we have faithful people who are doing the Lord's work. Don't assume that all their financial needs are being met. Like the Philippian church with Paul, take the initiative to support them. If you're not sure of their need, ask them. Keep in contact and direct some of the resources God has entrusted to you to help support them in His work.

2. Faithful giving should be focused on the furtherance of the gospel.

Paul was "preaching the gospel" (4:15). He had given each church where he worked an example of his hard work and his freedom from greed (Acts 20:33-35; 1 Thess. 2:5; 2 Thess. 3:7-9). There are those who claim to be serving the Lord, but they are lazy and greedy. Don't give to them. If a TV or radio preacher pleads for money, saying that his ministry will go under if you don't send your gift today, let him go under. He's not trusting God. Look at his lifestyle. If he's living in luxury, let him sell some of his junk and give it to his ministry. The Scriptures warn us about men who are in ministry for the money (1 Tim. 6:5; Titus 1:11; 2 Pet. 2:3, 14, 15).

The famous British preacher, C. H. Spurgeon, once received a request from a wealthy man to come to their town and help them raise funds for a new church building. He told Spurgeon he could stay in his country home there. Spurgeon wrote back and told him to sell the home and give the money to the project.

Give to those who emphasize ministry, not money. Paul's focus was on preaching the gospel, not on his need for money. While he genuinely appreciated the gift from the Philippians, he was more excited about what it signified about their heart for God, that it represented fruit accruing in their account in heaven (4:17). As for himself, Paul lived by faith and was content with whatever God provided. But he never made strong appeals for funds for himself.

Paul did, by the way, make a strong appeal for funds *for others*. In 2 Corinthians 8 & 9, he appealed strongly to them to give generously to meet the need of the poor Christians in Judea. Of course he would never stoop to some of the fund-raising gimmicks used by various ministries and churches in our day--sending out "prayer cloths" in exchange for your contribution, church raffles, bingo games, and the like. He appealed to them to give based on God's gracious gift of His Son for us (2 Cor. 8:9; 9:15). He was always scrupulous not to take advantage of anyone in financial matters, but to keep his focus on ministry (2 Cor. 7:2; 11:7-12; 12:18; 2 Thess. 3:8). So look for faithful servants or ministries who are focused on the furtherance of the gospel and give faithfully to them.

3. Faithful giving is investing in eternity.

Paul says, "I'm looking for the profit that increases to your account" (4:17). These terms were common accounting words. Paul is saying that when you give to the Lord's work, you're putting money into your account in the Bank of Heaven, and it pays guaranteed high interest for all eternity. If you have any money invested in stocks or mutual funds, you realize that the more risky the investment, the greater the chance that you can make high returns, but also the greater the chance that you can lose a lot. And, even the "safe" investments have no guarantees. But when you invest in God's work, there is no risk and you get the highest possible return on your investment, guaranteed by the very Word of God!

In Luke 16:1-9, Jesus tells the parable of the crooked steward. He was being called on the carpet for squandering his master's possessions. He knew he would lose his job and he didn't want to become a beggar or to dig ditches. So he quickly called his master's debtors and reduced their bills. Since he knew that his time was short, he made friends for himself in high places, so that in the future they would welcome him. Jesus isn't praising the steward's dishonesty, but rather his foresight. He is telling us for the short time we have left on this earth to use our Master's money to make friends for eternity, to see people come to Christ. Then, when we step into heaven, they will welcome us. By giving to the Lord's work, you are investing in souls for all eternity. It's the smartest investment you can make.

4. Faithful giving should be motivated by worship.

Paul calls their gift "a fragrant aroma, an acceptable sacrifice, well-pleasing to God" (4:18). These terms come out of the Old Testament where they describe the sacrifices that worshipers offered to God. They also are used in the New Testament to describe Christ's offering of Himself for our sins (Eph. 5:2). The point is, you aren't giving to the pastor or to the church; you aren't giving to the missionary or mission organization. You are giving to God Himself. If Jesus Christ bodily walked into this church, if He was the usher handing you the plate, and you saw the nail scars on His hands that were pierced for you, and if they money was going to Him personally for His support, would you give any differently than you do now? Would you grudgingly say, "All right, here's a few bucks!" Or, would you give gratefully out of a heart of love and worship because He gave Himself for you?

Suppose I gave my wife a gift on Valentine's Day. How would she feel if I said, "I didn't really want to, but I hadn't gotten you anything for quite a while, and I was feeling kind of guilty. I know that our neighbor got his wife something and I know it's my duty as your husband to give you something." She wouldn't be "well-pleased," because my motive was wrong. But if I said, "Honey, you deserve even more than I can give, but I love you so much and I was thinking of how much you mean to me when I bought this," the very same gift would be accepted as well-pleasing to her. That's how we should give to God, out of a heart of love and gratitude, to glorify Him (4:20).

If our giving is done as an act of worship to glorify God, then we won't want it advertised how much we're giving. Many Christian ministries cater to the flesh when they put up plaques or memorial books with the names of donors. The best plaque I've ever seen is one at the village at Campus Crusade's Arrowhead Springs that reads, "This village was donated by five businessmen who want the glory to go to God." Amen!

Thus we are to give faithfully to the Lord's work of furthering the gospel, out of a heart of worship to our Lord who gave Himself for our sins. If we do, God promises something:

THE PROMISE FROM OUR FAITHFUL GOD:

Faithful givers can count on the faithful God's faithful supply: "My God shall supply all your needs according to His riches in glory in Christ Jesus" (4:19). What a magnificent promise!

1. The source of the promise is our God with whom we are in union in Christ Jesus.

"My God," "in Christ Jesus." Here again is Paul's intimate, personal relationship with his Savior. Giving to the Lord's work is not for anyone who does not know Him through the cross. If you know Him as "my God," if you know that by faith you are "in Christ Jesus," then the privilege of giving and the promise of God's faithfulness apply to you. If you do not know Christ, you can't give to Him until you receive from Him His gift to you.

It is none other than the God who spoke the universe into existence who promises to supply your needs when you give faithfully. Even though, as Paul himself experienced, you may suffer some tight times, your needs (not luxuries--this isn't prosperity theology!) will be met, and you will have far more, namely, the great joy of fellowship with the Creator and Savior.

2. The sufficiency of the promise is the riches of God for all my needs.

He promises to supply all our needs according to (not "out of") His riches in glory in Christ Jesus. What a staggering promise! The God who owns the whole earth says that He will meet our needs if we give faithfully, and it is a blessed thing to know this in your experience as you watch Him do it.

The American pastor Wilbur Chapman had a family tragedy occur that made it necessary for him to travel to the West Coast. A banker who attended his church visited with him just before he left. As they talked, the banker took a piece of paper out of his pocket and slipped it into his pastor's hand. Chapman looked at it and saw that it was a blank check made out to him, signed by the banker. Momentarily stunned, he asked, "Do you mean you are giving me a signed check to be filled out as I please?" "Yes, exactly," said the banker. "I don't know how much you might need, and I want you to draw any amount that will meet your need." Chapman gratefully took the check, but he didn't need to use it on his trip. Later he commented, "It gave me a comfortable, happy feeling to know that I had a vast sum at my disposal." Our supply is as sufficient as the Bank of Heaven, a blank check for all our needs. But how do we know the check is good?

3. The certainty of the promise depends on God Himself.

Blank checks are no good if the person who signs them is destitute or a crook. But if the check is signed by "my God," the God I know personally, the God who is also our Father (4:20), the God who has never in human history failed His children, the God who demonstrated His great love for us by giving His only Son on the cross, then the check is good! "He who did not spare His own Son, but delivered Him up for us all, how will He not also with Him freely give us all things?" (Rom. 8:32). If we meet the condition by giving faithfully, the promise is certain--our God and Father will meet all our needs. You can count on it!

Conclusion

There is probably no more accurate gauge of your spiritual life than your giving to the Lord's work. Do you give only grudgingly and under pressure? Then you're not focused on the abundant grace of our Lord in your life. Are you hit and miss about your giving, doing it once in a while, but not systematically? Then you're probably not faithful in other disciplines of the Christian life, such as devotions. Are you stingy and tight with your giving? Then your love for the Lord is probably cold and sterile. Do you religiously give ten percent and take pride in it? Then you're probably legalistic in your spiritual life, judging yourself and others by the performance of certain duties rather than by a heart of love for the Savior.

The reason your giving is a pretty good gauge of your spiritual life is that your heart is bound up with your treasure. Jesus taught, "Where your treasure is, there will your heart be also" (Matt. 6:21). If you want your heart to be with the Lord, put your money in the Lord's work. If you want your heart to be in this evil world, put your money in the things of the world. It's a simple principle to state, but not so simple to implement, because it requires faith.

To give generously to the Lord's work requires that you believe that there really is a heaven ahead. Since you plan to spend eternity there, you put your money over to the other side in advance, where it's earning interest in heaven's bank, awaiting your arrival. Jesus called it "laying up treasures in heaven" (Matt. 6:19).

It's like the story of the sailor who was shipwrecked on a South Sea island. He was seized by the natives who carried him to their village and set him on a crude throne. They treated him as royalty. Soon he learned that their custom was once each year to make a man king, king for a year. He thought this was a pretty good deal until he started wondering what happened to all the former kings after their year was up. He found out that after the year, the king was banished to a deserted island where he starved to death. That worried him, but he was a smart king, so he put his carpenters to work making boats and his gardeners to work transplanting fruit trees and other crops to the island where he would be banished. His carpenters built a nice home there. So when his year was over, he was banished, not to a barren island, but to an island of abundance. In the same way, if we really believe that this life is temporary and eternity is ahead, we will be sending our treasures over to that side by our giving, so we'll have something there waiting for our arrival.

Giving generously also takes faith because you have to trust that when you give away your money, God is going to make up for it by providing for your immediate needs. What if I give and then some unexpected emergency comes up? What if I give and lose my job? I heard of a fellow who was struggling with the idea of giving ten percent of his income to his church. (I believe ten percent should be the base, not the ceiling.) He told his pastor that he didn't see how he could do it and keep up with his bills. The pastor replied, "If I promise to make up the difference in your bills if you should fall short, do you think you could try tithing for just one month?" After thinking about it for a moment, the man replied, "Sure, if you promise to make up any shortage, I guess I could try tithing for one month."

The pastor responded, "Now, what do you think of that? You say you'd be willing to put your trust in a mere man like myself, who possesses so little materially, but you couldn't trust your Heavenly Father who owns the whole universe!"

That's the issue at the heart of this matter of faithful giving. Will you trust the living God who gave His Son for you by giving generously and systematically, out of a heart of gratitude, love, and worship? If you do, He promises to meet all your needs according to His glorious riches in Christ Jesus.

Application Questions

1. Should a Christian who is in debt give to the Lord's work or first pay off his debts?

2. In light of all the needs, how can we know where to give and how much to give?

3. Is it a lack of faith for Christians to have savings and investments? Should we give everything and trust God for the future?

4. Is tithing the standard of giving for those in Christ? If not, how do we know how much to give?

WHERE SHOULD YOU GIVE?

How should we determine *where to give*, since we are confronted with so many ministries and needs worldwide? Of course, waiting upon the Lord in *prayer* is crucial for determining where to give and how much to give. But also, there are some guidelines. The *local church* is God's ordained means for propagating the gospel (Matt. 16:18), and so you ought to support its ministries. Beyond that,

. (1) Support individuals whom you know personally to be faithful.

. (2) Consider giving to those who are serving in difficult places.

. (3) Consider whether a person is helping reach those with no gospel witness. They may be serving at the home office of a mission, but if they are part of an outreach to those who have no indigenous church in their midst, they ought to be higher priority for support than those who are reaching the already reached.

If you're giving to a Christian organization (rather than an individual), ask some questions:

. (1) What is the organization really aiming for? Is their doctrinal statement sound? Are they using biblical methods? Is their focus on the gospel as essential, and not social ministry for its own sake?

. (2) Is the organization using sound financial methods? Do they belong to the Evangelical Council for Financial Accountability? If not, are their books audited? Will they send you a financial statement? Do they use proper fund-raising methods?

. (3) Do you know and trust any of the leaders in the organization? Are they godly people of integrity? Is the leader accountable to a board, or is the board a rubber stamp?

. (4) How does the organization function? Do they strive for excellence without extravagance? How much of their income goes to overhead and fund-raising (more than 25% is suspect)? Do the leaders live simply or in luxury?

Greet every saint in Christ Jesus.
The brethren who are with me greet you.
All the saints greet you, especially those
of Caesar's household. The grace of the
Lord Jesus Christ be with your spirit.

† Philippians 4:21-23

THE FELLOWSHIP OF THE SAINTS
Philippians 4:21-23

Bruce Larson observed,

> The neighborhood bar is possibly the best counterfeit
> there is to the fellowship Christ wants to give His church.
> It's an imitation dispensing liquor instead of grace, escape
> rather than reality. But it is a permissive, accepting, and
> inclusive fellowship. It is unshockable. It is democratic.
> You can tell people secrets and they usually don't tell
> others or want to. The bar flourishes not because most
> people are alcoholics, but because God has put into the
> human heart the desire to know and be known, to love and
> be loved, and so many seek a counterfeit at the price of a
> few beers. (Source unknown.)

It is clear from the Bible that Christianity is essentially relational.
The two greatest commandments call us to be right related to God and to
one another: "You shall love the Lord your God with all your heart, and
with all your soul, and with all your mind"; and, "You shall love your
neighbor as yourself" (Matt. 22:37, 39). Even though we all desire close
relationships, because of the fall we tend to act in ways that put distance
between us. When sin entered this world, Adam and Eve lost the intimacy
they had formerly known. They covered their nakedness and started what
continues to this day, blaming the other person for the problem. Their
family life was permanently shattered when Cain murdered his brother
Abel. And so the human race that longs for fellowship is marked by a
breakdown of it.

This means that true fellowship doesn't just happen; we have to
work at it constantly, both in our families and in the church. I've said it
before, and I'm only half joking, that if you get involved in the life of this
church, I can guarantee that you *will* be offended at some point! I quote
again the verse, which is not Scripture, but is true to it, "To dwell above
with the saints we love, O that will be glory! But to dwell below with the
saints we know, well, that's a different story!"

Paul closes his letter to the Philippians with a few words of greeting and a brief benediction. We tend to skip verses like these. But they show us Paul's theology in shoe leather. His theology, as I've said, was not abstruse intellectual stuff for theologians to debate. It was written to common people to show them how to live godly lives. Even the deepest theology in Philippians, where Paul deals with the *kenosis* or "emptying" of Christ when He took on human flesh, is written to show us how to be humble and selfless toward one another (2:3-11). So here at the end of the letter we see that his theology was not divorced from real people for whom he cared. These verses tell us,

It is vital that we be committed to the fellowship of the saints.

Someone has written concerning the early church,
> What that first century world saw was the phenomenon of people of all walks of life loving one another, serving one another, caring for one another, praying for one another. Slaves and free men were in that community. Rich and poor were in the fellowship; Roman citizens and non-Roman citizens were in that community. Members of the establishment and those violently opposed to the establishment were part of that community. The intelligencia and the illiterate were members of that community. To the utter amazement of the world outside they were bound together in an inexplanable [sic] love and unity. (Source unknown.)

These few verses bring out seven marks of the fellowship of the saints which we must strive for as we seek to grow in love:

1. The fellowship of the saints is an inclusive fellowship where every person matters.

"Greet every saint ...." The NIV mistranslates, "Greet all the saints," as if it were a blanket greeting. But Paul uses the singular, meaning, "Greet each one individually." It's not generic; he doesn't want anyone excluded. He wants to greet Euodia and those who may have sided with her; but he also wants to greet Syntyche and those who may have sided with her (4:2-3). He wants to greet each of the church leaders, but also each of the slaves who has come to know Christ. Each person counts. None are to be excluded.

Saints are not saved en masse, but one by one. There is no family or group plan to come into the true church, the company of those whose sins are forgiven through faith in Jesus Christ. Your parents may be godly people who raised you in the church. That's a wonderful advantage, but it won't get you into heaven. You must come before God and acknowledge your sin and your need for the Savior. You must realize that Jesus Christ shed His blood as the only way that your sins can be forgiven. Throwing off all trust in your own good works or self worth, you must trust in Jesus Christ as the One who by His perfectly righteous life and substitutionary death provided all that is needed to make you right before God. Then you join the fellowship of the saints.

At the moment you trust in Christ, the Holy Spirit baptizes you into the one body of Christ, made up of every person worldwide who believes in Him (1 Cor. 12:13). The Holy Spirit sovereignly places you in Christ's body as a member with a vital function to perform. Some have more visible gifts, such as preaching or leadership. Others have less noticed gifts, such as helps or encouragement. But as Paul spells out so beautifully (1 Cor. 12:12-31), no member is unnecessary. Just as in the human body, so in the church: Those members we may tend to despise are essential for the proper functioning of the body. You probably haven't thought much this past week about your pancreas (unless you were having problems with it), but you can't live if it stops working. Even so in the church, each member is vital for its proper functioning.

2. The fellowship of the saints is a holy fellowship, set apart from the world.

"Saints" means "holy ones." Due to the wrong teaching of the Catholic Church, we tend to think of saints as super-Christians who have distinguished themselves by their dedication or noble service. "But me? I'm just your average, run-of-the-mill Christian." But the New Testament is clear that every believer in Jesus Christ is a saint. Paul even addressed the immature Corinthians as "saints by calling" (1 Cor. 1:2). It is important that we view ourselves as such. It means that God has set us apart from the world unto Himself. We are to be *in* the world, having contact with worldly people. But we are to be *distinct from* the world, bearing witness by our godly behavior and by our words to the good news of Jesus Christ.

A little boy used to attend a church which had beautiful stained-glass windows picturing St. Matthew, St. Mark, St. Luke, St. John, St. Paul, and others. One day he was asked, "What is a saint?" He replied, "A saint is a person whom the light shines through." Not bad!

Being a saint is a *position* that is to result in appropriate *practice*. Our position is in Christ, set apart unto God. Our practice is to grow in godly behavior. Of course, the church is both a fellowship of sinners in need of constant grace (4:23) and of saints. We must hold both truths in tension, that we are saints set apart unto God who are to grow in holiness; and, sinners who must receive God's grace and show it to others.

3. The fellowship of the saints is a Christ-centered fellowship.

"Greet every saint *in Christ Jesus* ...." That is to say, we are set apart unto God through our being in union with Christ Jesus. His righteousness is imputed to us when we believe, and we are placed in Him so that all that is true of Him is true of us. Apart from Him we would not be saints at all. He is our Lord, our everything, our all in all. Everything we do must be centered on the Lord Jesus Christ. As we've seen throughout our study, Christ was central to Paul, as He must be to us. Bishop Handley Moule observes,

> The mere number of mentions of the Saviour's name is remarkable. More than forty times we have it in this short compass [in Philippians]; that is to say, it occurs, amidst all the variety of subjects, on an average of about once in every two or three verses. This is indeed perfectly characteristic, not of this Epistle only but of the whole New Testament. What the Apostles preached was not a thing but a Person; Christ, Christ Jesus, Christ Jesus the Lord (*Philippian Studies* [Christian Literature Crusade], pp. 255-256).

The local church is not just to be a social club, where we converse about the same sorts of things worldly people talk about. Our supreme desire and goal is to know Christ more deeply (3:10).

When we come together, He should be the focus of our fellowship. The things of Christ draw us together.

4. The fellowship of the saints is a family fellowship.

"The brethren ... greet you." We have a common Father through the new birth, so that we are now members of the same family. Every person born of God through faith in Christ is a member of this family that transcends social barriers, racial barriers, and national barriers. The saints in Philippi and the saints in Rome were brothers and sisters, even though they may never have met face to face. It included slaves and free-born, poor and wealthy.

Human families are a place where everyone belongs just by virtue of who they are, not by what they do or what they have accomplished. The elderly are in the family, and even though they can no longer work or have a career, they are valuable to the family. They are the ones who begot us and reared us. They have handed off their values and wisdom to us. Babies and young children are in the family. They make for a lot of work, always needing attention and care. But they are the hope of the future. We marvel at each one, uniquely created in the image of God, each with a different bent right from the womb. Everyone in between, from teenagers trying to establish their identity to the middle-aged, who are feeling their bodies beginning to wear out, are a part of the family.

Families aren't perfect. Everyone is in process. But you hang together and care for one another because of the family bond. Families don't get together to watch programs; they just get together because they're family, to find out what's going on in one another's lives. The church should be the same. The American church has become too entertainment-oriented. You can draw a crowd if you put on a good program, but if you announce that the church family is just getting together to meet with the Lord and one another, not many show up. It ought to be enough just to gather with the brothers and sisters and share in the things of Christ.

5. The fellowship of the saints is a supportive fellowship.

"The brethren who are *with me* greet you." Where was Paul? In prison. It wasn't a great place to hang out. Besides that, as we saw in chapter 1, some of the Christian leaders in Rome were criticizing Paul and using his imprisonment as a way to put him down and advance themselves. So to be with Paul in his imprisonment meant to expose yourself to the criticisms of these selfishly motivated preachers. But some--Timothy, Epaphroditus, and a few others-- were there with Paul, standing with him in his time of need.

Paul was strong and able to stand alone for the Lord when he needed to (2 Tim. 4:16-17). But he also appreciated the ministry of those who sometimes put their reputations or even their lives on the line to minister to him. During his second imprisonment, he wrote to Timothy, "The Lord grant mercy to the house of Onesiphorus for he often refreshed me, and was not ashamed of my chains; but when he was in Rome, he eagerly searched for me, and found me--the Lord grant to him to find mercy from the Lord on that day--and you know very well what services he rendered at Ephesus" (2 Tim. 1:16-18). Years before Paul and Barnabas had gone their separate ways because Barnabas wanted to give Mark a second chance after he deserted them on their first missionary journey. But as he sat in prison facing the end, Paul told Timothy, "Pick up Mark and bring him with you, for he is useful to me for service" (2 Tim. 4:11).

The point is, even though we sometimes have our differences with other Christians, we need each other. We are to bear one another's burdens. We are to stand with those who are hurting and give support, just as these brethren did with Paul.

6. The fellowship of the saints is a growing fellowship.

"All the saints greet you, *especially those of Caesar's household.*" The term does not necessarily mean Caesar's immediate family, although it could include such. It refers to those in civil service to Caesar. Some of these could be in the list of Romans 16, which Paul had written a few years earlier (see J. B. Lightfoot, *Saint Paul's Epistle to the Philippians* [Zondervan], pp. 171-178). In this case, they would have been Christians before Paul's arrival. But others, no doubt, were those in the Praetorian Guard and in other positions who had met Christ through Paul's witness as a prisoner (1:13). But in either case, the gospel was spreading to the most pagan corners of that society.

The emperor when Paul wrote Philippians was the notoriously wicked Nero. He had come to the throne at 17 after his mother had poisoned her third husband Claudius, who also happened to be her uncle. Five years later Nero had his mother killed because she was getting too pushy. Three years after that he had his own wife killed so that he could marry another man's wife. He murdered many of his top officials in the military and in the Roman senate. With that kind of court intrigue going on, working for Caesar would have been a corrupt environment, to say the least. And yet the gospel spread there.

God may have you working in a wicked environment. You may be thinking, "I wish I could work in a more godly, or at least, a neutral place where I wasn't surrounded by such raw paganism." But you need to view it as your mission field, a great opportunity for the light of the gospel to shine into that dark place through your witness. To bear witness effectively, you must live with integrity, not compromising the gospel by joining the world's ways. You are being watched, and those in the world will try to get you to mar your testimony, because then they have an excuse for not repenting of their sins. When you get opportunities to speak, you must not be ashamed of the gospel, but remember that it is the power of God to salvation to everyone who believes.

The church should always have an influx of new babes in Christ through the faithful witness of its members. But, remember, babies are cute, but they are also totally self-centered. They dirty their diapers, they wake you up in the night when they think they have a need, they throw up on your clean clothes, and they make a total mess out of meals. But no family should be without them. And no church should be without those from Caesar's household who are coming to faith in Christ.

7. The fellowship of the saints is a grace-oriented fellowship.

"The grace of the Lord Jesus Christ be with your spirit." This is a closing benediction, but it is more than just a nice way of saying, "Good-bye." The grace of the Lord Jesus Christ is crucial to the entire gospel. Grace means God's unmerited favor shown to us who deserve His judgment. Without grace, we could not receive the gospel, because none of us can ever earn or deserve it. Without grace, we could not grow in holiness, because we are so selfish and sinful that if God gave us what we deserve, we all would have been wiped out long ago. His grace is the motivation to deny our sinful selves and live to please and glorify Him. We stand daily, constantly in need of God's grace. Without it, we would be quickly consumed.

God's grace is something we all want for ourselves, but we don't want to extend it to others, especially to those who have offended or wronged us. When I get angry, I have good cause and, besides, I'm only human. So I claim God's grace. But when my wife or children get angry, they need to deal with it and not make excuses! Don't misunderstand--I'm not suggesting that we take advantage of grace by being sloppy about sin. We all need to judge our sin and turn from it. But I am suggesting that we're all quick to apply grace to ourselves and to be judgmental toward others, when we need to be quick to judge ourselves and show grace to others.

Grace ministers to the spirit (4:23), or inner person, our essential being. It is in our spirit that we commune with God. So many of our troubles can be traced to being defiled in spirit (2 Cor. 7:1), whether by bitterness, greed, lust, envy, or malice. But if the grace of the Lord Jesus Christ dwells in our spirit, so that we thankfully, joyfully live each day in the sweet awareness of His unmerited kindness toward us at the cross, then we can extend that same sweet graciousness toward others. Our homes and our church should be marked by grace-oriented fellowship.

Conclusion

Three concluding applications:

(1) Commit yourself to the fellowship of the saints by getting involved in some sort of small group. You can't experience true fellowship if you aren't connected to other Christians who know you personally and whom you know. It may just be one other believer, but commit to meet and build one another in Christ.

(2) Commit yourself to the fellowship of the saints by working through relational problems. The church isn't perfect. You will bail out with hurt feelings if you don't commit to work through problems.

(3) Commit yourself to the fellowship of the saints by ministry to the saints. Every believer is gifted for service. Rather than being self-focused ("Nobody said hello to me; this is an unfriendly church"), be focused on others ("There is a person who seems to need a friend; I'll go over and reach out to him"). Take the initiative.

Remember, Philippians tells us how to know God's joy in every circumstance. We will know joy by knowing the grace of our Lord Jesus Christ through the gospel, so that we grow in fellowship with Him; we will know joy by getting our focus off ourselves and onto others, so that we fellowship in God's grace with other saints; and we will know joy by bearing witness of His glorious gospel to those who are lost, so that they can enter the same joy of fellowship with God and with His saints.

Application Questions

1. How can [our church] strengthen true fellowship? Do we need new programs to facilitate it or just a renewed focus?

2. Friendships tend to be exclusive and yet fellowship is inclusive. How can we promote both without diminishing either?

3. Must an introverted loner-type be committed to fellowship? How does personality fit in with the biblical mandate?

4. How can we develop a grace-orientation and yet not grow sloppy about sin?

Made in the USA
Las Vegas, NV
20 June 2023

73688617R00173